THE SMELL OF SWEAT

GREEK ATHLETICS, OLYMPICS, AND CULTURE

BY

WM. BLAKE TYRRELL

Bolchazy-Carducci Publishers, Inc.
Wauconda, Illinois USA

General Editor
Laurie Haight Keenan

Typography and Page Design
Larry J. Bennett

Cover Design
Adam Phillip Velez

The Smell of Sweat
Greek Athletics, Olympics, and Culture

by Wm. Blake Tyrrell

Bolchazy-Carducci Publishers, Inc.
1000 Brown Street
Wauconda, IL 60084 USA
www.bolchazy.com

Printed in the United States of America
2004
by United Graphics

ISBN 0-86516-553-X

Library of Congress Cataloging-in-Publication Data

Tyrrell, William Blake.
  The smell of sweat : Greek athletics, Olympics, and culture / by Wm. Blake Tyrrell.— 1st ed.
    p. cm.
Includes bibliographical references and index.
  ISBN 0-86516-553-X (paperback with CD)
  1. Athletics—Greece—History. 2. Sports—Greece—History. 3. Games—Greece—History. I. Title.
GV21.T97 2003
796'.09495—dc22

2003023038

For B. W. T. and F. T.

parentibus carissimis

τῆς δ᾽ ἀρετῆς ἱδρῶτα θεοὶ προπάροιθεν ἔθηκαν
ἀθάνατοι.

The immortal gods have made it so: to achieve excellence, we first
must sweat.

Hesiod *Works and Days* 289

Αἱ περιστάσεις εἰσὶν αἱ τοὺς ἄνδρας δεικνύουσαι.
λοιπὸν ὅταν ἐμπέσῃ περίστασις, μέμνησο ὅτι ὁ θεός σε
ὡς ἀλείπτης τραχεῖ νεανίσκῳ συμβέβληκεν. ἵνα τί;
φησίν. Ἵνα Ὀλυμπιονίκης γένῃ· δίχα δ᾽ ἱδρῶτος οὐ
γίγνεται.

Difficult situations are what reveal men. Thus, whenever a difficulty
befalls, remember that the god matched you with it like a trainer with a
rough young man. For what purpose? He says: To become an
Olympic victor, and that does not happen apart from sweat.

Epictetus *Discourses* 1.24.1–2

ἐκ δὲ μετώπων
θλιβομένων καμάτοιο προάγγελος ἔρρεεν ἱδρώς.

From their foreheads
pressed against each other, sweat, harbinger of toil, began to flow.

Nonnus *Dionysiaca* 37.566–567

Contents

List of Illustrations ix

List of Maps x

List of Tables x

Preface xi

Introduction: The Myth of Amateurism xiii

1. The Warrior and the Funeral Games in the *Iliad* 1
    The *Aretê* of the Warrior 2
    The Hoplite Race 6
    The Funeral Games for Patroclus 8
    Alkinoös' Contests for Odysseus 27
2. Early Olympia 31
    Geographical Setting 32
    Religious Setting 35
    Setting Worth Fighting For 36
    Mythic Setting 38
    Setting for Lacedaemonians 45
    Setting for Growth 49
3. The Panhellenic Cycle of Athletic Festivals and Their Poet 57
    Olympic Games: The First Events 59
    Pythian Games: Horse Racing 74
    Isthmian Games 87
    Nemean Games 94
    Pindar's Epinician Odes 98
4. The Heavy Events 105
    Wrestling 107
    Boxing 118

Pankration 133
5. Athletics in Athens 141
   Panathenaic Games 145
   The Gymnasion and its Culture 156
   The Critics 175
6. Olympic Festival 181
   The Sanctuary during the Classical Period 181
   The Games: Making Ready 188
   The Five Days of Competition 197
   Pentathlon 204
   Discus 204
   Jump   210
   Javelin 213
   The Sequence of Events in Pentathon 216
   Determining the Winner of Pentathlon 218
   Glorious Day, Day of Glory 224

Bibliography 227

Index   253

List of Illustrations

1. Bronze statuette of a female runner, ca. 580 B.C.E. Br. 208. © The British Museum, London, England. *51*

2. Bronze statuette of a male runner, ca. 480–470 B.C.E. Courtesy of the Archaeological Museum, Olympia, Greece. *61*

3. Starting gate with *balbides*. Reproduced from Oscar Broneer, "Excavations at Isthmia: Third Campaign, 1955–56." *Hesperia* 27 (1958): 1–37, Plate 5 d. Courtesy of Professor Elizabeth R. Gebhard, Director of the University of Chicago Excavationis at Isthmia. *64*

4. Red-figure Panathenaic amphora, ca. 460 B.C.E. Attributed to the Achilles Painter. Pell. 12, inv. 18040, Side B: footrace. Courtsey of the Archaeological Museum of Bologna, Bologna, Italy. *68*

5. Black-figure Panathenaic amphora, 530 B.C.E. Attributed to the Euphiletos Painter. Accession number 14.130.12. Side B: footrace. Courtsey of The Metropolitian Museum of Art, Rogers Fund, New York, New York, U.S.A6. *68*

6. Black-figure Panathenaic amphora, 333 B.C.E. B. 609, Side B: footrace. © The British Museum, London, England. *73*

7. Black-figure amphora, ca. 540 B.C.E. Courtsety of Staatliche Antikensammlungen und Glyptothek, Munich, Germany. *81*

8. Black-figure Panathenaic amphora, ca. 420–400 B.C.E. Vase 606, Side B: four horse chariot. © The British Museum, London, England. *82*

9. Red-figure amphora, ca. 450 B.C.E. Courtsey of the Staatliche Antikensammlungen und Glyptothek, Munich, Germany. *112*

10. Attic psykter, ca. 510 B.C.E. Attributed to Euthymides. Vase 4123. Courtsey of the Museo di Antichità, Turin, Italy. *114*

11. Attic amphora, ca. 525 B.C.E. Attributed to the Andocides. Painter. Vase F 2492. Courtsey of the Bildarchiv Preußischer Kulturbesitz, Berlin, Germany. *115*

12. Attic cup, ca. 500 B.C.E. Of the proto-Panaetian Group. Vase 523. Bibliothèque Nationale, Paris, France. *117*

13. Red-figure amphora, early fifth-century B.C.E. Vase 1689. Courtsey of the National Archaeological Museum, Athens, Greece. *119*

14. Bronze statue, first century B.C.E. Courtsey of the Museo Nazionale Romano, Rome, Italy. *121*

15. Detail of bronze statue, first century B.C.E. Museo Nazionale Romano, Rome, Italy. *126*

16. Attic red-figure kylix, ca. 490 B.C.E. Attributed to Duris. Vase E 39. The British Museum, London, England. *135*

17. Attic cup, ca. 480 B.C.E. Attributed to the Foundry Painter. Vase E78. © The British Museum, London, England. *137*

18. Roman bronze statuette, first century C.E. Item BR 1067. Photo credit: Hervé Lewandowski. Copyright Réunion des Musées Nationaux / Art Resource, NY. *144*

19. Black-figure Panathenaic amphora, ca. 480–470 B.C.E. Attributed to the Berlin Master. Vase C.959.53. Courtsey o f the Hood Museum of Art, Darthmouth College, Hanover, New Hampshire; gift of Mr. and Mrs. Ray Winfield Smith, Class of 1918. *146*

20. Detail of C.959.53, Hood Museum of Art, Darthmouth College, Hanover, New Hampshire; gift of Mr. and Mrs. Ray Winfield Smith, Class of 1918. *147*

21. Black-figure Panathenaic amphora, ca. 500 B.C.E. Attributed to the Painter of Wurzburg 173. Side B: racing chariot. The Art Museum, Princeton University. Bequest of Mrs. Allan Marquand. Photo Credit: Bruce M. White. *154*

22. Red-figure bell krater, ca. 430–420 B.C.E. In the manner of the Pelius Painter. Courtesy of the Arthur M. Sackler Museum, Harvard University Art Museum. Bequest of David M. Robinson. Photo credit: Michael Nedzweski. *172*

23. Attic red-figure kylix, ca. 520 B.C.E. Vase E 6. © The British Museum, London, England. *172*

24. Attic black-figure lekythos, sixth century B.C.E. Attributed to the Michigan Painter. Item 06.1021.60. Courtsey of The Metropolitan Museum of Art, New York, New York. Rogers Fund, 1906. *205*

25. Attic black-figure lekythos, sixth century B.C.E. Attributed to the Michigan Painter. Item 06.1021.60. Courtsey of The Metropolitan Museum of Art, New York, New York. Rogers Fund, 1906. *205*

26. Copy of the Discobolus by Myron, mid-fifth century B.C.E. Courtsey of the Museo Nazionale Romano, Rome, Italy. *208*

27. Attic black-figure neck amphora, ca. 575 B.C.E. Vase B 48. © The British Museum, London, England. *211*

28. Red-figure amphora, ca. 500 B.C.E. Vase A Tf.204, 1f. Courtsey of the Staatlich Antikensammulungen und Glyptothek, Munich, Germany. *215*

29. Attic black-figure amphora of Panathenaic shape. Vase B 138. © The British Museum, London, England. *224*

List of Maps

Early Olympia *31*
Olympia at the End of the Fourth Century *182*

List of Tables

Lacedaemonian Victors at Early Olympia *47*
Lacedaemonian Victors in Horse Racing *85*

Preface

This study surveys Greek athletics and the changes it underwent through the Archaic and Classical periods. This endeavor is not without difficulties. The casual way in which Athenian tragedians and writers of comedy, poets working in popular media, incorporate the language of athletics leaves no doubt that the Greeks were familiar with the events of their athletic program. But that same familiarity has left the modern investigator, someone trying to imagine the shape and look of a particular event or institution, at sea. One must, as it were, piece together the ship from the flotsam, the event from references scattered hither and yon in sources from the sixth century B.C.E. to the fifth century C.E.and later. The result has been to make difficult the examination of the changes that happened through time to individual events and contests.

No source is more essential to this task than Pausanias' *Description of Greece*. Pausanias wrote a guide for tourists about the Greek world of the second century C.E. He talks about the history and topography of cities, records local myths and rituals, and dwells upon sanctuaries, temples, and images of gods and goddesses. His willingness to ponder inscriptions written on statues at Olympia, many of them faded and in an ancient dialect or script, bequeathed to scholars a rich heritage of names and achievements, vignettes of the athletic scene. His work has become a goldmine for scholars at their desks who, like his first recorded reader, the grammarian Stephanos of Byzantium (sixth century C.E.), probe it for information. I refer to him often, always grateful that he is there.

Among the modern authorities that I have consulted, a few stand out. In matters of archaeology, I have rarely strayed from Alfred Mallwitz's chapter "Cult and Competition Locations at Olympia" and Catherine Morgan's *Athletes and Oracles: The Transformation of Olympia and Delphi in the Eighth Century BC*. The works of Oscar

Broneer on Isthmia and Stephen G. Miller on Nemea are essential for investigating those sites. Any reader familiar with the evidence for the heavy events of the Greek athletic program will realize my debt to Michael B. Poliakoff's *Combat Sports in the Ancient World*. No account of athletics at Athens may be written without profiting from Donald G. Kyle's *Athletics in Ancient Athens*.

Unless otherwise indicated, all dates relating to the ancient Greeks are B.C.E. Dates are given the first time an ancient author or event is mentioned. For familiar names, I have retained the Latinized spellings; for others, I have approximated the Greek orthography. Translations from the Greek and Latin are mine. The text for Pindar is Bruno Snell's *Pindari Carmina cum Fragmentis* (Leipzig: B. G. Teubner, 1959). References within parentheses in the text are to works listed in the bibliography. The letter M enclosed in brackets with a number and following the name of an athlete, for example, Koroibos [M 1], indicates the number of the entry for that athlete in Luigi Moretti's *Olympionikai, I Vincitori negli Antichi Agoni Olimpici* (Rome: Accademia Nazionale dei Lincei, 1957), which has become a standard reference work.

Packaged with the *Smell of Sweat* is a CD-ROM that contains an extensive, but not exhaustive, collection of sources for the study of Greek athletics. These sources are meant to be read in conjunction with the text but also offer the student and instructor resources for independent research.

I would like to acknowledge the help I received from the Interlibrary Loan Department of Michigan State University in researching this project. Its staff responded promptly and accurately to my requests for books and articles, many of them rare, arcane, and difficult to locate. Gerald V. Lalonde, Professor of Classics, Grinnell College, advised me on matters of archaeology; any infelicities in this regard are mine. I express my thanks to my friends and coauthors, Larry J. Bennett for producing the book CD, and Frieda S. Brown, Professor Emeritus of Romance Languages and Literatures, Michigan State University, for her careful and insightful reading of the manuscript.

Introduction

The Myth of Amateurism

The dependency of modern scholars upon post-classical sources for understanding the Archaic (eighth to sixth centuries) and Classical (fifth to fourth centuries) periods pertains generally to the study of Greek history and not less to the study of Greek athletics. In the latter instance, the subject of this book, the sustained acceptance of late nineteenth- and early twentieth-century advocacy of amateurism, supported by the erroneous attribution of amateurism to the ancient Greeks and rooted in the radical classism of the Victorian Age, continues to distort our view of Greek athletics and the ancient Olympic Games.

While amateurism has its own complex history, neither the word nor the concept existed among the ancient Greeks (Young 1985, 7). The word "amateur," derived through French from the Latin *amatorem*, accusative case of *amator* (lover), appeared first in the late eighteenth century to denote a person who pursued a passion in painting, for instance, or architecture, or natural science, or any such endeavor without expectation of monetary compensation. The man who applied himself to a specific activity for material gain was a "professional." Until the mid-nineteenth century, athletic professionals were working men whose livelihood involved an activity that came into play in a race or match. In rowing, for example, disputes broke out between rowers from Cambridge and Oxford Universities and watermen when the latter, who worked near and on the water, were barred from rowing, because their daily converse with boats gave them advantages over the collegians in strength and knowledge of the river. The amateur engaged in an activity as a pastime and, although he may have trained, he did not apply himself with the devotion that marked one a professional—even if that devotion was spent in earning a living. The amateur's dilettantism, in turn, accounted for his contempt for skilled play as the nineteenth-century novelist Anthony Trollope illustrates with billiards: "To play billiards is the amusement of a gentleman;—to play billiards pre-eminently well is the life's work of a man who, in learning to do so, can hardly have continued to be a gentleman in the best sense of the word" (5). While not above accepting a valuable prize in a competition or profiting from betting on a game, the English amateur spurned the professional's dedication and steadfastness as work, a thing beneath him.

By contrast, and generally speaking, Greek athletes who contended for a crown of olive branches at the Olympic Games or of parsley at the Nemean Games or for amphoras of olive oil in the Panathenaic Games at Athens dedicated much of their time and effort to training for the competitions (Plato *Laws* 807C) in a way that may be described as professional. Those who won received great wealth for their victories, which enabled them to pursue lives devoted to athletic competition. But athletics were part of a Greek's life, especially the aristocratic Greek, who defined himself not as an amateur but as *aristos* (best) in all areas of society. To be best entailed serious competition, and all were competitive. That some were more so than others—that some were what scholars have deemed professionals— did not mean to the others that they were amateurs.

E. Norman Gardiner, who promoted the idea of ancient Greek athletes as amateurs, believed that the athlete was "one who competes for something" but never for the material worth of a prize and always for "the honour of victory" and out of "the desire to put to the test his physical powers, the desire to excel." This desire turns "his effort into joy." The athletic spirit can exist and flower "only in physically vigorous and virile nations that put a high value on physical excellence" (1930; reprint, 1980, 2). Physical training, however, cannot replace sport, because "it cannot import those higher qualities—courage, endurance, self-control, courtesy—qualities which are developed by our own games and by such manly sports as boxing and wrestling when conducted in the true spirit of manly rivalry for the pure joy of the contest: it cannot train boys 'to play the game' in the battle of life" (1980, 98). Many an Englishman went out into the world to cure its ills by "the simple expedient of propagating the public school ethic of playing the game" (Mangan, 202). Gardiner would have Greeks train boys along the lines of Montagu Butler's appeal to Harrovians, young and old:

Play the Game! Play the Game!
Boys of Harrow, Men of Harrow,
  Play the Game.
End each Match as just beginning,
Bowl and field as sure of winning!
Meet your Fate, but meet it grinning
  Play the Game (Mangan, 201).

It was a call to decency and modesty and to a dislike of everything
mean and fraudulent (Mangan, 201), but Greeks rarely played the
game for the playing and little countenanced the chagrin of defeat.

We need only contrast Butler with the lyric poet Pindar (518–438)
who wrote epinician odes, songs of praise to be sung by choruses for an
athlete's victory in the Panhellenic games, to appreciate the chasm that
separates these views. In an ode for the boy wrestler Aristomenes of
Aigina, an island in the Saronic Gulf off the coast of Attica, Pindar
comments on the diverse fates of the four whom Aristomenes
vanquished in wrestling in the Pythian Games and of the victor himself:

You fell from on high
on four bodies, harboring ill intent,
and no happy homecoming was declared
in Pythia for them as it was for you.
And when they returned to their mother,
no sweet laughter stirred a welcome.
But down alleys,
evading their enemies,
did they cower, bitten with defeat.
He who has gained a new success,
in his great prosperity,
takes flight in his hope
on soaring wings of manhood, with
his thoughts on more than wealth (*Pythian Ode* 8.81–92).

No smile but utter humiliation befalls the defeated, while for the victor,
there are exhilaration, hope, and plans for the future, as if defeat were
death, and victory, life. Greeks competed in a contest for the prize.
Anything short of winning that prize meant nothing. The creed that
Pierre de Coubertin, considered the founder of the modern Olympic
Games, adopted for the modern Olympic athlete—"to participate is
more important than to win"—would be incomprehensible to the
ancient Greek (Pleket, 52).

1.
The Warrior and the Funeral Games in the *Iliad*

During the second half of the eighth century B.C.E., the Greeks burst forth from the isolation of their regional confines to spread across the Mediterranean (Snodgrass 1971, 402–436). Groups of families left their homes and emigrated to far-off places in Ionia and southern Italy where they colonized new territory and founded cities, established the Panhellenic shrine at Delphi where Apollo would soon have his oracular seat, and organized the first games at Olympia, traditionally dated to 776, which testified to the widening interest that attached to earlier festivals and their games. Foremost among the many factors contributing to this explosion of energy and the ensuing effusion of confidence and creativity was the shift from herding and hunting to arable farming as the primary means of sustenance. The individual farmer now plowed his fields and stored his grain, supporting a larger family and bringing about an increased population. Regions were unified under cities, as towns and villages scattered across a territory surrendered their autonomy for greater security, power, and influence. In this way, the *polis* (city-state; pl. *poleis*) came into existence and, with its surrounding territory, provided the breeding grounds for the expanding awareness by Greeks of their uniqueness and worth among the older peoples of the Mediterranean. Thus, two conflicting forces swept among the Greeks beginning around 750: one widened their outlook to include a Panhellenic perspective held by the elite of the city-states and the other narrowed their ambitions to local concerns and rivalries.

At the same time, Greeks turned their eyes back to the heroes and lost ways of a culture that moderns call the Mycenaean civilization (1600–1100) after the monumental ruins of Mycenae. The Greeks drew their knowledge from poetry that had breached the gap of some three hundred years by being carried on the lips of generations of oral poets. These poets acquired the tools of their craft—themes, diction, and sound patterns—from other poets who, in turn, had been taught by still others as apprentices became masters. They told and retold the story of Achilles' wrath, reaching over time a high level of poetic skill and content (Edwards, 15–54). They preserved the past, even elements from the Mycenaean period, and incorporated the present to form both a language and a world that embraced many different dialects and local customs but were peculiar to no specific area in Greece. The poets traveled among the *poleis*, synthesized local traditions, and melded them into a Panhellenic voice that aided in unifying Greeks.

The *Aretê* of the Warrior

The Greeks believed in the reality of the world depicted by Homer and looked to his poems as a repository of information and truths about themselves and the past (Havelock, 61–96). They admired and strove to emulate the values of the Homeric warrior, chief among which was his valor, his *aretê*. *Aretê* meant excellence in whatever task was undertaken, and for the warrior, that was war. His *aretê* therefore resided first and foremost in his bravery in battle. He fought man-to-man out in front of the other warriors against someone similarly armed and motivated for the reputation of being, and the right to boast that he was, among the best. It was a style of fighting that harkened back to the Mycenaean period and that had vanished with its *wanax* (king). The men who listened to the poets during the eighth century and afterwards fought battles in a different fashion. Their *aretê* comprised the courage to don heavy armor, stand in the line alongside their fellow combatants, and face an enemy with similar weapons and organization in a clash of formations. These men, many of them farmers, could not practice on their fields of war the grander and individualistic *aretê* of the Homeric warrior, but they found the tales of such men inspiring.

This study of Greek athletics begins with the warrior's *aretê* because in many ways his values continued to impel men to pursue through athletics the glory no longer obtainable in war. Sarpedon, lord of the Lycians and ally of the Trojans, gives the clearest expression of the warrior's *aretê* in the *Iliad* as he tells Glaukos, his companion and second in command, what they must do to remain lords and commanders of Lycians:

Glaukos, why are we two most held in honor (*timê*)
with place at table and meats and more cups
in Lycia, and all men look upon us as gods,
and we possess a large portion of land beside the banks
of the Xanthos good for orchards and fields of wheat?
Now in the forefront of the Lycians
we stand and meet the burning battle
so someone of the armed Lycians may say:
"Surely, no ignoble kings of ours rule
throughout Lycia and eat the fatted flocks
and drink the choice honey-sweet wine. Their might
is good since they fight in the forefront of the Lycians."
Man, if, escaping this war,
we would remain ever ageless and immortal,
I myself would not fight in the forefront,
nor would I send you into the fight that glorifies a man.
Now, as it is, the spirits of death stand about us,
countless, whom no mortal can flee or avoid.
Let us go and offer our boast to someone or he to us (12.310–328).

Lycians honor Sarpedon and Glaukos, that is to say, they assign a value to them and express their estimation with the finest land and conspicuous amenities. The Greek *timê* denotes value and worth as well as the respect and esteem that great worth commands. The Lycians prize their chieftains for their courage and ability—their *aretê*—in fighting the enemy out in front of the mass. Sarpedon earns the *timê* they pay him by engaging an enemy warrior in a contest in which each man seeks the other's life. Though at the risk of his own, it is the offensive that counts. Let boast confront boast, he says, as he prepares to reenter the fight where the winner takes all and the loser yields all. It is the zero-sum game that demands for every gain a corresponding loss: "someone can win only if someone else loses" (Gouldner, 49). It is the game played by the Homeric warrior and, as Alvin W. Gouldner implies, by the Greek athlete as well:

> This, of course, is manifest in the case of victory won by "wars" and "threats"; but it also seems to be the case in "competitions," especially by the standards of a "shame culture," which defines any kind of defeat as shameful regardless of circumstances; here a loser does not leave the contest with as much fame as he enters. Losing in such a competition, therefore, does not simply mean a prize foregone but a loss suffered: someone is the loser (49).

A man's worth in the shame culture of the *Iliad* depends upon what others say of him. Defeat diminishes his fame and threatens his value in the eyes of others. Such a man may become hesitant to compete unless convinced of his chances to win and will often stoop to any means to that end (Gouldner, 52–55). There are no fun runs or personal bests among the Greeks. The zero-sum game does not recognize second place or more than one winner, since wealth is limited, and for it to be gained by one, it has to be lost by another. Although in this system brave men tend to be wealthy, and the wealthy tend to be brave, material gain is not the essence of the warrior's life. Neither does Sarpedon relish the fight for its own sake. If he could escape death, he admits, he would not enter battle. But death comes to all men, warrior and carpenter alike, and only the warrior can elude its finality by winning imperishable glory in battle. Through fighting, he becomes like a god among men and achieves the mediated immortality of his culture, remembrance through songs like Homer's. To have his name resound upon the ears of men born long after his death—that is the motivation that drives more than the Homeric warrior; that is the ideal sought by every Greek.

Emerging with the rising prosperity of the late eighth and seventh centuries was a new type of warfare. The hoplite phalanx developed slowly as new elements were added to old to form its panoply and techniques of battle (Snodgrass, 1965). Once in place, the hoplomachy (battle by hoplites) remained the dominant mode of fighting battles among Greeks until the fourth century. The hoplite wore a breastplate, greaves (shin protectors), and a helmet which was especially bothersome as it restricted his vision to the field immediately before him. His weaponry was expensive and heavy; the shield gave him his name. The *hoplon* was a heavy, round, convex, wooden shield with a strap in the center and one on the right rim. By the fifth century, it was covered with a thin layer of bronze which offered no protection but, when highly polished, was thought to intimidate the enemy (Hanson, 65). The hoplite inserted his left arm in the center grip and grasped the outer strap with his hand. In this position and because of the shield's weight, he had little choice but to hold the shield with his upper arm parallel to his body and bent inward at the elbow. As a consequence, the left half of his body was protected by the right semicircle of the shield. His right side was exposed, and the left semicircle of the shield projected past his body, offering him no benefit. Drawn up next to other hoplites, however, he gained some protection from the left side of the shield belonging to the man on his right and offered protection to the man on his left. The success of the phalanx depended upon its cohesiveness, and that required that each man remain at his assigned place in the line. The poet Tyrtaios thus exhorts the Lacedaemonians in the formative days of the seventh century to "Let the man stand firm and remain fixed with both feet on the ground, biting his lips" (10.31–32, in Edmonds 1:70).

Drawn up in lines as far across as possible and ranks of eight deep or as deep as the circumstances demanded and resources allowed, the hoplites approached another phalanx of Greeks. Both sides had agreed upon the site for the battle, a level area usually near the grainfields that were often the object of contention, and both followed the simple etiquette of this brutal affair. As the men marched, the *aulos* player marked the cadence with an oboe-like instrument. The same sounds accompanied the dancers of tragic choruses, which must have sent chills up the spine of many a veteran seated in the theater. At the right moment, the hoplites charge. They may throw a spear, but they hold one for thrusting. It is the main weapon for the killing zone. The first lines collide; spears strike on shields and armor and flesh, and men fall. Then the murderous work gets under way as men try to strike over the enemy's shield and into his neck or under his shield and into his groin. Meanwhile, the rear ranks have fit their shields into the backs of the men in front and are pushing them forward (Hanson, 169–177). The phalanx that weakens before the push and jab, that panics and breaks into flight, suffers terrible losses.

The battle was usually fought to the finish in as short a time as an afternoon. Winners and losers were easily distinguished: the former controlled the battlefield, picking up their dead first, collecting their armor and possessions as spoil, and setting up a trophy. They then departed, leaving the field for the losers. Hoplomachy was stylized, almost ritualized, and was fought with particular intensity by the defenders. Its participants, mainly citizen farmers who could afford the equipment, drove off assaults on their fields with more success than they invaded the fields of others. They fought to get the battle over and return to fields left unworked and undefended. Aristocrats participated, perhaps even riding their horses, emblems of their status, to the field and there dismounting and joining the line, but individual glory of the kind sought by Sarpedon was impossible, a thing of the past for the hoplite farmer or aristocrat. The phalanx depended upon cooperation among men, another of the many ironies of ancient Greek culture, for men who strove to be known with a personal renown that all would envy devised a way of fighting that rendered all equal and the same. The desire for personal glory and the need to erect differences among men moved elsewhere, to the courts and assemblies, the theater, and athletics.

The Hoplite Race

For over one hundred and fifty years, the hoplite's panoply and way of fighting remained unchanged. Then, towards the end of the sixth century, the Greeks began to introduce changes that seemed to be directed toward increasing his mobility. Anthony Snodgrass, pointing out that "it is in the nature of military technology to be more than usually sensitive to external developments, since they present a potential threat," suggests that the fall of Ionian Greek cities to Cyrus of Persia alarmed the Greeks (1980, 151). In addition, around 520–510, the Etruscans and Carthaginians wiped out a fleet of Greeks from Phokis who had settled in Corsica. Whatever the stimulus, Greeks developed a new type of breast protection, a metal-studded cuirass of leather, that was lighter and offered greater freedom of movement. Around the same time, the Eleans, organizers of the Olympic Games, inaugurated an event for the sixty-fifth Olympiad (520), namely, the hoplite race, which was won by Damaretos of Heraia (Pausanias 3.14.3; 6.10.4). Later, during the classical period, runners carried a round shield, possibly covered with bronze (Pindar *Pythian Ode* 9.1–4), and wore a helmet and shin guards. All ran in the nude, the custom for athletes in all contests except the horse races. Over time, the Eleans dropped the helmet and greaves from the race at Olympia (Pausanias 6.10.4). Philostratos (ca. 170–249 C.E.) states that the race held in the Boeotian city of Plataea was the best because the racers ran in full armor over a long distance (*Gymnastic* 8).

At Olympia, Athens, and Nemea, the race was a *diaulos* or double-channel race (Pausanias 2.11.8; Aristophanes *Birds* 291–292), that is, the runners ran for two laps, down the course, around a turning post from right to left, and back to the starting point. Rounding a marker (*kamptêr*, *terma*), the universal method for conducting races of a length greater than one stade, roughly 600 ancient feet, has presented the problem of how several closely bunched runners managed a post without fouling and why the sources are silent about the turn in footraces when they describe the same move in horse racing at length (Harris 1964, 71). Stephen G. Miller (1980) has offered a convincing solution. From the remains of the stadium at Nemea, Miller reasons that runners had individual lanes (grooves), marked by lime spread on the ground, and separate turning posts. Each runner set forth from the starting line in a lane to the right of the *kamptêr* down the course and turned the *kamptêr* into an open line on its left. Every other lane was open, an arrangement that precluded the collisions that marked chariot races.

While the hoplite race "suggests an interest in the training of mobile infantry" (Snodgrass 1980, 152), it was also connected with warfare through foundation myths, myths of origins, that tell of a hoplite in full armor who comes running to the city with news of a victory in the field (Philostratos *Gymnastic* 7). Further, its positioning as the last event of the Olympic Games might well have signaled, as Philostratos speculated, the expiration of the armistice declared for the period of the games (*Gymnastic* 7; Artemidorus *Interpretation of Dreams* 1.63).

The hoplite race evokes the initial stage of battle when the hoplite ran to meet the enemy. Once the phalanxes collided, the fighter was rooted to his place in the line for the duration. Before then, however, he ran for some two hundred yards, exposed to the rain of enemy missiles, as fast as he could and still maintain formation, given the weight and constrictions of his panoply (Hanson, 144–151). Every hoplite surely prayed to get across that distance quickly and arrive at the enemy line with sufficient breath and energy to fight for his life. The race, it seems, recognizes this desire by celebrating swiftness of foot. Athletes in hoplite armor displayed the speed of the runner, mediating the unhampered speed of the naked runner who ran unencumbered by armor and the leaden discomfort of the hoplite traversing no-man's-land.

The question of the use and contribution of athletics to military training and fighting continued to be debated throughout the classical period and later, but war and athletics were undoubtedly associated in the Greek mind from the first. Homer's athletes were warriors; they played games—chariot racing, boxing, wrestling, foot racing, and spear throwing—that derived from warfare. Earliest criticisms of athletics contrasted the athlete with the warrior:

> Neither would I recall a man or put him in my tale
>   whose valor lies in his feet or in wrestling
> . . . .
> not if he had every fame save that for impetuous might.
>   For a man does not prove to be brave in war
> unless he has seen and endured bloody slaughter,
>   and, standing close by, reaches out to strike the foe.
> This is valor, the best prize among men
>   and the most beautiful thing for a youth to win.
> This is the common good for a city and all its people,
>   when a man standing firm remains among the front men
> incessantly and forgets disgraceful flight altogether,
>   committing his life and spirit and

encouraging the man that stands at his side with his words.
    This man proves to be brave in war
(Tyrtaios 12.1–2, 9–20 in Edmonds 1:74).

The athlete won an *aretê* of his own, one sufficiently honored and
widespread to arouse the ire of Tyrtaios, voice for the war craft of the
Spartan hoplite. The striving for individual honor, forced out of war by
the hoplite mode of fighting, moved to other competitive arenas, among
them, the contest (*agôn*) of the athlete. Michael B. Poliakoff has aptly
proposed that the change in warfare from the individual to the phalanx
"gave impetus to organized competitive athletics" (1987, 114). But if
war fed athletics, the converse issue of the use and relevance of athletics
for war nagged the Greeks.

The Funeral Games for Patroclus

    Homer's *Iliad* is an epic poem that tells the story of the warrior
Achilles' wrath against Agamemnon, leader of the Greeks who were
besieging Troy. It opens with an old man, a priest of Apollo, imploring
Agamemnon to accept the ransom he brought and return his daughter
to him. Agamemnon favors the girl but, as a gift given him by the army,
she serves as visible proof of his *timê*. He spurns her father's request
and dismisses the old man with a threat against returning. The priest
prays to Apollo, and the god sends a plague up through the Greek army
that first destroys the animals and then the men. Achilles convenes a
meeting to confront the issue and, discovering that Agamemnon's denial
of the priest has angered Apollo, appeals to Agamemnon to give back
the young woman. Agamemnon agrees but, uncertain of his position
and fearing loss of face, demands a replacement prize, which would
have to come from another warrior. Achilles accuses Agamemnon of
cowardice and greed in wanting to seize from others their hard-won
prizes, and a quarrel ensues between the men. Achilles, enraged at
Agamemnon, quits the camp and the fighting. Deprived of his aid, the
Greeks suffer defeat against the Trojans. In an attempt to reverse the
tide of battle, Achilles allows Patroclus, his closest companion, to enter
the fighting wearing Achilles' armor in order to deceive the Trojans
and relieve the struggling Greeks. Victorious at first, Patroclus kills
Sarpedon, but, forgetting his promise not to extend the fighting to the
walls of Troy, he is slain by Hector, war leader and foremost warrior of

the Trojans. Achilles returns to the fighting and slaughters Hector but cannot find solace in revenge or let go of Patroclus whose corpse he refuses to bury. Finally, Patroclus' ghost appears to Achilles, requesting the burial that would allow it to enter the world of the dead. Achilles heaps up a huge pyre and cremates Patroclus' body. Afterwards, in the presence of Agamemnon and his fellow warriors, he gathers the bones into a golden jar and declares contests to honor the dead:

> Achilles
> held the people and had the broad assembly sit down.
> He brought up prizes from the ships, cauldrons and tripods
> and horses and mules and heads of stalwart cattle
> and lovely girdled women and gray iron (23.257–261).[1]

Neither Homer nor Achilles needs to give a reason for the games, a common feature of funerals for prominent men. The Kadmeians held a boxing contest for Oedipus (23.679–680). The old man Nestor speaks of the games the Epeians hosted for their dead lord Amarunkeus (23.634–642) and bids Achilles: "Come, pay your companion funerary honors with *aethla*" (23.646). The word *aethla* denotes contests and/or prizes, depending upon the context which often supports a double meaning. For example, in the *Odyssey*, when he describes the games celebrating the slain Achilles, Agamemnon's ghost uses *aethla* to refer to the "very beautiful prizes" (24.91) laid out for the competitors but extends its meaning to include both prizes and contests as the young men prepare for both:

> In the past, you [Achilles] have been present at the funeral of many
> men, warriors, when, because a chieftain has died, the young men
> gird themselves and make ready for the prizes and contests
> (24.87–89).

Prizes go with games as the language itself reveals. Moreover, both serve an important social function. The living honor the dead with prizes (*aethla*) that are distributed in contests; in turn, the contests (*aethla*) attract competitors because of the worth of the prizes. The host of the contest wins by inducing others to honor his dead, and the competitors win by carrying off things of great value.

The Homeric warrior gains fame, social position, and wealth by displaying his valor, by being the best, before the enemy. To be best means killing the man before him and taking his life and armor as his prize. The warrior enters the athletic contests with the same outlook.

---

1 Unless otherwise indicated, all references in parenthesis are to Homer's *Iliad*.

He intends to prove his *aretê* and to be the best. Achilles speaks of the valor of his horses (*Iliad* 23.276) and Menelaus of his own (23.578) and that of his horses (23.571). Epeios claims to be best in boxing (23.669). Achilles calls Eumelos best (23.536), challenges the best men to compete (23.659, 802), and recognizes that Agamemnon is best in the spear throw (23.891). In the contests, however, the warrior strives not for a life but for a prize, a difference Homer highlights in an extended simile that compares Achilles and Hector to prize-winning horses in a chariot race:

> A good man [Hector] was fleeing, and a far better man [Achilles] was pursuing him rapidly, since neither a sacrificial victim nor an ox-hide were they trying to win, which are prizes for men's speed of foot, but they were running for the life of Hector, tamer of horses. As when prize-winning ungulate horses run swiftly
> around the turning posts, and a great prize lies forth,
> a tripod or a woman, in honor of a dead man,
> so the two whirled three times around Priam's city
> on rapid feet, and all the gods were looking on (22.158–166).

Homer cuts abruptly away from the pursuit to a chariot race like those he may have seen in his own life. Similes frequently open glimpses to the everyday world of ordinary men of the poet's time (Edwards, 103). With a few words, the poet conjures the scene: racing horses careering around the post, lap after lap, and spectators looking on to see who will carry off the valuable prize. However hotly contended and dangerous at the turns, the race cannot have the seriousness of the run for Hector's life which surrounds the simile. The games for Patroclus also lack that deadly purpose, but the athletes, being warriors, pursue the prize in the games with the same thirst for honor as they fight.

The games for Patroclus, Oedipus, and the others exist in a narrative created by the skills and techniques of the oral poet. They are variations of one another on the theme of games. Had Homer wished, he could have amplified the games for Amarunkeus or abbreviated those for Patroclus. The games are what they are for narrative, not historical or biographical, reasons, and their referent, what they refer to, is not a historical event but the rest of Homer's story. Throughout Book 23, Homer alludes to the events of the first and second books. An intratextuality of recurrent allusions, themes, and language binds the games to earlier events and sets up contrasts and comparisons between Achilles then and now. In this way, the games advance the theme announced in the very first line of the poem: "Sing, goddess, the wrath of Peleus' son Achilles." When Achilles places among the prizes "the heads of stalwart cattle" (23.260), for example, the experienced listener of epic would not wonder why the cattle are stalwart, but rather he would recall that Achilles' wrath "sent forth many stalwart ghosts of warriors to Hades" (1.3) and brought about the death of the friend (18.98–100) whom he now honors with cattle as a prize for warriors like those sent to Hades.

In announcing the funeral games, Achilles acts as their director. He establishes the prizes for the chariot race, has the contestants step forward, and determines their positions on the starting line by lot. First to leap up to compete in the chariot race is Eumelos whose horses are the best horses by far of the men who followed Agamemnon. "Swift like birds," they were nurtured in Eumelos' native land by Apollo (2.763–767). Arriving with Agamemnon and in command of eleven ships, he should, it seems, have been an important man, but he plays no part in the action of the *Iliad* until the call for charioteers. The lot gives him the most favorable combination of horses and position, one to the right of Antilochos, Nestor's son, and the listener of epic does well to remember Eumaleos' relationship with Apollo. The prominent Greek warrior, Diomedes, the second to come forth, who receives the far right, and worst, position for turning a post to the left, has challenged Apollo's divinity (5.432–442). The Trojan pedigree of his horses brings back the events of their capture, his near slaying of their driver, Trojan Aeneas, and the latter's rescue by his mother, Aphrodite, and Apollo (5.297–317). Diomedes had recently suffered a wound to his foot (11.376–377; 19.47–49), so that ancient critics wondered how he could compete (23.291 in Erbse, 414). Homer evidently wants him for his narrative and conveniently forgets the wound. As for his audience, well, the virtue of a retentive memory in listening to epic is perhaps best balanced by the virtue of selective forgetfulness. Menelaus enters next with one of Agamemnon's horses, a reminder of the brothers' closeness.

Homer interrupts the catalog of contestants at the mention of the fourth driver, Antilochos, with a lengthy narrative of the advice of Antilochos' father, Nestor. The technique of breaking away from, or temporarily halting, the action draws special attention to the character or event described. Antilochos plays a prominent part in the games which foreshadows his role in the epic poem *Aithiopis,* extant only in summary, that continued the story of Troy after the *Iliad*, but it is Nestor, the Gerenian horseman and scion of Poseidon, god of horses, who, having given advice judged best in the past (7.324–325), now takes over the poet's voice. The old man had raced in, and fought from, chariots in his youth (11.736–748) and later instructed his men on chariot

warfare (4.301–309). His counsel for Achilles to respect hierarchy, and
for Agamemnon, regarding the army's distribution of prizes, fails to
forestall the conflict between them (1.274–284), but he is later vindicated
by Agamemnon's admission of madness in dishonoring a warrior of
Achilles' stature (9.115–118). Now he advises his son not about
horsemanship itself but of the need to apply ingenuity (*mêtis*) against
his competitors in the race:

> Antilochos, in truth, although you are young,
> Zeus and Poseidon have loved you and taught you
> horsemanship of every sort. Thus, I do not need to teach you.
> You well know how to wheel around the turning posts. But your
> horses are very slow in running, and so I think that will plague you.
> Their horses are faster, but even so, they themselves
> do not know more than you about employing ingenuity.
> Come now, dear son, lay up in your mind ingenuity
> of every sort so that the prizes may not flee out from before you.
> With his ingenuity, a feller of oaks is much better than with brute
> force. With ingenuity, the helmsman on the wine-colored sea
> guides the swift ship as it is buffeted by storm blasts.
> With ingenuity, a charioteer outstrips another charioteer.
> The man who trusts himself to his horses and chariots wheels
> mindlessly around the turn, swerving this way and that, and his horses
> wander outside the course, and he does not control them
> (23.306–321).

Mêtis embraces a kind of thinking identified by Marcel Detienne
and Jean-Pierre Vernant as "an informed prudence" (11). It comes into
play, they explain, in situations like that facing Antilochos. Despite
the formulaic "swift of foot" (23.304), his horses are very slow, sure to
be outstripped by other teams. He must use his ingenuity to watch how
the race develops, keeping his eye on the man in front of him, and be
flexible and ready to act in an instant. Antilochos has already displayed
mêtis in saving Menelaus from a fatal mistake when the latter pitied
two youths who were killed by Aeneas. Menelaus sets out against
Aeneas, "mindful that he might be subdued beneath Aeneas' hands"
(5.564), but Antilochos foresees what may happen and moves to prevent
it. Together with Menelaus, he forces Aeneas to back down (5.565–
572). Thinking about what lies ahead is a hallmark of *mêtis* (Detienne
and Vernant, 14). When Antilochus thinks ahead in the race, however,
he outmaneuvers Menelaus, leaving Menelaus to cry foul in protest
against the very intelligence that saved his life.

Nestor's instructions help his son to win second place in spite of
his slower horses, but they fulfill other functions of epic poetry as
well, acting as "a sort of encyclopedia of ethics, politics, history and
technology which the effective citizen was required to learn as the core

of his educational equipment" (Havelock, 27). Within the immediate context of the narrative, they give the essentials for rounding a mark in a 180-degree turn in a chariot that slides around the post. The driver must pull back on the inner or left horse to keep the chariot close to the post, preventing it from going wide—the result of the horses' momentum and natural inclination to be mindful of their own safety—and let out the outer or right horse so it can move ahead and inward and force the chariot nearer the post:

> Approach it tightly, driving your horses and chariot near it.
> You yourself lean over in your chariot with wickerwork sides
> a little bit to the left of your horses, but cry out to the horse
> on the right and spur him on, and let out the reins with your hands.
> At the turning point, let the left horse approach it tightly
> so that the hub of your fitted wheel seems to reach
> the edge, but stay clear of touching the stone
> for fear you wound your horses and shatter the chariot.
> That will be a joy for others but a disgrace for you yourself
> (23.334–343).

Homer thrives by repeating words, lines, even whole passages, but he triumphs in his silences. Nestor's direct speech permits the poet to forgo description of the turn in the race itself, while the audience hears the wise voice of experience and feels the intensity of the father who has a stake in the race.

Meriones, henchman of Idomeneus, leader of the contingent from Crete, completes the field. He wins in archery with a magnificent shot (23.874–877, 883), but he lacks skill in driving and has the slowest horses (23.530–531). He takes fourth prize, mainly by staying the course (23.614). Homer probably includes him in the contest, as ancient critics surmised (23.351, in Erbse, 425), as a motive for his chieftain's special interest in the race (23.450–451), since, if he were not in the race, he would not be missed. Any of the other entrants—all experienced horsemen—could win: Eumelos, with the best horses, the best track position, and Apollo on his side; Diomedes, "best by far" (23.357), the model warrior with Athena as his protector; Menelaus, the brother of Agamemnon, whose chariot will be pulled by Agamemnon's mare, avidly yearning to run, as well as his own swift horse; or Antilochos, with his youth and Nestor's wise and wily counsel.

The race begins. The horses rush over the sand, away from the sea, with headlong abandon. Up and down lurch the chariots as they bound over the rough course:

362–At the same time, they raised their whips high over the horses
363–and shook them with the reins and cried out
364–eagerly. The horses made their way quickly across the plain
365–far from the ships. Beneath their breasts, dust
366–lifted up, rising like a cloud or storm wind,
367–and their manes flowed out with the blasts of wind.
368–Sometimes, the chariots came near the earth that feeds many,
369–other times they shot up into the air. Their drivers
370–stood in the chariots, and the spirit of each was throbbing
371–as he yearned for victory. Each kept calling out
372–to his horses, and they flew, lifting dust over the plain.

Speed is the thing that counts as man and beast explode from the starting line, and Homer mimics that movement by his frequent use of the run-on line (enjambment), a poetic device that lessens the usual pause between lines and allows closely related words to fall in different lines, leaving the full sense of one line to be completed in the next. Here, six lines (363, 364, 365, 369, 370, 371) of eleven run on to create the impression of speed. Against the expectation of a completed thought in a line of verse, the listener is forced to move forward rapidly with the poet—and the racer.

All make the turn safely. In the final lap of the race, Eumelos is in front but so hotly pursued by Diomedes and his Trojan stallions that:

Now, either they would have passed him or effected a dispute,
had not Phoebus Apollo been angry with Tydeus' son
(23.382–383).

The inference is clear: Diomedes, the supreme warrior, should win or at worst finish in a dead heat with Eumelos, but no sooner is the expectation proffered than it is retracted. Athena intervenes, as the gods often do at such junctures to forestall or alter an event, in this instance, the outcome of the race.

Apollo, who probably would favor Eumelos in any case since he raised Eumelos' horses, has a score to settle with Diomedes. In the great battle fought on the day after Achilles' withdrawal, Diomedes comes very close to mortally offending Apollo's divinity. Athena has temporarily lifted the mist from Diomedes' eyes, and he is able to discern the gods. She also gives him permission to wound Aphrodite should that goddess enter the war (5.131–132). As it turns out, Diomedes wounds Aphrodite's son, Aeneas, and when she moves to protect him, Diomedes grazes her hand with his spear (5.334–337). Aphrodite drops Aeneas and retires, and Apollo throws his hands around Aeneas "lest someone of the Danaans with fast horses / strike him in the chest and take the life spirit from him" (5.345–346). Disregarding Athena's orders and though he sees Apollo, Diomedes does not relent but attacks three times, only to be thrice repulsed. On the verge of a fourth attempt, the god warns him:

> Consider, son of Tydeus, and give way. Do not presume
> to think yourself equal to the gods, since never the same is
> the tribe of immortal gods and men who trod the earth (5.440–442).

Still, Diomedes draws back but a little, avoiding "the wrath of far-darting Apollo" (5.444). His actions risk no ordinary anger but a god's righteous indignation over an insult to his divinity that wreaks destruction upon any and all, innocent and guilty, who are associated with the offending party, here, the Argive army (Muellner, 8). By attempting to equal Apollo, he imperils the cosmic hierarchies that separate immortals and mortals. Diomedes escapes, but the god remembers and sends his brother Ares to stir the Trojans against him.

In the race, Diomedes suffers Apollo's anger only as the loss of his whip, and Athena is there to aid him by returning it and inspiring his horses (23.389–390). Diomedes would win anyway—he is *aristos*. For worse or better, gods attend Diomedes; they enhance his prestige and confirm him a winner. The god who helps him balances the god who hinders him and, with that "magic," his victory reassures order as the poet comes through with the comfort of an established winner winning. After all, a nobody like Eumelos could not be allowed to win, however swift his horses or skilled his touch on the reins. The race, then, reinforces the superiority of the *aretê* of the *aristos* over *aretê* alone.

Out on the back lap, Menelaus still has the lead over Antilochos when the latter sees an opportunity as the road ahead narrows. "Get going, you two," Antilochos cries out to his father's horses, "Stretch out as fast as you can" (23.403). He calls for them to extend their bodies completely, a position reached at top speed in full gallop when the horses' feet leave the ground with each stride. To spur them on, he shames them with a man's embarrassment in being bested by a female and threatens them with the sword and death (23.404–414). The horses hear his tone of voice and run faster for a short time (23.417–418), playing their part in what ensues as the driver will play his. Quickly, Antilochos seizes his opportunity. By trickery rather than speed, he passes Menelaus:

> There was a gully in the ground where winter water had pooled
> and broken out part of the road and hollowed out the whole place.
> Menelaus clung to the road, seeking to avoid driving side-by-side,
> but Antilochos turned aside and guided his ungulate horses

off the road. He swerved a little bit and kept in pursuit.
The son of Atreus was alarmed and cried out to Antilochos:
"Antilochos, you are driving foolishly. Hold up your horses.
The road is narrow. Soon it will be wider for passing.
Be careful not to hit my chariot and destroy us both."
    So he spoke, and Antilochos drove still harder,
urging his horses on with his whip like someone who does not hear.
As far as the distance covered by a discus swung from the shoulders
that a vigorous man throws in testing his youth,
so far did they run. The mares of Atreus' son gave way
and fell behind, since, of his own will, he let up on urging them
for fear the ungulate horses would collide in the road
and overturn the chariots with wickerwork sides, and the men
themselves, pressing hard for victory, fall down in the dust.
Fair-haired Menelaus spoke to him and upbraided him:
"Antilochos, no one else among men is more reckless than you.
Damn you. We Achaeans spoke falsely in saying you have sense.
Yet you will not carry off the prize this way without an oath"
(23.420–441).

While Menelaus continues on the road, Antilochos leaves it and from the side pulls up next to the older man who eschews driving side-by-side. Antilochos must come back on the road to traverse the narrow section. Menelaus yields for fear of a collision. When Antilochos cuts back in, he has free rein to take the lead down the stretch.

With a familiar shift from action to words, Homer leaves Menelaus facing defeat and reduced to profanity and technicalities to turn to the spectators. Things begin innocently enough. The Cretan war lord, Idomeneus, perched high in a lookout, has espied Diomedes and his chestnut stallion out in front. His eyes have scanned the plain of Troy and cannot see Eumelos. Eumelos had been leading into the turn but must, Idomeneus reckons, have encountered disaster there. He calls down to the others for confirmation: "Am I the only one to recognize the horses and discern them, or do you also?" (23.458). Perhaps because of the gray hair of middle age sprinkling Idomeneus' head (13.361) but certainly not because of failings in battle (4.250–260), a younger man, Ajax, son of Oïleus, chooses to taunt the older without provocation:

Idomeneus, why are you ever mouthing off?
The horses with fast-stepping feet have much plain still to cover.
You are not the youngest among the Argives,
nor do your eyes look out from your head most keenly.
Still, you are always mouthing off. You should not be
a loud-mouth, because others are better than you.
The same mares are in front as before,
Eumelos', and he himself is behind them, holding the reins
(23.474–481).

This Ajax, not to be confused with Telamon's son, has trouble controlling his lip, and though he survives Athena's hatred and the war, he perishes, ignominiously drowned at sea on the homeward voyage, after he boasts of surviving the deep against the gods' will (Homer *Odyssey* 4.504–511). He soon receives his comeuppance in the footrace for his abuse of Idomeneus. But, it seems, Idomeneus has been modest about his eyesight. He is proposing a wager on which horses are in front when Achilles steps in:

> Do not any longer exchange harsh words,
> Ajax and Idomeneus, ugly words, since it is not seemly.
> You are offended by another who acts this way.
> Sit now in the gathering, and watch
> the horses of the Argives. The ones who are driving themselves
> for victory will come here. Then each of you will know
> the horses who are second and those who are out in front
> (23.492–498).

The quarrel of an older and younger man returns the listener to the beginning of the story of Achilles' wrath. An old man is walking along the beach toward the ships of the Achaeans. From his robes and the god's woolen ribbons wound around a scepter, he looks to be a priest. Indeed, Apollo's priest Chryses has come with "countless ransom" to redeem his daughter from Agamemnon (1.13). But Agamemnon, a young man, prefers her to his wife at home. Moreover, the girl constitutes a *geras*, a prize given by the army outside of the distribution of booty, that validates his *aretê* and secures his *timê* among the host. He cannot let her go without suffering loss of face. He sends the old man away abusively. The priest stands on the shore where sea and land, divine and human, intermingle, and prays to his god for vengeance. Apollo hears and responds with plague, "and always the fires for the corpses burn thickly" (1.52). Hera, concerned for the Greeks, places the purpose in Achilles' breast to convene an assembly and seek a solution for the plague from the interpreters. Hera could not have sent a less suitable man from among those besieging Troy. Vernant has eloquently captured this Achilles:

> Dedicated from the outset—one might say by nature—to a beautiful death, he goes through life as if he were already suffused with the aura of the posthumous glory that was always his goal. That is why he finds it impossible, in applying the code of honor, to negotiate, to compromise, to yield to circumstances or power relations; craven settlements are, of course, out of the question, but he cannot make even the necessary adjustments without which the system can no longer function. For Achilles every insult is equally intolerable and

unforgivable, no matter where it comes from and however high above him the agent's position on the social scale. Any apology, any honorable offer of compensation (no matter how satisfying to his pride it might seem from its size and public nature) remains empty and ineffective (1991.51).

The story of Achilles' wrath traces this man's journey to the man of the games and beyond to their closure with another redemption, the Trojan king Priam's of his son Hector's body. This man, however, is never far from sight and must be remembered in watching the director of the games. And yet, the Achilles of the games is not the same man, if only because the man of the games no longer enjoys the company of Patroclus. Still, he intervenes again in a quarrel between an older and a younger man, a quarrel like that between Apollo's priest and Agamemnon. His task, the ancient commentators say, is to keep "good order" (23.491, in Erbse, 443), and this he does with his presence and the reasonableness of his request: quarreling is unseemly; wait, and soon you will see.

The race ends abruptly in a cloud of dust from Diomedes' horses' hooves that pelts the driver while his speeding chariot barely skims the beach, leaving scant trace of their passage. First to finish, Diomedes pulls up amid the assembly, springs from his chariot, and, as if to demonstrate the race is over, leans his whip against the yoke. His companion, Sthenelos, claims the prizes (23.499–511). Homer then reproduces the language of pillaging as others *lead away* the woman and *carry off* the tripod that are the victor's prizes (23.512–513). These details suggest how far behind Diomedes has left the other drivers (Richardson, 226). Antilochos and Menelaus arrive. Menelaus has caught up with Antilochos but failed to pass him in time. Clearly, Antilochos' horses are slower, for the poet reminds his listeners that he passed Menelaus "by trickery, not by speed" (23.515). Meriones comes in fourth and leaves with his gold (23.528–529, 614–615). Eumelos was snatched up in the rivalry between Apollo and Athena. The goddess shattered the yoke on his horses who ran off the road. The pole, no longer supported by the yoke, fell to the ground, with the result that the driver was jerked out of the chariot alongside the wheel, suffering cuts and bruises (23.392–397). Now Eumelos limps in, last of all, "dragging his beautiful chariot and driving his horses before him" (23.533). The sight moves Achilles to pity:

On seeing him, brilliant swift-footed Achilles took pity on him,
and, standing up among the Argives, spoke to them with winged words:
"The best man drives his ungulate horses last.

Come, let us give him a prize, as is seemly,
for second place, but let the son of Tydeus carry off first"
(23.534–538).

The ancient commentator explains Achilles' reaction: Eumelos "teaches one to pity those who suffer misfortune in violation of their just deserts and not to allow fortune to triumph over *aretê*" (23.536–537, in Erbse, 450). Eumelos is "the best man" with the best horses in the race, and Achilles moves to correct his misfortune with a prize worthy of his valor. Achilles pities him, but line 534 suggests so much more in that it repeats verbatim Achilles' earlier reaction when he sees Patroclus. Patroclus has witnessed the destruction caused the Greeks by Achilles' withdrawal from the fighting and approaches Achilles concerning it. "Seeing him, swift-footed Achilles took pity on him" (16.5). This repetition of line five of Book 16 infuses the pity at seeing Eumelos with the pity Patroclus stirred in Achilles. Achilles can feel pity again as he did before Patroclus' death robbed him of such feelings (21.100–105).

Antilochos challenges the giving of the second prize to Eumelos, and the episode of the chariot race ends with Achilles' awarding Eumelos a supernumerary prize from his hut, the breastplate he stripped from Asteropaios (23.558–562). Again, Homer speaks a language of pity. Asteropaios confronted Achilles after the river Xanthos had instilled him with courage. Xanthos was angry over the young men that Achilles had slain in battle beside his streams and had not pitied (21.145–147). Now Achilles bestows the armor of a man who perished for unpitied others upon the first man who has stirred him to pity since Patroclus' death. He releases part of his rage at the death of his companion whom he realizes he was obligated to protect (21.135) and recovers a part of himself. Another man will appeal to that pity when Priam asks, "respect the gods, and pity me" (24.503).

It was Antilochos who brought Achilles the message that Patroclus had fallen before Trojan Hector and who remained with him, holding his hands for fear he would end his life "with iron" (18.34). A close companion before Patroclus' death (23.556), he becomes closer during the months before Achilles' death. Homer's audience surely knew that Antilochos would be killed by the Ethiopian king Memnon and avenged by Achilles (Apollodorus *The Library,* Epitome 5.3; Quintus Smyrnaeus *Fall of Troy* 2.244–259). In post-Iliadic tradition, Antilochos reprises Patroclus' role, but Homer's Antilochos brings to mind the Achilles of Book 1.

Antilochos resents the awarding of second prize to Eumelos. It is his. He pleads his case directly and succinctly: I will be angry if you take away my prize; Eumelos should have prayed to the gods; reward him, if you pity him, from the many possessions stored in your hut (23.543–552). His language echoes the taunt aimed at Agamemnon by the common soldier, the ugly and impudent Thersites: "Your huts are filled with gold. In your huts / are many choice women" (2.226–227). Antilochos digs in, prepared for a fight: "I will not yield her. Let someone try / who wishes to fight with me hand-to-hand for her" (23.553–554). He is talking about the prize of a pregnant mare, but Homer's words echo those of Agamemnon in refusing to ransom Chryseis, daughter of Apollo's priest (1.29). Moreover, Homer recalls Achilles' language when he declared he would fight anyone who tried to carry off his possessions against his will (1.300–303). Antilochos is no rabble-rousing Thersites; rather, Homer has him play Achilles, a hot-headed youth. But unlike his model, Antilochus pleads a case before a man who knows what it is like to lose a prize (Eustathius *Commentarii* 4.1315.53–54). A friend of Achilles, he raises a smile from the man, perhaps, as Eustathius thought, because Achilles sees himself in the son of Nestor (4.1315.31–32). Yet Antilochos is trying to carry off one of those possessions that Achilles once would have shed blood to keep but no longer esteems as tokens of his, or any man's, worth (9.401–409). And Antilochos succeeds for that very reason, and for another. When Agamemnon demanded compensation for the loss of Chryseis, there were no available possessions, but Achilles has possessions in abundance. With the breastplate, a prize of greater value than the mare, he circumvents the zero-sum game by giving Eumelos a prize above those set forth for the contest. His solution satisfies Antilochos who remains unaware that it renders the mare a mare, emptying her of symbolic value to represent his worth.

Achilles' only Homeric smile is short-lived as Menelaus, obviously in a rage, gets to his feet and, by requesting the scepter, signals that he is about to deliver a formal speech. He is angry with Antilochos but also saddened, it seems, that someone he esteemed would do this to him (23.566–567). "One senses that their former friendship and Menelaus' admiration for Antilokhos' qualities . . . made the situation even more distressing for him" (Richardson 230). Menelaus chastises Antilochos:

Antilochos, prudent before, look at what you have done.
You have brought shame upon my valor and thwarted my horses
by throwing yours in front of them, though yours are inferior by far.

> But come, leaders and counselors of the Argives,
> judge this for us both impartially and without favor for either,
> so that no man of the Achaeans armored in bronze may say:
> "Menelaus, after coercing Antilochos with falsehoods,
> goes off, leading the mare, even if his horses were far inferior,
> but he himself is greater in valor and in force."
> If I myself shall offer judgment, I say that no other
> of the Danaans will gainsay it for it will be straight.
> Antilochos, come now, beloved of Zeus, as is meet and right,
> stand before your horses and chariot, but take the slender whip
> in your hands with which you drove them before,
> and touching your horses, swear by him who holds and shakes the
> earth that you did not bind my chariot by means of deceit
> (23.570–585).

Menelaus shares with Achilles the precedence of *aretê* and believes
that he has been shamed. He bemoans Antilochos' departure from his
prudent good sense, evidently not appreciating the subtleties of *mêtis*
in overcoming the handicap of inferior horses. He calls upon Antilochos
to swear an oath that he did not willfully use deceit to hinder his chariot.

Antilochos now finds himself facing a different man, one of stature
but a touchy Atreid like his brother, Agamemnon. Antilochos, however,
is not the hot-headed Achilles; he is the son of Nestor, and, forthwith
and gracefully, he begins to backpedal by opening with a colloquialism
intended to shift the tone:

> Hold on now. I am much younger than
> you, lord Menelaus, and you are before me in place and in valor.
> You know what transgressions come to rise in a young man.
> His intelligence is impetuous and his ingenuity lightheaded
> (23.587–590).

Antilochos, whose agility Menelaus valued in the fighting (15.569–570),
excuses his actions as those of an impulsive young man. He claims no
disrespect was intended toward his elder and greater. He capitulates in
regard to his intelligence, specifically deprecating his *mêtis* as "light" or
"unsteady." And although he still refers to the mare as his own, "the
one I won," he offers to give her to Menelaus (23.591–592). He would
give anything Menelaus wanted from him, he avers, "rather than for
all my days, beloved of Zeus, / fall from your favor and be culpable
before the gods" (23.594–595). In avowing his unhesitating generosity,
Antilochos skirts around the notion of culpability toward the gods. He
could not very well swear an oath that he did not use deceit in passing
Menelaus, for he pretended not to hear the older man's cries of fear
and exasperation (23.430). By giving back "his" mare, he dodges the

oath, which would, if taken, not only have perjured him but exposed him to divine retribution.

Menelaus is overwhelmed with gratitude by the younger man's respect and concession and lets Antilochos keep the horse, "though she is mine" (23.610), but with a stern reprimand not to repeat such behavior. Nevertheless, Menelaus is fully aware how much Nestor and his sons have suffered and labored for him (23.607–608). *Aretê* aside, the husband of Helen of Troy can never be free of responsibility for the Trojan War. He cannot defend himself in the end before those who have toiled for their own honor to his benefit.

Antilochos hands the mare over to his companion, Noëmon, a name as pregnant with meaning as the mare with her foal. Noëmon, a name based on *noêma* (purpose, understanding) and derived ultimately from the verb for "discerning with the eye" and "thinking," provokes the listener to suspect that the son of wily Nestor has bamboozled the pompous son of Atreus. But their exchange has implications that go beyond the encounter between the players. "The competition . . . suddenly shifted from deciding who is the fastest to determining who is the most fair-minded. . . . Doing and saying the right thing have suddenly become far more important than the actual prize for the race" (Kitchell, 169). The lesson here is for Homer's ancient audiences, men for whom, in the heat of competition, the prize often overshadowed what was right.

The fifth prize laid out by Achilles, an unfired cauldron with handles, remains. Achilles picks it up and carries it through the large assembly of Achaeans to give it to Nestor:

> Here, now, take this, old man, and let it be a treasure
> laid away for you in memory of the funeral of Patroclus.
> You will no longer see him among the Argives. I give this
> prize to you for the same reason. You will not box or wrestle
> or enter the contest in spear throwing or run in the footrace,
> for harsh old age is already pressing upon you (23.618–623).

Neither Patroclus nor Nestor will appear again in the ranks of competitors for prizes. In memory of his companion, Achilles presents the jar, a gesture meant to recognize Nestor's worth as an old man, for old men in this society speak with wisdom, and none is older or wiser than Nestor (1.250–252). But this gift may serve another purpose as well. Achilles has never apologized to Nestor for ignoring his advice during the quarrel between Achilles and Agamemnon (1.277–279). Indeed, in the world of Homer's warriors, there can be no apology that admits wrong on the part of the doer, since that would entail an irreparable loss of face (Dodds, 18). Yet Achilles can, and does, use prizes to show respect and convey honor, even if they hold no such meaning for him. There is in his thoughtfulness an honesty and sincerity that someone like Nestor's glib son lacks for all his attempts to convey respect. Achilles has become what he will again prove to be in telling Priam the story of Niobe (24.602–613), a wise elder, for only wise men of years and experience tell *mythoi* in Homer's world.

For his part, Nestor acknowledges that his athletic days are over and laments those times when, young and strong, he "stood out among the heroes" (23.645) and "[t]here was no man like me" (23.632). He accepts Achilles' gift with joy and gratitude:

> I accept this gratefully, and my heart rejoices that you are always
> mindful of me as a friend, and do not forget the honor with which
> it is fitting that I be honored among the Achaeans.
> May the gods give you what satisfies your heart in return for this
> (23.647–650).

The narrative of the most important contest thus closes with the honeyed words of a favored character recounting his own *ainos* (tale, tale of praise). With his concessionary tale of praise (23.795), Antilochos persuades Achilles to add a half-measure of gold to the half set forth as third prize (23.796). Nestor and his son have done well, as may be expected from men who have the knack of telling *ainoi*.

Achilles next sets out the prizes for "painful boxing," a jenny for the winner and a two-handled goblet for the loser (23.654–656). Epeios, "a good and huge man" (23.664), stands up and, placing his hand upon the female donkey, declares that his opponent had better be content with the goblet, since he is the best—intimations, so to speak, of John L. Sullivan's boast, "My name's John L. Sullivan, and I can lick any son of a — here!" (Dibble, 209), and every other boxer's predictions of doom for his hapless opponent. Curiously, Epeios belittles his prowess as a warrior: "Am I not lacking something in fighting? There was no way / for a man to be master of every enterprise" (23.670–671). Perhaps Epeios is content with being a carpenter rather than a warrior. It is he who will later build the Trojan horse (*Ody*ssey 8.492–493; 11.523). On the other hand, Homer may be reflecting the reality that boxing skills were of little value in combats between men encased in helmets and breastplates, as well as the tensions, noted earlier, between athletics and the military.

Epeios' boasts that he "will bash his [opponent's] body and bust his bones" (23.673) silence the assembly. Euryalos stands up; he is

Diomedes' cousin, which explains the latter's interest in his winning and his words of encouragement. An ancient scholar noted that "The poet knows the pep talks of trainers" (23.681–682a, in Erbse, 472). Epeios supports his boasts with an uppercut to Euryalos' jaw, and then:

> Not for long did
> Euryalos stand, for his shining limbs collapsed on the spot.
> As when a fish leaps up from under water stirred by the north wind
> along the shore covered in weeds, and the black wave covers it over
> again, so he leaped up when struck, but great-hearted Epeios
> caught him in his arms and set him up straight (23.690–695).

Epeios' sportsmanship holds "none of that contempt for the defeated that the Greeks are supposed to have felt" (Dickie, 15). On the other hand, Epeios may well exemplify how a victor should act.

The third contest, wrestling, takes the form of a confrontation between two great warriors, the *aristoi* Ajax, son of Telamon, and Odysseus. Both have immense physical strength, but Odysseus possesses cleverness as well, so the conflict becomes one between *bia* (bodily force) and *mêtis*. Ajax participates in three contests and is bested in all, although Achilles pronounces the first, this wrestling match, a draw. Good at everything, Ajax excels in nothing. The audience for whom Homer may have intended his poem cannot listen to the wrestling match against Odysseus without thinking of the contest both will soon wage for the weapons of the dead Achilles. Failing again, Ajax will go mad and kill himself (Apollodorus *The Library*, Epitome 5.6–7).

"They girded themselves and walked into the middle of the assembly" (23.710). The rhetor and historian Dionysius of Halicarnassus (first century) understands from this line that Odysseus and Ajax wear a loincloth while competing (*Roman Antiquities* 7.72.3). Cyrus H. Gordon (1950–1951) suggests that they donned a belt for belt wrestling, a popular activity in the Mediterranean (Poliakoff 1987, 31–33). The boxers are said to gird themselves in language (23.685) that is nearly identical to that used of wrestlers (23.710). Homer does not distinguish between a loincloth for the boxers who do not wrestle and a specialized belt for the wrestlers that was sufficiently strong to be seized and twisted. The girdle is the same for both pairs of athletes and was intended for covering and protection.

The two men wrestle from the standing position; to win, one must throw the other to the ground and remain standing. In the opening, they probe one another for weakness and to gain leverage:

They grappled each other in the bend of each other's arms with their
stout hands as when rafters that the renowned carpenter has interlocked
in a lofty house ward off the strength of the winds.
Their backs cracked as they were constantly wrenched
beneath their bold hands (23.711–715).

Their jostling comes to naught, and Ajax proposes a solution: "Brilliant
son of Laertes, much-devising Odysseus, / either pick me up, or I pick
you up. All else will be in the care of Zeus" (23.723–724). Ajax tries to
lift Odysseus who brings them both to the ground by craftily knocking
Ajax's knee out from under him with his foot. Odysseus then attempts
to raise Ajax off the ground but without much success. He trips Ajax's
foot again, but both fall, this time side-by-side. Although they are
prepared to continue, Achilles stops the match and bids them take "equal
prizes" (23.735–736). Richardson proposes a sensible reading of this:
"Akhilleus does not want to see Odysseus the victor by guile" (246).

The footrace again illustrates the cleverness of Odysseus who is
introduced with the formulaic epithet, "of much *mêtis*" (23.755). He
runs against Oïleus' son, Ajax, who could fly like no one else in running
down a panicked enemy (14.520–522), and Antilochos who always
defeated the young men in running (23.756). The footrace is reminiscent
of the chariot race. The leaders, Ajax and Odysseus, jump off to a fast
start and run very close to one another until the back lap, a narrative
ploy that allows the lead to change suddenly. The return lap is ending
when Odysseus prays silently to Athena. The goddess has aided and
protected him before (e.g., 2.169–181; 5.674–676). Now she quickens
his limbs (23.772) and when they are about to sprint for the prize, she
makes Ajax slip and fall on dung from the sacrifices for Patroclus; he
ends up with his nose and mouth full of dung (23.773–777). Ajax
receives just retribution for the insults he hurled at Idomeneus. "The
goddess thwarted my feet, she who ever before / like a mother stands
by Odysseus and helps him" (23.782–783), he complains, only adding
to the mirth the Achaeans feel at his distasteful rout. The *aristos* with a
god's aid defeats the swifter man. Antilochos, who finishes third behind
the older men, remarks how "the immortals still honor elder men"
(23.788). Odysseus, he says, is a "spry old man" whom the Achaeans,
except for Achilles, of course, would be hard-pressed to keep up with.

Most listeners would agree that Telamonian Ajax gets the worst in
the wrestling match, for despite Achilles' awarding of equal prizes, he
is twice toppled by Odysseus. He now stands to contest in armor against
Diomedes. Ajax is a defensive fighter, invaluable to the Greek effort
against the Trojans and instrumental in securing the safety of many of

his fellow warriors. He attacks simply, straight against Diomedes' shield with his spear. It penetrates the shield but does not reach Diomedes' vitals, the measure of success that would have brought him Achilles' prize, Asteropaios' "silver-studded sword, a beautiful Thracian thing" (23.805–808). But Diomedes goes for a "dirtier" but cleverer tactic, reaching over the shield and into the neck, a technique suggestive of the hoplite's approach (23.818–819, in Erbse, 493). The horrified Achaeans stop the contest, bidding the two men "carry off equal prizes" (23.823). Homer leaves undecided how the weapons Patroclus stripped from Sarpedon were divided, but Achilles presents Diomedes with Asteropaios' sword. To all appearances, Ajax has lost.

In the next contest, Ajax outstrips the first three contestants in throwing a lump of iron. Then, Polypoites comes from nowhere—his is not a common name in the ranks—and hurls the iron not only farther than Ajax but even outside the area set aside for throwing (23.836–847). Achaeans shout, and "the companions of strong Polypoites stood up / and carried the prize to the warlord's hollow ships" (23.848–849). Homer seems to suggest in the speed with which Polypoites' comrades seize the iron away the rapidity and finality of Ajax's defeat.

Teukros and Meriones set up to shoot an arrow at a pigeon tied to a ship's mast by a cord. Teukros wins the draw and lets fly his arrow in haste. He misses the bird but cuts clean through the tether. The bird soars up to the clouds where she circles. Meriones seizes the bow from Teukros' hands, nocks his arrow, and strikes the bird beneath her wing:

and the shaft went straight through her and again impaled itself
in the earth at Meriones' foot. But the bird,
coming to rest on the mast of the dark-prowed ship,
let her neck fall, and her thick wings drooped.
The spirit quickly fled from her limbs, and far from the mast,
        she fell. The people stared and wondered (23.876–881).

Meriones takes first prize, ten double axes, because he killed the bird. Hitting the tethering cord may be the more difficult shot, but the contest is modeled on the hunt. Teukros must settle for second, a fate he holds in common with his half-brother, Ajax, son of Telamon. The pigeon shoot itself seems out of place in the pantheon of games for Patroclus, but together with the armor fight, it probably represents the kind of contest that would appeal to warriors and their admirers in Homer's audience.

Achilles then presents the prizes for the spear throw, a long spear and a very beautiful cauldron decorated with flower designs. When

Agamemnon stands, however, Achilles concedes the lord's supremacy over all without his having to compete:

> Son of Atreus, we know how much you surpass all others,
> and how much you are the best in power and in throwing.
> Well, take this prize, and go to your hollow ships,
> but let us give the spear to the warrior Meriones
> if you agree in your spirit, for I urge you so (23.890–894).

Achilles grants Agamemnon that he is *aristos* in power, alluding to his supremacy in the Greek army as well as to his prowess with a spear. Behind Achilles now is the once angry and disillusioned challenge to Agamemnon's authority or his own resentment over the lord's gathering of booty without having to fight (1.163–168). Achilles has secured his *kalos thanatos*, his beautiful death, the refuge from all that would trespass upon his glory; he need only wait. The quarrel is ended and the games conclude when, in a tacit acknowledgment of the wrong done Achilles, Agamemnon gives the prizes, the spear to Meriones and the cauldron to Talthybios, immediately redistributing the wealth as befits the foremost leader of warriors.

Alkinoös' Contests for Odysseus

In the *Odyssey*, Laodamas, the son of King Alkinoös, Odysseus' host among the Phaeacians, challenges Odysseus to join in the games that Alkinoös calls for as a demonstration of "how much we surpass others / in boxing and wrestling and leaping and in speed of foot" (8.102–103). When Odysseus first appears among the Phaeacians before the hearth with Athena's aid, Alkinoös raises him from the ashes and, dislodging his son, inappropriately seats him in his son's chair (7.168–171). On the next day, Laodamas, who is supposed to protect his father's guest, exposes him, perhaps out of pique, to embarrassment by challenging him to join in the games:

> Come now, you also, father stranger, make trial of the contests,
> if you have skill in any. You seem to know contests,
> for no glory is greater for a man while he is alive
> than what he accomplishes with his feet and his hands.
> So come, try them, and scatter those cares from your spirit
> (8.145–149).

Odysseus demurs. He cannot understand why Laodamas wants to make fun of him, since he has more on his mind than games, namely, past hardships and the need for transportation home. But the Phaeacian Euryalos judges Odysseus' reluctance to be no more than an excuse to conceal Odysseus' identity as a pirate and man of trade:

> Stranger, I do not have you as a man learned in contests
> of the sort that are found everywhere among men,
> but as a man who haunts the sea in a ship of many oar locks,
> the captain of sailors who hustle others,
> with his mind on freight and watchful of payloads
> and covetous of profits. You do not look like a man of contests
> (8.159–164).

With the charge that Odysseus resembles a pirate, adventurer, and sharpster, Euryalos has thrown down the gauntlet. At stake is a ship homeward or confinement on an island among xenophobic strangers who worship Poseidon, the god most angered at Odysseus, and people ignorant of the suffering that makes a human being a man. At the break of this day, Athena had prepared him, for she knew he would face "the many contests / with which the Phaeacians would test Odysseus" (8.22–23). He now must rise to the challenge because, amid the pleasantries of the Phaeacians, there has always been the implied test of his worthiness. Does he merit transportation across the sea by these seamen gifted by Poseidon, god of the sea, with "ships as swift as a bird on the wing or a thought?" (7.36). Odysseus acknowledges, "I am not without skill in games, / as you say, but I think that I have been among the foremost / as long as I have confidence in my vigor and hands" (8.179–181). Then, with crushing superiority in throwing a heavier discus farther than his competitors do a lighter stone, he demonstrates his skill. He boasts that he will reach another mark still farther out if a Phaeacian should match this throw. He is now incensed, ready to take on all—in boxing, wrestling, or running—all except Laodamas: "He is my host, and who would fight with someone to whom he is obligated?" (8.208). Odysseus passes the test, leaving Alkinoös no choice but to disclose:

> We are not outstanding boxers or wrestlers,
> but we run swiftly and are best at ships
> and always dear to us are feasts and the lyre and dances and
> changes of clothing and hot baths and beds (8.246–249).

For Gardiner, this "delightful" passage has value because it shows "that Homer regards sports as a natural part of everyday life" (1980,

19). The Phaeacians' games, like all games in Homer, manifest "the true spirit of sport, the joy in the contest" (1980, 27). But do they? Though "impromptu" and without prizes, these games are not played for pleasure. They are motivated first by a desire to impress Odysseus and distract him from his grief and then by resentment and a wish to embarrass him. Athletics here serve Homer as a means of proving his hero worthy of Poseidon's seamen. Odysseus is no tradesman but an aristocrat whose life has enabled him to learn the discus and other athletic activities. He must prove through athletics that he is such a man and therefore a guest deserving of treatment as an equal, someone to whom gifts can be given in the expectation that the obligations to repay imposed by the gift and the ties created by the gift have been negotiated with an equal.

Homer's games tell us that chariot races, boxing, wrestling, footraces, and discus and spear throwing belong to the panoply of athletics throughout Greek history, and that these activities occupied the men of the eighth century, the time when Homer composed the poem known today as the *Iliad*. They imply that Homer's audience knew the rules and the conditions for each event, since the poet does not explain a turning post or how to win in boxing or wrestling. The games reflect ways of imaging the world, such as the contrast between *bia* and *mêtis* and *aristos* and commoner that pervade Greek culture in all its aspects. But, in the end, Patroclus' and the games of the Phaeacians belong to the epic.

2.
Early Olympia

Ancient Olympia lay in a spacious, verdant valley in the western Peloponnesian district of Elis. Wild olive and pine trees speckled the fertile soil that supported wheat fields and vineyards. Low hills embraced the valley; the mountains of Arcadia towered over its eastern horizon. The Altis, the sacred precinct, was enclosed on the south by the Alpheios, "a large and very pleasant river" (Pausanias 5.7.1), and bordered on the north by the Hill of Cronus, low, steep, and wooded with pines and shrubs. On the west, the Kladeos River flowed southward to its nearby confluence with the Alpheios. "The whole aspect of the scene, without being grand or impressive, is rich, peaceful, and pleasing" (Frazer, 3: 482; Map1).

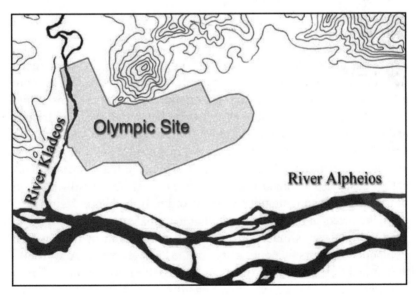

Map 1. Early Olympia

Such a description does not, of course, tell the whole story. By contrast, when the neighboring peoples gathered in the Altis at Olympia, they sweltered in the heat of high summer (Epictetus *Discourses* 1.6.26) and suffered under the swarms of flies spawned by its low marshes. With no end of prayers to Zeus as the Averter of Flies, they appealed to the god to drive them out of his sanctuary (Pausanias 5.14.1). But they came to the god's chosen place for the same reasons that brought other peoples to the banks of their rivers. The synergy of natural landscape, piety toward the god who had made his presence known, and attraction among people for their kind had marginalized the setting, separating it from profane space and moving it toward the divine. Mortals, those condemned to death, communicated there with undying Zeus Olympios. In turn, the physical and religious settings inspired visitors to impose social, political, mythological, and athletic values upon the Altis and its environs. Oldest of the Panhellenic shrines, Olympia was the first to provide a sacred place for athletic contests. It is the design of this chapter to investigate the Olympia of the eighth and seventh centuries, its implications for Greek culture, and the earliest athletic events conducted there, in order to appreciate more fully the birthplace of the Olympic Games.

Geographical Setting

The first archaeologists at Olympia discovered a dark substratum deep beneath the Altis that covered a large portion of the precinct's northern third. The substratum, probably a dump site for one or more altars, consisted of charcoal and bones and, among other items dating from the tenth to the eighth centuries, broken and dismantled tripods and thousands of shattered offerings in terra-cotta and bronze depicting animals and men. Terra-cotta figurines of Zeus that date to the tenth century confirm the presence of a cult of Zeus at the sanctuary. This early Zeus was worshiped as a god of the weather, specifically, the god of the rain, wind, and thunder, who, accordingly, had his cult sites near or on the peaks of mountains and other marginal areas open to the sky.

Olympia was situated in remote Elis, a region in the western Peloponnesus sparsely populated from the Protogeometric Age (1050–900) into the eighth century (Morgan, 26–28). Removed from the forces that elsewhere in Greece were uniting villages and small communities with a capital city to form *poleis*, Olympia remained free of outside control throughout most of the eighth century, but because it lay near routes of travel, it was readily reached by individuals. During this time, piety and pilgrimage were matters of individual, not state, concern (Snodgrass 1980, 57). The combination of religious sanctity, political independence, and accessibility allowed the shrine to serve as a center where chieftains and others of the elite from the west could gather to exchange information and renew ancestral family ties, assert their status, exercise rivalries, offer sacrifice, and compete for prestige through the splendor and expense of their offerings to the god (Morgan, 28–29).

This conspicuous consumption of wealth helps explain a peculiarity of the archaeological record at Olympia, namely, the near absence of pottery in the substratum in favor of metal, bronze, and iron (Morgan, 28–29). Metal commanded respect by virtue of its expense and the labor and skill required to work it. Small figurines of animals were cast at the shrine by itinerant craftsmen who came for the festival of Zeus Olympios. Iron tripods, too elaborate to be fabricated during the festival, were likely brought to the shrine as offerings. These activities imply that the shrine had an altar and some means of storing and protecting the votive offerings. On the other hand, as a sanctuary free of control by any one city, Olympia did not participate in the building programs of the eighth century when emerging *poleis* asserted their selfhood and the inviolability of their territory by erecting temples. At this stage in their development, *poleis* had nothing to gain by investing their resources to glorify a sanctuary that was not under their sway and catered to social and religious needs of those beyond their borders.

In the last quarter of the eighth century, activity at Olympia increased. More elaborate votives were offered from a wider geographical area that evidenced more complex craftsmanship and greater expenditure of materials and labor (Morgan, 30). More people, from more widely spread communities, visited the sanctuary. At the same time, the population of Elis began to recover from the dramatic decline of the previous centuries. Settlements were concentrated in the valleys of the Alpheios River in the south and the Pheneios in the north. Although ceramic evidence suggests the local Eleans used the shrine for sacrifices year-round (Pausanias 5.13.10; Morgan, 55–56), the history of the Olympic Games indicates that Eleans in the north controlled the sanctuary. By the end of the eighth century, however, the participation of western cities in the sanctuary had been augmented by the involvement of the elite from other Greek states, and the role of Olympia as a Panhellenic meeting ground had been established forever.

The festival at Olympia may have begun as an annual celebration, perhaps of one or two days and been held, like later festivals, in the high summer after the solstice. If so, the time of the festival, falling during the lull in agricultural activity that followed the grain harvest, reveals what appears a deliberate attempt to avoid periods of intense agricultural work (Morgan, 41). Farmers, released momentarily from the toil of the farm, could journey to the sanctuary, by ship if they desired, since the seas were best for sailing in the heat of the summer (Hesiod *Works and Days* 663–668). Consequently, Olympia could not have been an agricultural festival; its games did not celebrate a new harvest. Celebrants might have competed at earliest times in the range of athletics described in epic and practiced at the funerals of historical men (Roller), but the fact is that no archaeological evidence testifies to contests at Olympia in the early eighth century. None should be expected: the transient use of the sanctuary for the festival precluded the construction of a stadium or other facility from durable, expensive materials.

Throughout its history, Olympia confronted its visitors with a hot and thirsty setting for their celebrations. A modern visitor remarks: "The heat is massed in Olympia as if it came from the force of all the bodies that ever existed" (Storace, 58). Parched mouths and sweating brows seek water, and as more celebrants arrived at the sanctuary, more water was needed. The Eleans began digging temporary unlined wells. About two hundred wells have been discovered. Of these, none lies in the west, that is, in the vicinity of the Altis, and only nine date from the end of the eighth century. The wells are concentrated in the area of the stadium, built later, and their placement on the eastern portion of the sanctuary shows that the cult of Zeus predates the contests and that the contests themselves date from the end of the eighth century (Mallwitz 1988, 96–101). The wells evidently supplied water for athletes and spectators. An increase in the number of wells should reflect an increase in demand caused by an increase in attendance at the contests. It is not surprising, then, that the wells are most numerous after the Persian War (480–479) when the shrine blossomed with the construction of the Temple of Zeus (ca. 468) and the expansion of the stadium. The earliest wells, on the other hand, were dug toward the end of the eighth century when the Eleans began offering prizes for the *diaulos* (724), the *dolichos* or long race (720), the pentathlon and wrestling (708), boxing (688), and four-horse chariot races (680) (Pausanias 5.8.6–7). The accuracy of these dates aside for the moment, the fact that they cluster near the end of the eighth century, taken in conjunction with the innovation of wells, indicates that more people were coming to Olympia to participate in, and watch, the games. Moreover, the wells, clustered away from the Altis and its altar of Zeus, demarcate a separation of the athletic events from the religious, a separation of nearly two hundred meters. Alfred Mallwitz concludes, "we cannot doubt that in Olympia the Games did not begin until about 700, but that the cult is considerably older, as shown by the finds dating back to the Protogeometric period" (1988, 99).

Religious Setting

When Pausanias (second century C.E.) visited Olympia and wrote about what he saw in the Altis, the grove was resplendent in a garb of temples, numerous altars of gods and heroes, and nearly countless statues of gods and athletes, but in the eighth century, he would have seen little more than altars. Excavators have found nothing dating from the Mycenaean period in the Altis. As a northern god, Zeus came to Olympia with the Eleans in the early tenth century when they emigrated from Aetolia into the Peloponnesus (Jeffery, 167). The epithet Olympios implies that Zeus was associated with Mount Olympus in Thessaly. From the tenth century, in any event, the god received the offerings of devotees among the trees of the Altis. The setting befit the early Zeus who was worshiped at Dodona in Epirus as Zeus in the Trees, an oracular god who lived in trees and spoke through their rustling leaves (Farnell,1:39). Indeed, Zeus had an oracle at Olympia that athletes and visitors surely consulted concerning the contests (Strabo *Geography* 8.3.30; Pindar *Olympian Ode* 8.1–2; Hönle, 16–17). But his powers are more evident in his care of the wind, rain, and thunderbolt in which the god descended to claim Olympia as his own. The remains of dedications prove cult activity which must have included sacrifices to Zeus at his altar and to any other deities whose altars or shrines stood in the Altis. Themis, Gaia, and Hera are most often mentioned (Drees, 13–16).

"Within the Altis is also a precinct dedicated to Pelops. Pelops is honored by the Eleans above the heroes in Olympia as much as Zeus is above the other gods" (Pausanias 5.13.1). The Pelopion stood north of the Temple of Zeus Olympios in the Altis of the early fourth century. It was surrounded by a pentagonal wall of ashlar construction and enclosed within were trees and statues. The Eleans worshiped Pelops as a hero, a mortal man who they believed retained the power after his death to aid or harm them. Consequently, they had to sacrifice to him at his grave, where the hero's potency was strongest, or risk his fury. Because Pelops was dead, they approached him as a chthonic deity, upholding the strict separation of the realm of chthonic gods and heroes who belong to the earth from that of Olympian gods who dwell in the ether of Mount Olympus.

As long as scholars followed Martin P. Nilsson's 1927 analysis (584–615) and regarded hero cults as a continuation of Mycenaean cults of the dead, the fourth-century Pelopion was considered a descendant of a Mycenaean mound and the grave site that held Pelops' bones. No bones were found, but what was discovered proved far more damning for a Mycenaean origin. The northern half of the Pelopeion rests upon the black stratum. Pious Greeks could never have spread the remains of altars over an ancient site revered for generations upon generations (Mallwitz 1988, 85–87). Mallwitz affirms that "there was no such cult place" (87) in the late eighth century. Pelops must have arrived at Olympia during the seventh century or even later. Greeks had turned to the worship of heroes during the eighth century. Hero cults proliferated with the growing popularity of epic poetry whose poets depicted a world of men stronger and braver than the men who heard their songs. These lesser mortals prized the prestige of having a Homeric warrior as an ancestor (Burkert 1985, 204). Hero cults bound citizens together politically through rituals performed for a communal ancestor that promoted the interests of the *polis* over those of its families of *aristoi*. An independent sanctuary like Olympia did not need a hero cult for the reasons that prompted leaders of *poleis* to encourage such cults among their citizens. Olympia in the early seventh century, however, had become something worth fighting for, and during its struggles, Pelops entered as a figure of compromise between rivals as religion among the Greeks served as a tool for political ends.

Setting Worth Fighting For

Pheidon, hereditary king of Argos, wrested control of his *polis* from the Argive aristocracy by relying upon hoplites, a strategy that apparently led Aristotle (384–322) to deem him a tyrant (*Politics* 1310b 27-29). He won control over most of the northeastern Peloponnesus (Wade-Gery, 539–543; Andrews, 31–42). The sources agree that Pheidon seized Olympia, expelled the Eleans, and presided over the games (Herodotus

Histories 6.127.3; Strabo *Geography* 8.3.33; Pausanias 6.22.1–2). Strabo (64 B.C.E.–21 C.E.) and Pausanias place him about 748, while Herodotus (fifth century) dates him around 600–570. Herodotus' chronology is clearly too late, since Argive dominance of Greece occurred in the seventh century (Jeffery, 134–136; Coldstream, 154), and the mid-eighth century too early for games at Olympia. In 669, the Argives crushed a force of invading Spartans at Hysiai in the southern Argolid (Pausanias 2.24.8). Seeing Pheidon's hand in this victory, scholars have accepted an emendation that changes Pausanias' eighth Olympiad[1] to the twenty-eighth (Burn 1960, 177–179, especially 178 n. 11; Coldstream, 154–156). Pheidon's intervention in Olympia thus falls in 668 when, with the Spartans defeated, he was free to answer the call of the Pisatans through whom he could claim Olympia, a worthy addition to his holdings and a foothold in the western Peloponnesus.

Pindar refers interchangeably to Olympia and Pisa in his victory odes, implying that Pisa was sufficiently near the sanctuary to be synonymous with it. Pisa may have been the name of a spring (Strabo *Geography* 8.3.31) or a city that has disappeared. Although Pindar calls the mythic king Oinomaos and his daughter, Hippodameia, Pisatans (*Olympian Ode* 1.70), he never refers to contemporary Pisatans or speaks of their earlier differences with the Eleans over Olympia. Pisatans do not appear in the sources until the fourth century when the Arcadians occupied Olympia and wanted to celebrate the games "with the Pisatans who, they say, were first to be in charge of the sanctuary" (Xenophon *Hellenica* 7.4.28). The struggle for Olympia between Eleans of the Peneios River Valley and those living in the Alpheios Valley was, it would seem, related later as a conflict between Eleans and Pisatans.

According to Strabo, "after the twenty-sixth Olympiad [676], the Pisatans, receiving back their homeland, began celebrating the Olympic Games when they saw that the contest was held in esteem. But in later times, Pisatis succumbed to the Eleans, and the presidency of the games again fell to them" (*Geography* 8.3.30). Eusebius (260–340 C.E.) has the Pisatans holding the games of the twenty-eighth (668) and the thirtieth (660) Olympiads, from which time they presided for the next twenty-two Olympiads (*Chronicles,* in Schoene, 1:197). Pausanias reports that the Pisatans, led by King Pantaleon, seized control of the twenty-eighth and thirty-fourth (644) Olympiads. Disputes over the sanctuary

---

1 The term Olympiad is used as the name for a festival, the tenth Olympiad, for example, and for a period of four years, the year of the festival and the three successive years. With the fifth year, a new Olympiad, the eleventh, begins.

continued with Pantaleon's sons, Damophon and Pyrrhos, under whom the Pisatans took up arms against the Eleans and were annihilated. Pausanias' account reflects Elean sources which, not surprisingly, deny that the Pisatans ever possessed the games for the length of time maintained by Strabo and Eusebius.

H. T. Wade-Gery (546) proposes that Pantaleon and his sons, supported by the powerful Corinthian tyrant, Kypselos, championed the Eleans living near Olympia against rival Eleans from the north. Those nearest the sanctuary perhaps resented the fact that others living far off possessed this gem in their neighborhood. Struggle for dominance began when Pheidon and his Argive hoplites, a foreign power, sought to break the chains of tradition and allow the local Eleans to assume the presidency. Under their tenure, Hera and Pelops were imported as a means of asserting their presence through the establishment of new deities. The black substratum, then, bears witness to a reorganization of the Altis when an existing ashen altar of Zeus and altars of other gods were demolished to make way for the introduction of the cults and their sites for Hera and Pelops (Mallwitz 1988, 102–103). Promotion of Hera culminated in the construction of her temple in the early sixth century. For the games of the fiftieth Olympic festival (580), the Eleans replaced the single president with "two men selected by lot from all the Eleans" (Pausanias 5.9.4; Harpokration on *Hellanodikai,* in Keaney, 91–92). The struggle for the sanctuary among the Eleans ended in a joint presidency whose makeup was left to the lot, the voice of the gods.

Mythic Setting

Greeks learned the myths of their gods and heroes early in life and throughout their lives told them and heard them being told in manifold forms and variations. Their myths contained a common body of knowledge that helped form them as Greeks as opposed to gods, animals, or foreigners, and as Argives as opposed, for example, to Athenians or Corinthians. Myths defined a group of people as a community and provided a verbal discourse with which its members spoke through the past about the present. Although myths belonged to every Greek, they were told in formal situations by poets and political leaders. More than most, these men knew the normative codes of their society and used myths to express the opinions, beliefs, prejudices, and principles held by the majority. As long as a particular story obtained the desired effects from its listeners, a mythmaker—a tragedian entertaining and instructing his audience, a statesman appealing to his fellow citizens, or, in the day-to-day world, a mother cautioning her child—would tell it. As a story was repeated, its beginnings were lost in time, and it became a traditional tale, one that had always been told. Its power to move an audience, however, did not lie in its longevity or in the plot of the story itself but in the listeners' responses to it. Within the dynamic of Greek culture as a system, mythmakers and audiences as senders and receivers, respectively, of messages communicated truths about that system through tales. As long as a myth served in this dialogue to organize, explain, and mitigate experience, making order out of chaos, it was told. Greeks, knowingly or unknowingly, confronted problems and flaws in their culture and faced the existential variables of birth, coming of age, and death, in part, by telling myths. Myths, in turn, came at them with other worlds lived by beings that were superior versions of themselves, creations of the same culture that produced audiences, mythmakers, and the needs addressed by myths. In this way, Greek myths both defined and defended Greek culture against disorder and the forces of entropy (Tyrrell and Brown, 8–11).

Myths account for the world by rooting the present onto the formative past through words that name a place or custom and its founding god or hero and by relating the events that changed the place or invented the custom (Dowden, 74–89). By the same token, mythmakers tell myths to use the power of words to form the world of the past as they and their audience would have it. This mythic past consists of events that occurred *in illo tempore*, in that time of first beginnings when the cosmos or some aspect of the cosmos was being created by a god or a hero. Contestants at the Olympic Games, for example, are called athletes after Aethlios who founded the games as a means for testing his sons (Eusebius *Chronicles,* in Schoene, 1:192). As a mythic setting, Olympia is overdetermined, having a superabundance of conflicting and competing foundation myths. Long before men came to Olympia, gods and heroes had competed there, sanctioning Olympia as a place for games. When men held their own games, they did so in imitation of their gods and heroes. This continuity from the divine occupation of Olympia to human occupation was preserved by myths and revivified each time the myths were told.

Pausanias admits that when he began to write his account he thought the stories of the Greeks were "more than silly," but, nearing the end of his travels, he came to realize that the wise Greeks of old couched their wisdom in riddles (8.8.3). Although apparently skeptical about their veracity, he reported myths because they were what was being said by his informants. Pausanias cites "those among the Eleans who recall the most ancient things" (5.7.6) as his authority for the following foundation myths:

> Those among the Eleans who recall the most ancient things say that Cronus first held the kingship in heaven, and a temple was made for Cronus in Olympia by the men of that time who were named the Golden Race. When Zeus was born, Rhea entrusted the watching of the child to the Daktyloi, who are also called Kouretes, from Mount Ida. They were Herakles, Paionaios, Epimedes, Iasios, and Ida, and they came from Ida in Crete. Herakles, for he was the eldest, feeling playful, set a footrace for his brothers and crowned the winner with a branch of wild olive. There was such an abundance of the olive that they spread out its fresh foliage for beds while sleeping. The wild olive, they say, was brought to the Greeks by Herakles from the land of the Hyperboreans, the men who live beyond Boreas, the north wind. . . . The glory of first holding the contest at that time and of giving Olympia its name belongs to Idaean Herakles. He established the custom of celebrating the games every fifth year, because he and his brothers were five in number. Some say that Zeus wrestled there with Cronus for the supreme power. Others say that Zeus presided over the game in honor of the vanquished Cronus. Apollo, others say, outran his rival Hermes and defeated Ares in boxing. For this reason, they say that the Pythian flute song was introduced to the jumping event in the pentathlon, since the flute song was sacred to Apollo, and Apollo had won Olympic victories.
>
> Later than these events, they say that Klymenos, son of Kardys, arrived from Crete in about the fiftieth year after the flood came upon the Greeks in the time of Deucalion. He was related to Idaean Herakles and held the contest in Olympia and founded an altar for the other Kouretes and for his ancestor Herakles whom he surnamed Parastates [One Who Stands by Another's Side]. Endymion, son of Aëthlios, put an end to Klymenos' supreme rule and set the kingship up as a prize for his sons in a footrace at Olympia. About a generation later than Endymion, Pelops made the contest for Olympian Zeus in a style far more memorable than that of his predecessors. When Pelops' sons were outside Elis and scattered across the whole Peloponnesus, Amythaon, son of Kretheus and cousin of Endymion on his father's side—for they say that Aëthlios was the son of Aiolos, a surname of Zeus—Amythaon held the Olympic Games. After him, Pelias and Neleus held them in common. Augeas held them, and likewise Herakles, son of Amphitryon, who captured Elis. Among the victors whom Herakles crowned is Iolaos who raced with Herakles' mares. There was from ancient custom the practice of competing with another's horses. Homer, in the games held for Patroclus, made Menelaos use Agamemnon's horse Aithe and the other from his own horses. Iolaos won the chariot race, and Iasios, an Arcadian, the single horse race. The sons of Tyndareos won, the one [Kastor] in the

footrace and Polydeukes in boxing. It is said of Herakles that he
carried off victories in wrestling and *pankration* (5.7.6, 9–5.8.4).

Like Greek mythology itself, Pausanias' brief outline of founders,
presidents of the games, and athletes abounds in names. Names attribute
actions to specific persons who come from specific parents and
homelands that, in turn, convey authority and persuasiveness.

Men appeal to foundation myths like these to support their claims
of ownership to a place or legitimacy for what they do. Menelaos is
justified in racing with Agamemnon's horse, for example, because Iolaos
raced with another's horses. Olympia derives its authority as a place
for games, in part, from the tale that gods competed there: Zeus wrestled
Cronus for the kingship of the universe; Apollo and Hermes raced; and
Apollo and Ares boxed. These pursuits they shared with Homeric and
other *aristoi*. The footrace surely owes its prominence in the myths to
its reputation as the first contest of the games. A Herakles from Crete,
not the son of Zeus, held the first game, a footrace, and crowned the
victor with an olive branch. The olive, flourishing across the Alpheios
Valley, was used to crown victors, a custom that had to be accounted
for by a hero's founding deed. The games were celebrated every four
years, but the Greeks, counting the first year of the next Olympiad as
the fifth of the present Olympiad, sometimes spoke of holding them
every five years as well as every four. Their calculation is then derived
from, and justified by, the number of Herakles and his brothers. Some
mythmakers said that Herakles was the Idaean from Crete, while others
said he was the son of Zeus and Alcmena, wife of Amphitryon. Their
uncertainty cannot be eradicated from the myths, since the past to which
the mythmakers refer is a past existing in hearsay—hence, the repeated
expressions "they say" and "some say." They have no way of proving
the truth other than revising it with a story asserted on their own authority
as Strabo attempts to do for the origin of the Olympic Games:

> The Eleans above all deserve the credit for the splendor of, and the
> honor paid to, the temple at Olympia. . . . Moreover, the Olympic
> contest is an invention of the Eleans who completed the first
> Olympiads. One must let go old things about the founding of the
> temple and the establishment of the games—some say that one of the
> Idaean Daktyloi, Herakles, was their founder, while others say it was
> the son of Alcmena and Zeus who was the first to complete and win
> the games. Such things are said in many ways and are not at all to be
> believed. Nearer to something trustworthy is to say that from the first
> Olympiad [776] in which Koroibos the Elean won the *stadion* [a running

event] until the twenty-sixth [676], the Eleans held the presidency
over the temple and the contest (*Geography* 8.3.30).

Strabo does not attack either Herakles as non-historical. Since both had
been spoken of in myths since olden times, they must have existed.
Instead, Strabo tries to cleanse the myths of Olympia by denying a role
to either Herakles in the belief that, once such errors are removed,
what remains is the truth (Veyne, 59).

Pausanias cites as his authority the "continuous records" (5.8.6)
kept by the Eleans for the report that Iphitos, their king, restored the
contest and festival at Olympia after a long interruption (5.4.5):

> When Greece was perishing from civil discord and plague, the notion
> came to Iphitos to ask the god in Delphi for release from these evils.
> The Pythian priestess, they say, enjoined Iphitos himself and the
> Eleans to renew the Olympic Games. Iphitos also persuaded the Eleans
> to sacrifice to Herakles whom before they regarded as an enemy (5.4.6).

Pausanias later elaborates that Iphitos held one contest alone, the *stadion,*
won by the Elean Koroibos [M 1] (5.8.6). Thereafter, other events
were added piecemeal, so the story continues, as men remembered the
ways of the older games, those before the hiatus, which they had
forgotten during the time of suspension.

Phlegon (second century C.E.), a freedman of the Roman emperor
Hadrian, reproduces the Elean version of the founding of the Olympic
Games in this fragment of his lost *Olympiads*, a lengthy account of the
history of the games from the their beginnings to 140 CE:

> I think that I should give the reason why the Olympic Games came to
> be organized. It is this. After the time of Peison and Pelops, and then
> Herakles, the first ones to establish the festival and contest at Olympia,
> the Peloponnesians at some time abandoned the celebration until
> twenty-eight Olympiads from Iphitos to Koroibos the Elean had been
> numbered. After the Peloponnesians neglected the games, sedition
> arose across the Peloponnesus. Lycurgus the Lacedaemonian, son of
> Prytanis—the son of Eurypon, son of Sous, son of Prokles, son of
> Aristodemos, son of Aristomachos, son of Kleodaios, son of Hyllos,
> son of Herakles and Deianeira—and Iphitos, son of Haimon or, as
> some say, of Praxonides, a descendant of Herakles and an Elean, and
> Kleosthenes, son of Kleonikes, a Pisatan, wished to restore the
> populace to concord and peace. They decided to celebrate the Olympic
> festival according to ancient customs and to complete an athletic
> contest. They sent men to Delphi to inquire of the god whether he
> approved of their doing this. The god replied that things would be
> better for them doing this. He also ordered them to announce a truce
> to the cities that wished to participate in the contest. After this had
> been announced throughout Greece, a discus was inscribed for the

Hellanodikai, judges of the Greeks, according to which they must conduct the Olympic Games. Since the Peloponnesians did not pursue the contest eagerly but instead were put out about it, they were ravaged by plague descending upon them and by the withering of their crops. They again dispatched ambassadors under the leadership of Lycurgus to Delphi and asked for surcease from the plague and some cure. The Pythia gave this oracle:

> O elders, best of men, who dwell
> in Pelops' citadel renowned everywhere,
> you ask from me that I tell you the god's oracle.
> Zeus bears wrath against you over rites that he revealed,
> because you dishonor the Olympic Games of Zeus, Lord
> of All. As an honor for him, Peisos first founded and
> established them. After him, Pelops, when he came to the
> land of Greece, ordained a festival and games for the dead
> Oinomaos. Third over them was Amphitryon's son,
> Herakles, who conducted a festival and contest for his
> maternal uncle, son of Tantalos, who died, a festival you
> now somehow are neglecting along with the rites.
> Angered in his heart over them, Zeus sent evil famine and
> plague upon you which it is possible to end once you
> have restored the festival for him again.

They listened and reported this reply to the Peloponnesians who disbelieved the oracle and in accord with a common resolve sent men back to inquire of the god more attentively. The Pythia gave the following oracle:

> Inhabitants of the Peloponnesus, gather around an altar
> and sacrifice and believe whatever the prophets say.

After this oracle was delivered, the Peloponnesians entrusted to the Eleans the management of the games and announcement of the truce to the cities. And the Eleans, wishing to aid the Lacedaemonians when they were besieging Helos, then sent to Delphi and consulted the oracle. The Pythia declared this oracle:

> Ministers of the Eleans, by making straight the law of your
> fathers, save your own fatherland, and stay away from
> war, conducting an impartial friendship for the Greeks,
> whensoever the fifth year with welcome of friendship
> arrives.

After the oracle was delivered, the Eleans refrained from making war and took care of the Olympic Games. No one was crowned for five Olympiads. In the sixth, they resolved to consult the oracle to ask if they should place fillets around those who won, and they sent King Iphitos to the god's oracle. The god said the following:

> Iphitos, do not place the fruit of the apple for winning,
> but put around the wild fruitful olive
> that now is embraced by the gossamer webs of a spider.

> Coming to Olympia, where there were many wild olive trees in the sanctuary, Iphitos found one embraced by spiders' webs. He fenced around it, and a crown from this tree was given to those who won. Daikles, a Messenian, who won the *stadion* in the seventh Olympiad [752], was first to be crowned (Jacoby 1962, 1160–1162).

These myths, probably invented by the Eleans after the eighth century to justify their claims to Olympia, neatly accommodate the independent tradition that Herakles established the games much earlier than they. The myths lay down the rules for the Hellanodikai who managed the games and explain the reason for the addition of events. Phlegon's version reflects, it seems, the influence at Olympia of Lacedaemonians whose athletes dominated the games after 700. It portrays the Lacedaemonians and the northern Eleans and those from the south (Pisatans) as founders of the games that were abandoned. The break in celebrating the games allows the parties to act not only as founders of the games but also as advocates of peace across the Peloponnesus. They take credit for the truce among competing cities and laud their own neutrality as guardians of the games. Visible proof of the tradition, furthermore, was offered in the inscription on the discus of Iphitos that Pausanias saw: "Iphitos' discus has the truce which the Eleans announce for the Olympic Games" (5.20.1). The Delphic oracle, the usual solution in myths for release from plague, authorizes the Eleans' claim to be founders and implies that the Olympic Games, the premier athletic event, owes its establishment to Delphi. The Peloponnesians' impiety in refusing to celebrate the games casts the Eleans as the deliverers of the Peloponnesus from certain destruction unleashed by Zeus. This role explains why they are the sole custodians of the games. In the Elean version, their king trumps Herakles, who is given credit for bringing the olive to Olympia, by inventing its use in crowns for victors. With regard to the Eleans, it is difficult to imagine a more powerful and self-serving myth for the origin of the games at Olympia.

By modern reckoning Iphitos' restoration of the games falls in the year 776, a date which has become traditional for the inauguration of the Olympic Games. One of the few fixed dates for the eighth century, it was established originally when the Elean sophist Hippias (ca. 485–415) published it in the late fifth century. Hippias drew up a list of victors in the *stadion* for each Olympic festival that later writers adopted as the basis for a chronological system for reckoning dates. From the start, Hippias' list was defended and attacked vigorously (Golden, 43–45, 63–65). Hippias had no archival records at his disposal; his and the lists of archons at Athens and ephors at Sparta were unprecedented. Epigrams, poetry, and the memoirs of the Eleans supplied him with data, but how he constructed the list will never be known (Mosshammer, 93–96). Modern historians, Alden A. Mosshammer insists, "must combine skepticism about the existence of early lists with confidence in the authenticity of the first lists that finally were published" (1979, 96). Since they cannot escape relying upon Hippias' registry for dates and events in Olympic history, especially those before the fifth century, they must emend and challenge his dates in ways that do not destroy fundamental confidence in his registry. Yet Hippias' assumption that the games and the festival were coeval—that they were linked from the outset—is not supported by the testimony of the site itself. He would have had neither evidence to believe nor means to ascertain otherwise, but the stone, ash, ceramics, and metal that comprise the archaeological record yield no information about the games, while the bronze figurines of horses and two-horse chariots contradict the records of the Eleans who contend that races with four-horse chariots were not introduced until 680 (Mallwitz 1988, 96).

Setting for Lacedaemonians

Those Dorian Greeks who would become Spartans first appeared in Laconia, the territory occupying the western half of the southern Peloponnesus, toward the end of the eleventh century. During the next century, four villages along the west bank of the Eurotas River united under the leadership of two royal houses, and the aggregate that they named Lacedaemon but others came to call Sparta was born. It added a fifth village but remained close to its humble beginnings throughout the classical period (Thucydides *Histories* 1.10.2). Its inhabitants, arms-bearing citizens who called themselves Spartiates, displayed a lust for conquest from the outset. By 750, in the face of vigorous resistance, they had gained control over all of Laconia and divided the land among themselves. They reduced the indigenous Mycenean people to Helots, a population bound to the land who "worked the land for them, paying them in kind a specified amount" (Plutarch *Lycurgus* 24.2). They made the other Dorians whose *poleis* surrounded much of the land owned by the Spartiates into partial citizens called *perioikoi*, "those dwelling about." *Perioikoi*, although considered Lacedaemonians, were required on demand to serve in the army and allowed to govern themselves locally, but they had to pay tribute to the Spartiates and lacked full participation in the government of the *polis*. In this way, the Spartiates created a three-tier social structure with the lower tiers supporting the upper one, a system that henceforth distinguished and flawed their society.

From earliest times in the eighth century, Lacedaemonians journeyed to Olympia for personal reasons. Spartiates evidently engaged in the social and religious activities afforded by the Panhellenic shrine and formed private alliances through gift exchanges with aristocrats of other *poleis*. Metal workers, who may have themselves been disenfranchised Spartiates, sought out markets for their wares and skills. Olympia offered them not only profits but also the opportunity to meet with fellow artisans from other cities. Many of the finds dug up at early Olympia came from the hands of men trained in Laconia (Cartledge, 174–176). While at Olympia, some, whether they came for that purpose or not, competed in the games to prove themselves the best. The list of victors in the *stadion* records the Elean Koroibos as the winner at the first Olympic festival (Pausanias 5.8.6). His triumph was not followed by another Elean victory until that of Agis [M 93] in 572 at the fifty-second Olympic festival, and the olive crown for the *stadion* of the ensuing ten festivals went to foreigners, seven of them Messenians, neighbors of the Lacedaemonians to the west. The Messenian Leochares [M 11] claimed the last of these victories at the eleventh Olympic festival (736). Soon afterwards, the Lacedaemonians invaded the rich fields of his fatherland in what is known as the Second Messenian War, and by the end of the eighth century, Messenia had ceased to exist as an independent *polis* (Fine, 139–142). The Spartiates shared out its bottomland among themselves, and those Messenians who survived and failed to escape they made into Helots. With the subjugation of Messenia, the Spartan system was complete, and the conquerors forever tied their fortunes to those they suppressed. "The Helot danger was the curse Sparta had brought upon herself, an admirable illustration of the maxim that a people which oppresses another cannot itself be free" (Ste. Croix, 292).

The Lacedaemonians proved their athletic prowess in the competitions of early Olympia, and from the time of Kleptolemos' victory in the *stadion* at the twenty-fourth Olympic festival (684), they dominated this event for almost a century:

Olympiad	Year	Athlete	Moretti Number
24th	684	Kleoptolemos	30
25th	680	Thalpis	32
26th	676	Kallisthenes	34
28th	668	Charmis	40
29th	664	Chionis	42
30th	660	Chionis	44
31st	656	Chionis	46
33rd	648	Gylis	50
35th	640	Sphairos	55
36th	636	Arytamas	57
37th	632	Eurykleidas	59
38th	628	Olyntheus	62
39th	624	Rhipsolaos	65
40th	620	Olyntheus	67
42nd	612	Lykotas	72
44th	604	Gelon	76
46th	596	Chrysamaxos	78
47th	592	Eurykles	80
50th	580	Epitelidas	91

Table 1.

The list is impressive by any reckoning of an athletic dynasty; yet after 580, the next Spartan victorious in the *stadion* does not come until Ladromos [M 108] in 552 at the fifty-seventh Olympic festival. Over the next century, Spartans post fewer than ten victories in the athletic contests [M 149, 160, 211, 237, 1024?] and none after 448 until 316 [M 478]. Why?

Questions are far more easily asked of things Spartan than answered. Sparta appeared to the French scholar François Ollier like a mirage refracted by the evidence. His expression and the title of his study, *Le mirage spartiate*, aptly denote the idealization of Spartan life and manners created and revised by Lacedaemonians and accepted and embellished by others. With a mirage, the phantom waters in a desert prove illusionary as they vanish into sand. Historical Sparta cannot be so easily separated from the evidentiary fantasy whose qualities are suggested by the words "Spartan" and "laconic." Lacedaemonians promoted the view that they were simple, virtuous men, austere in their daily needs, physically courageous, dedicated to a military regimen, selfless before the needs of the community, and obedient to laws, elders, and generals. Their *polis* was consequently free of the internal strife that plagued other Greeks. Yet, glimpses appear through the evidence that Lacedaemonian aristocrats of the later seventh century conducted themselves like other Greeks of their position. Their town, it seems, was a "Big Easy" where, like New Orleans, foreign musicians and song writers, *poêtai* in Greek parlance, as well as architects and philosophers could readily find a patron and get a gig (Tigerstedt, 1:39–44). Spartans were famed for their appreciation of the musical forms developed by visitors in their midst, while their native artists working in metal excelled over those of other *poleis*. By the mid-sixth century, however, they had forsaken their cultural interests and changed everything about their city and themselves. Although the defeat of the Messenians left them at a peak of prosperity, with victory came the burden of maintaining hold on the fertile fields to the east across the Taygetus mountain range and of keeping their grip on the Helots. To this end, they began to avoid warfare, since a major loss incurred by aggressive actions threatened their control over the Helots, and adopted a strategy bent on shielding themselves through alliances (Tigerstedt, 1:61–70). They resolved long-standing and now potentially dangerous internal conflicts by imposing upon themselves a way of life that subordinated every aspect of their lives to the state and their bodies to a harsh discipline and constant military training and preparedness.

In the Classical period, laws forbade Spartiates from traveling abroad except on public business (Plutarch *Lycurgus* 27.5–7). Whether legal restrictions pertained earlier is unknown, but recorded athletic victories, though few, imply the lack of strict formal constraint. In all likelihood, Spartiates voluntarily forsook the Panhellenic contests. At any rate, the mirage has preserved an explanation for their withdrawal from the gamematures in this description of boxing:

> Boxing was a Laconian invention . . . The ancient Lacedaemonians used to box for this reason. The Lacedaemonians did not wear helmets, and they did not think a battle against an inferior was worthy of their country. For a man conducting himself skillfully, a shield served as a helmet. To ward off blows to the face and to endure blows when hit, they practiced boxing and trained themselves in protecting their faces. As time went on, they gave up boxing . . . , considering that the way these events were decided was shameful. Since one man acknowledge a defeat in these contests, it was possible for Sparta to be slandered as devoid of courage (Philostratos *Gymnastic* 9, in Kayser, 265).

Inventiveness followed by denial suggests the history of early Sparta, but Philostratos' report belongs to the ideal city where everything must be justified by a military motive, and defeat cannot be lightly risked.

With the shift inward, victory at local festivals surely conferred greater prestige and honor, since glory was gained over one's peers before the eyes of the whole community. At the same time, the Spartiates inaugurated the *agogê* or rearing (Scanlon 2002, 81), a system of education that held boys in thrall from the age of seven until their incorporation into adult status at thirty years. The *agogê* conveyed its lessons by deprivation and brutality, reinforced by the discipline and pederasty of older boys and men. Whatever athletic activities such as running and ball-playing that it entailed were subordinated to its initiatory purpose of shaping boys into Spartiates.

Setting for Growth

Olympia stood alone in offering athletic competitions at an independent sanctuary throughout the seventh century. By the early sixth century, the Pythian Games at Delphi, the Isthmian Games at Corinth, the Nemean Games at Nemea, would be established to become, with the Olympic Games, Panhellenic, that is, open to all Greeks.

The transformation that had already begun of Olympia into a Panhellenic sanctuary now continued with foreign investment in the form of treasuries (earliest ca. 600). Treasuries, which resembled miniature temples, had two columns on the front side, a central hall, and a roof. Some displayed sculptures in the pediment. They were constructed by Greeks living in the Isthmus of Corinth and by colonists in Sicily, Italy, and Illyricum on the eastern coast of the Adriatic Sea (Frazer, 4:56–71; Drees, 120–121). The Sikyonians appear even to have imported the materials for their treasury from their distant region in the northern Peloponnesus near Corinth, since the sandstone, found on no other building in the sanctuary, is common at Sikyon. Treasuries stood on a nine-foot-high terrace within the Altis that abutted the Hill of Cronus (Pausanias 6.19.1–15) and were reached by a staircase (5.21.2). Foundations for twelve treasuries have been discovered, but Pausanias describes ten (6.19), two having been destroyed before his time to open way for a road to the hill. The treasuries housed votive gifts, athletic equipment, and ritual implements. Some housed money, converting Olympia itself into a kind of treasury. Since the treasuries were themselves votives, their presence and splendor bore witness to the wealth of the colony or *polis* and asserted its prestige in the fatherland.

To the south and east of the treasuries lay the Heraion, temple of Hera, built in the Doric style near the end of the seventh or the beginning of the sixth century. Although temples were a prominent expression of

Greek piety, they were not necessary, and many sanctuaries did not
have them (Burkert 1985, 88–92). They were not places of worship but
served to shelter the deity's cult statue and secure the dedications.
Sacrifices took place at an altar before the entrance on the temple's
east side. The Heraion reproduces the common floor plan for temples,
and its ruins have enabled archaeologists to make useful deductions
about its appearance: the *pronaos* or porch on the eastern side led to
the door; the *cella* or inner chamber held the statues, raised on a pedestal,
of a sitting Hera and a standing Zeus, bearded and wearing a helmet
(Pausanias 5.17.1); and the *opisthodomos,* a chamber walled off from
the *cella,* occupied the west and rear. A peristyle of rather thick columns
characteristic of the Doric order surrounded this structure whose walls
were made of sun-dried brick. The columns, originally of wood—one
of oak was still standing before the rear chamber in Pausanias' time
(5.16.1)—were replaced as the wood decayed with stone fashioned in
the manner of the day. By the time of the Heraion at Olympia, wood
and clay were giving way to stone, but they may have been preferred
as less expensive materials for erecting a temple in an independent
sanctuary. In any case, the replacements explain the differences in size
and shape of the columns (Frazer, 3:585–586).

Pausanias is momentarily diverted from describing the contents of
Hera's temple by his mention of the Sixteen Women (5.16.2). Every
fourth year, these women oversaw the weaving of a new dress (*peplos*)
for Hera's statue and conducted the Heraia, an event dedicated to Hera
and celebrated by girls and maidens:

> The contest is a race for maidens, not all of whom are of the same
> age. The youngest run first, then the next oldest, and then the
> oldest. They run in this way: their hair is let down; their tunic comes
> down to a little above the knee; they reveal the right shoulder,
> exposing the breast. The Olympic stadium is reserved for them and
> for the contest, but they shorten the distance by about a sixth. To
> the victors, they give crowns of olive, a portion of the ox sacrificed
> to Hera, and the right to dedicate their images inscribed with their
> name. Those who wait on the Sixteen, like those who administer the
> contest, are married women. They trace the contest of the maidens
> back to earliest times, saying that Hippodameia founded it in
> gratitude for her marriage to Pelops and that she gathered the
> Sixteen Women and celebrated the first Heraia with them (5.16.2–4).

"Earliest times" and the marriage of Pelops and Hippodameia allow a
Mycenean or Protogeometric origin for the Heraia (Scanlon 2002, 112–
115). As with Pelops, however, the archaeological record fails to support
so early a presence for Hera at the sanctuary. Hera figurines are few

Illustration 1. Bronze statuette of a female runner, ca. 580 B.C.E. © The British Museum, London, England.

and do not constitute a notable number until the time of her first temple in the late seventh century (Morgan, 42).

The first quarter of the sixth century was a period of vigorous political and religious activity at Olympia. The Eleans to the north and those in the south, the so-called Pisatans, had resolved their struggle over the sanctuary. Major construction was under way on Hera's temple. Although the date when the Heraia was founded cannot be ascertained with certainty, a festival that presumably drew its celebrants from the families of the Eleans and Lacedaemonians and, hence, encouraged ties between the groups, is appropriate for the period, especially one that seems so Lacedaemonian. A bronze statuette, Spartan in origin and now in the British Museum in London, depicts a young female runner wearing a costume like that Pausanias describes (Illustration 1). Lacedaemonians were famous, even notorious, for a treatment of young girls that, in their view, prepared the girls to be wives of Spartiates. Xenophon (428–ca.

354), an Athenian political exile and ambassador for Lacedaemonians
visiting Olympia, contrasts their ways with those of other Greeks in his
Constitution of the Lacedaemonians:

> The rest of the Greeks feed girls who are going to become mothers
> and who are raised in respectable circumstances on as plain food
> and with as few treats as possible. They do not allow them wine at
> all or only heavily diluted wine. Just as many men of those who
> practice a craft are sedentary, so too are the girls whom the other
> Greeks prefer to sit and tend to their wool-working. How to expect
> girls nourished in this way to give birth to anything magnificent?
> Lycurgus, who thought that slaves were capable of supplying
> clothes, considered childbearing to be the most important task for
> free women. He first ordered that the female exercise no less than the
> male. Secondly, he held competitions in running and in strength for
> the females as for the males, against one another, thinking that
> stronger children are born from strong parents (1.3–4).

Plutarch (ca. 50–150 C.E.) adds that "Lycurgus trained the bodies of
maidens by having them run races, wrestle, and throw the discus and
javelin" (*Lycurgus* 14.3; cf. Philostratos *Gymnastic* 27). Running is a
feature of prenuptial rituals for girls elsewhere in Greece, notably at the
Brauronia in Attica (Parke 140). The races of the Heraia, celebrated
for Hippodameia's wedding to Pelops, have the appearance of puberty
rituals that conduct the initiates, here virgin girls, from childhood to
adulthood (Serwint, 419–422). In puberty rituals, adults of the same sex
guide the initiates through their ordeal and impart to them the wisdom
needed for their new life as adults. The Sixteen Women acted in these
capacities, watching over the initiates during the transition, a frightening
and exciting time that includes not only the race but the separation from
their families and instruction in "the secrets of fertility and sexuality and
. . . the accepted responsibilities of women" (Serwint, 420).

Most provocative of a puberty rite is the girls' garment. It has been
variously attributed to the Amazons and to the goddess and huntress
Artemis, but Nancy Serwint has properly identified it as a man's *exômis*
or "off the shoulder" shirt (416–417). The *exômis*, worn by workmen,
slaves, artisans, soldiers, and sailors, was attached over the left shoulder,
leaving the right arm free for heavy work. As a ritual garment, it
expresses the initiate's liminal status during her transition into
womanhood. She has been separated from her status as child, but while
she is running the race, she has yet to be reintegrated into society as an
adult. Socially, she has no sexual status, a blurring manifested by the
transvestism of a male dress worn by females. The London bronze
captures the moment. The girl, her hair let down, has a long face with

pronounced features and a slender body, stylistic indications of Laconian origin. She runs in full stride to the right on strong, sinewy legs. She is gracefully lifting her dress over her leading leg to speed her on her course while, at the same time, she looks backward to what has been left behind. Moreover, the dress, exposing the girl's right breast, reveals her in a way that will never again be the case in public. For this reason, men were most likely forbidden by taboo from watching the Heraia. Their exclusion as well as their disinterest in women's activities go far in explaining the absence of the Heraia from the sources until it was reported by Pausanias in the second century C.E.

Lying south of the temple of Zeus and outside the Altis, the council chamber or *Bouleuterion* housed the administrative offices of the sanctuary. A *bouleuterion* was one of the public buildings found in most cities; it provided an enclosed space where leaders and elders could deliberate in private (Wycherley 1976, 125). At Olympia, it consisted of three separate structures, built at different times but placed together in the shape of a three-sided figure ($\sqsubset$). The northern and southern wings were connected on the east by a rectangular edifice, perhaps an open shrine, that was faced by a colonnade. Scholars have differed on the chronology for the long parallel wings. The southern wing exhibits the more archaic design, but the northern wing seems to be older. Mallwitz dates the northern to the late sixth century (ca. 520), the southern to ca. 450, and the connecting structure to a time after 374 (1988, 83 Fig. 6.2). The long wings end at the western end in an apse, a semicircular roofed enclosure that is itself a feature of archaic architecture and may have served the Hellanodikai as a repository for their records.

Events continued to be added throughout the seventh century. Boxing was introduced at the twenty-third Olympiad (688); chariot races for four horses were added at the twenty-fifth (680); *pankration*, a form of fighting, and the *kelês*, a race for mature horses with a rider, at the thirty-third (648) (Pausanias 5.8.7–8). In the thirty-seventh Olympiad (632), the Eleans on their own authority introduced events for boys, *stadion* and wrestling. Pausanias states that they had no precedent for these (5.8.9); equally surprising is that they made no effort to invent a founder for them. At the thirty-eighth Olympiad (628), they added pentathlon for boys and immediately terminated the event after the festival (5.9.1). In the forty-first Olympiad (616), they added boys' boxing. The Eleans did not consent to *pankration* for boys until the 145th Olympiad (200) (Pausanias 5.8.11).

The events for boys originated during a time when athletes from all over the Greek Mediterranean were offering themselves for acceptance into the competitions. Crowns of olive branches and, with them, the prestige of victory were leaving Elis on the heads of foreigners. Something had to be done. Mark Golden astutely submits that the Eleans resorted to events for boys (107–110). An Elean, Polyneikes, won the first boys' *stadion* (Pausanias 5.8.9), and others, children of the local elite, proved to be overwhelmingly successful across the Olympiads. Although Elean men won about 10.5% of the 832 contests where the victor's city of origin is known, Golden observes: "Strong though this showing is, it falls far short of their dominance in boys' events: Elis produced 28 (22.5 %) of those 124 winners whose home-towns are known, nearby Lepreon 3 more; its closest rivals, Sparta and Miletus, had just 5 each" (107). Boys' competitions offered a way for Eleans to gain fame from their own games. Travel to Olympia was arduous, and accommodations at the sanctuary were primitive until Roman times. Many a local winner could not, or was not allowed to, travel to Olympia to compete. Pindar recounts the fate of Aristagoras of Tenedos, a winning athlete as a boy in Tenedos about 446 (*Nemean Ode* 11.22–29):

> Too fearful hopes of the boy's parents
> restrained his might from testing the games at Pytho and Olympia.
> On my oath, as I see it, had he come to Kastalia [Delphi]
> and Cronus' well-wooded hill,
> he would have returned home more nobly than
> his opponents who contended for the prize,
> after celebrating Herakles' solemn five-year festival
> and binding his locks with shining wreaths.

Aristagoras was surely not the only local victor whose parents shrunk from the dangers of travel to Olympia. The way was open for the boys of Elis to dominate the Olympic Games that, for them, were a local festival presided over by their citizens. The Eleans dropped pentathlon for boys after Eutelidas the Lacedaemonian took the olive (Pausanias 5.9.1). Perhaps the Eleans feared that their sons could not overcome strapping boys trained in the Spartan way. At any rate, Spartan men had repeatedly won Olympic victories, and it was apparently self-defeating to let them expand into boys' events. From earliest times, the games at the sanctuary served other, often less ennobling, purposes than athletic achievement.

Early Olympia emerged as one of several factors—alphabet, metalworking, hoplite warfare, the *polis*—that revolutionized Greece. It became a magnet for ideas and social interchange as well as a beacon for broadcasting those ideas and changes across an ever-widening swath of land. Olympia was both a means to change and a symbol of change. What it was historically was never apart from what "they" said it was. "They" are still talking. In a real way, what the Olympic Games were and are is synonymous with what has been, is, and will be said about them.

3.
The Panhellenic Cycle of Athletic Festivals and Their Poet

After the First Sacred War in the early sixth century, the administrators of the sanctuary at Delphi added athletic contests to its traditional musical contest for Pythian Apollo. In 582, the Corinthians established games for Poseidon at his sanctuary on the Isthmus and for Zeus a few years later (573) at Nemea on their southern border with the Argolid. By the end of the sixth century, these games had been institutionalized into a cycle or *periodos* of athletic competitions, and in time, an athlete who won at all four was known as *periodonikês*. Because of its antiquity, Olympia was the most prestigious and provided the model for others. Future games in the Roman period would be deemed isolympic, that is, like the Olympic Games, if they awarded only a crown for victory. Closely rivaling Olympia, Delphi received respect for its Pythian Games from its long-standing musical contest and the political influence wielded by its oracle. Delphi, like Olympia, attracted pilgrims and competitors from several districts of Greece from the beginning. Isthmia and Nemea remained local centers, but the Isthmian Games benefited from Corinth's wealth and appeal as a crossroads for travel and trade by land and sea.

These contests were Panhellenic. They were held during the spring and summer months and at regular intervals coordinated to the four-year Olympiad, the market strategy that made the *periodos* possible. It is important for the chronology of the *periodos* to realize that the spring and summer months in the ancient Greek calendar did not belong to the same year as they do in the modern solar calendar. The Greek year began with the new moon before the summer solstice, and its months overlap modern ones. For example, Hekatombaion, the first month in the Athenian calendar, consisted of days from the months June and July, and the calendar year extended from June/July through May/June.

The cycle of games for the seventieth Olympiad (500), for instance, occurred according to the following schedule:

1. Olympic Games	July/August 500
2. Nemean Games	August/September 449
Isthmian Games	April/May or May/June 499
3. Pythian Games	July/August 497
4. Nemean Games	August/September 497
Isthmian Games	April/May or May/June 497

The seventy-first Olympiad then began with the Olympic Games in July/August 496. The Olympic and Pythian Games had a solar year to themselves, and since the Isthmian and Nemean Games fell in different months in the same athletic season, athletes could participate in all the competitions.

All four sanctuaries conferred symbolic rather than monetary rewards: a crown of wild olive at the Olympic Games, bay laurel at the Pythian Games, wild celery at the Nemean Games (Lucian *Anacharsis* 9), and pine at the Isthmian Games from their foundation until the early fifth century, withered wild celery from then until the second century, and both thereafter until at least the end of the second century C.E. (Broneer,1962). Victory at a crown game or *stephanitês* brought the athlete more honor than victory at a *chrematitês*, a game awarding monetary prizes. Herodotus has the Persian Tritantaichmes point out to the Persian general Mardonius the folly of attacking Greeks: "Alas, Mardonius, what sort of men have you led us against to fight who hold contests not for money but for *aretê*" (*Histories* 8.26.3). Some six centuries later, Lucian (ca. 120–180 C.E.) echoes the ideology of *aretê* when the Scythian Anacharsis voices his wonderment at the punishments contestants endure for readily available celery, and Solon replies:

> Best of men, we do not look at the bare gifts. They are signs of victory, tokens to mark those who have prevailed. For those who have won, the reputation accompanying them is worth everything; even to be kicked is fine for those in the hunt for glory from their toils (*Anacharsis* 10).

The period festivals served as meeting places for Greeks from across the mainland, the colonies in Sicily and southern Italy, and cities in the Cyclades and Ionia. Visitors could be bitter rivals, even enemies, outside the festival. Panhellenic forces encouraged by, and embodied in, these festivals did not overcome the divisiveness inherent in the *polis* and its exclusive citizenship. In fact, the remains of trophies found at Olympia that once trumpeted the victory of Greeks over fellow Greeks belie the claims found in Phlegon that Olympia discouraged such fighting (Raubitschek 1988, 36). At the games, however, everyone had made a truce to set aside hostilities for the festival (Isocrates *Panegyricus* 43), and the athletes competed according to fixed rules in which every athlete had a fair chance at victory (Raubitschek 1992,185–186). Skill and physical ability in the contests provided the road to distinction, and success lay open to all who could make the grade. In reality, most athletes came from the elite who had the leisure and the means to train and travel to the competitions, and the games remained essentially aristocratic.

Herodotus pronounces Tritantaichmes' thought "most noble" (*Histories* 8.26.2), because it eschews money in favor of *aretê*; it also illustrates the Greeks' abiding confidence in athletics as training for war (Poliakoff 1987, 94–103). The decades on either side of 500 were beset with the rumblings of war from the mighty empire of the Persians and their king, Darius, in the east. Darius probably sought to expand westward into Greece and Italy before his subject Greeks in Ionia revolted in 500 (Fine, 276). The Ionians held out for six years, and then, with them subdued, Darius turned to the west for revenge. The Athenians and Eretrians who sent ships in aid of the Ionians became his special targets, but all Greeks surely feared the future. The games bolstered their resolve, as Herodotus makes clear by minimizing the threat that had already been surmounted by the time he came to write. Carried out regularly in two- and four-year rotations, the Panhellenic contests reassured the Greeks of their *aretê,* and that reassurance, in turn, reinforced the cohesiveness of the *periodos*.

Olympic Games: The First Events

Earliest among the contests at the Olympic Games were the *stadion*, *diaulos*, and *dolichos*, all running events. The word *stadion* denotes a stade, a distance of six hundred ancient feet, a race that is one stade in length, and a running track where the *stadion* is held. At Olympia, Herakles, son of Zeus, is said to have marked off the distance by putting his feet heel to toe six hundred times (Aulus Gellius *Attic Nights* 1.1). According to a myth preserved by Philostratos, the *stadion* began as a race toward the altar of Zeus:

> The *stadion* was discovered in this way. After the Eleans had offered the customary sacrifices, the offerings were laid out on the altar, but

the fire had not yet been kindled beneath them. The runners were a *stadion* away from the altar. The priest stood before the altar, with a torch, acting as umpire. The man who set the fire to the victims was the first to leave as an Olympic victor (*Gymnastic* 5).

The *stadion* was a sprint comparable to the modern 200-meter race. Runners ran at full speed for a short period from a starting point to a finish line across the stadium: "He was best in the *stadion*, running / a straight direction with his feet" (Pindar *Olympian Ode* 10.64–65). How exactly the race began remains a question. A bronze figurine from Olympia, a votive dedicated by the victor and having "I belong to Zeus" on the right thigh, depicts a runner's standing start (Illustration 2). His upright stance is similar to that of the hoplite runner in the bronze figure from Tübingen (Jüthner, Ill.XXI a; Yalouris 169, Ill.76).[1] In the latter, the runner extends his right arm forward and somewhat below the level of the shoulder. The left arm that carries the shield is bent at the elbow and drawn back. His feet are set in the same configuration as the figurine from Olympia, and both legs are slightly bent at the knee. A hoplite runner with a shield on a red-figure amphora (Yalouris 170, Ill.77) stands in the same posture as the Tübingen bronze. The technique is called red-figure, because the background is painted black, and figures are in the red of the baked clay of the vase with details highlighted with black and white paint.

The *stadion* was run from one line to another, east to west at Olympia, but athletes in the *diaulos* and in a *dolichos* consisting of an even number of laps finished where they started, at the west end. A *dolichos* of an odd number of laps would start at the east end and finish on the west. Runners stood behind a line (*grammê*) scratched in the earth and ran to the finish over another. The same word was used to mark the beginning and end of the race so that the comic poet Aristophanes (ca. 457–ca. 385) refers to the *grammê* as a starting line: "Step forward now, spirit. The scratch-line (*grammê*) is here" (*Archarnians* 483), while his contemporary, the tragedian Euripides (ca. 485–ca. 406), uses it as a finishing line:

Don't let a scoundrel think,
if he has run his first step well,
that he outrun Justice until he arrives
across the scratch-line (*grammê*) and makes
    the turn around the goal of life (*Electra* 953–956);

---

1 *The Eternal Olympics: The Art and History of Sport*," edited by Nicolaos Yalouris, is an excellent source for illustrations but is not widely available.

Illustration 2. Bronze statuette of a male runner, ca. 480-470 B.C.E. Courtesy of the Archaeological Museum, Olympia, Greece.

as does Pindar:

> In this way did Libyan [Antaios] give his daughter in marriage,
> joining a bridegroom to her. He dressed her in finery and stood her at
> the scratch-line (*grammê*) to be the far-end goal and said among
> them: "Whoever is first to run and touch the robes about her leads
> her away" (*Pythian Ode* 9.117–120).

The Scholiast comments: "Antaios stood his daughter at the farthest scratch-line (*grammê*) of the course, having arranged that the maiden standing still be the goal and end. They scratch a line which contestants have as the beginning and end. From this comes the saying: Do not move the scratch-line (*grammê*)" (on *Pythian Ode* 9.209, in Drachmann, 2:240). The meaning of *grammê* depends, therefore, upon the event and context of the reference. The same is true of *balbis* (pl. *balbides*). Theagenes, hero of the romancer Heliodorus (third century C.E.), "takes his stand at the starting line (*balbis*)" (*Aethiopica* 4.3), but Sophocles (ca. 496–406) has his chorus of Theban elders sing of Zeus who:

hurls the brandished fire at him
who was already rushing to scream victory
at his finish line (*balbides*) high on our battlements
(*Antigone* 130–132).

Improvement over the *grammê* came at some unknown time in the form of permanent starting and finish lines carved in stones set, but left raised, in the lightly sanded clay surface of the track. These sills extended across each end of the track in the stadia at Olympia, Delphi, Isthmia, and Nemea. (The northern line at Nemea has been lost with the erosion of that end of the stadium.) A sill of eighteen inches in width extended about twelve yards across the western end of the stadium at Olympia and about ten yards across the eastern end (Jüthner 1968, 58). The sills were placed twelve yards and ten and one-quarter yards from their respective ends. Incised across the length of the sill were two parallel grooves about seven inches apart and a fraction over one and three-quarters deep whose cross-section delineated an inverted triangle. Square sockets, cut into the sill at intervals of four feet, held vertical posts. This arrangement of posts divided the sill into twenty sections or starting positions on the west and twenty-one on the east, allowing those numbers of athletes to compete at any one time. Athletes stood on the sill, standing with the toes of their forward foot gripping the front groove, and those of the hind foot, the rear groove.

Allan Wells, 1980 winner of the Olympic gold metal in the 100-meters, had in mind modern sprinting when he said that "Sprinting has a bigger element of nervous tension and is more physical and explosive than the other track events" (Wells 94), but his assessment must have characterized the *stadion*. Both the 100-meters and the *stadion* feature speed, disciplined, no doubt, but equally vital is the athlete's ability "to move his arms and legs as fast as possible whilst at the same time taking as long a stride (and therefore fewer for the same distance) as he can" (Wells 16). Aristotle made the same observation: "The man who can somehow hurl his legs with force and move quickly is also a good runner" (*Rhetoric* 1361b 23–24), and "the runner runs faster by swinging his arms" (*Progression of Animals* 705a 18). Tensions bottled up at the start made for jockeying for position. As early as the seventh century, King Leo of Sparta, on seeing the runners at Olympia trying hard to gain some advantage at the start, remarked "How much more anxious are the runners about speed than about justice" (Plutarch *Moralia* 224F). False starts, "jumping the gun," so to speak, were common and met with caning from the official. On the eve of the battle of Salamis, the Athenian Themistocles was speaking at length before the assembled generals of the Greeks when the Corinthian Adeimantos interrupted: "O Themistocles, in the contests, those who start up before the rest are thrashed." Defending himself, Themistocles retorted with a reply that became famous: "But those who are left behind are not crowned" (Herodotus *Histories* 8.59). Gamesmanship, anything to get an edge, was endemic to the sprinter's explosive burst at the start.

The Roman epic poet Statius (ca. 45–96 C.E.) alludes to a device that furnished a "fair entrance" into the course for the runners:

> When the bar fell and left a fair entrance for all,
> they lightly seized the course, and their naked company
> glistened across the plain (*Thebaid* 6.593–595).

Statius' Latin phrase, *aequum limen*, denotes a free and open access to the racecourse for all runners and has no equivalent in Greek terminology. *Regula* or bar is synecdoche for a starting mechanism that the Greeks variously called *balbis* or *hysplex*. Aristophanes expected his audience to be familiar with *balbides* or bars. In *Knights* (424 B.C.E.), Sausage-Seller proposes a race: "Let me and him go from the *balbides*" (1159); in *Wasps* (422 B.C.E.), Philocleon begins his exposition from the *balbides* (548–549). *Hysplex*, on the other hand, denotes a snare or "a part of a spring or noose trap which slips down when touched" (Liddell, Scott, and Jones, 1905). Plato (ca. 429–347) relates the term to the hippodrome when he speaks of a charioteer recoiling from the *hysplex* (*Phaedrus* 254E). It does not seem to be associated with the stadium until an inscription from Delos (c. 166) specifying "pipes for the *hyspleges*" (pl.). This suggests that the cords for the *hysplex* for the games on the island sacred to Apollo were enclosed in wood pipes (Dürrbach, 1400.9). Another inscription lists "3 elbows for the *hysplex*; 4 posts for *hyspleges*" (Dürrbach, 1409 Ba II 43–44). Classical authors used *balbis* for a starting mechanism for runners, and *hysplex* for horses, but later authors like Lucian (*Timon* 20) used the terms interchangeably.

Everyone in Aristophanes' audience may have known how the bar fell, but its operation remained unclear from written sources until Oscar Broneer demonstrated how it worked as a starting gate for the games at Isthmia (1956, 268–272; 430–431). In its 1956 campaign at the Isthmian sanctuary at Corinth, the University of Chicago expedition encountered:

a triangular pavement of stone slabs, only 6 ins. thick, and lined at the base with a narrow course of stones nearly twice as thick. At the broad end of the triangle there is a pit cut through the pavement and extending down ca. 3 ft. From near the rim of this pit, eight deep grooves extend toward the base line. At either end of the grooves is a bronze staple fastened with lead to the pavement (Broneer 1956,430).

After clearing the area, the expedition realized that this exposed triangle was the northeast half of a larger triangle whose southwest half lay under a Roman foundation. Tunneling exposed this part, revealing it to be less well preserved but similar.

The starting mechanism consists of the triangular pavement whose base faces the racecourse, a sill at the base of the triangle through which sockets were cut, a starter's pit recessed in, but not at the peak of, the triangular pavement, and a series of grooves incised in the pavement connecting the pit with the sockets. The sockets held upright wooden posts that marked off the lanes which were an average of 1.049 meters (41.3 inches) in width. Hinged on the northeast side of each post was a crossbar, a horizontal piece of wood of the length to block the lane but fall freely between the posts. Cords were set in the grooves and held in place by a staple at the pit and another at the socket. These ran from the starter's hands to the socket where, pivoting

Illustration 3. Starting gate with *balbides*. Courtesy of Professor Elizabeth R. Gebhard, Director of the University of Chicago Excavations at Isthmia.

on the staple, they went up to the crossbars to which they were attached (Broneer 1973, 49–50) (Illustration 3). "As soon as he [the starter] let go of a string, the bar held by it in a horizontal position would fall of its own weight and hang vertically on the side of the post to which it was hinged. The gate was thus instantaneously opened" (Broneer 1973,50). Broneer's explanation concurs with the ancient scholars' comment on Aristophanes' *Knights* 1159:

> The *balbis* is the start for the runners. It is a word borrowed from those competing in the races at the contests. Lying transversely, the wooden bar at the beginning of the race is also called the starting line. After the runners were set, the bar was released, permitting them to run (in Dübner, 72).

The athletes for the final race in the *stadion* were summoned to the starting line by a herald (Plato *Laws* 833A). Up to twenty sprinters could compete in the race at Olympia. The number of sockets at Isthmia indicates that eighteen runners were the maximum. In modern racing, a series of heats eliminates athletes and narrows the field to a manageable number. A corrupted passage in Pausanias alludes to a system of preliminary heats at Olympia that is probably not unique:

> [The runners] were grouped together according to the lot, and were not started for the race all together. Whoever wins in each heat runs again for the prize. And thus, the man crowned in the *stadion* will win two victories (6.13.4).

Runners were perhaps selected for each heat by lot (Gardiner 1910, 278) with a system similar to that used in matching opponents in wrestling and *pankration* and described by Lucian:

> A silver urn, sacred to the god, is set forth. Into it are thrown small lots, about the size of beans, with letters written on them. Alpha is written on two lots, and on two lots, beta, and on two others, gamma, and so forth in the same way if there are more athletes. Each of the athletes approaches in turn, offers a prayer to Zeus, puts his hand into the urn, and draws out one of the lots (*Herotimus* 40).

An official would then "go around and look at the lots of those standing in a circle and join the one who has the alpha with the other who drew the alpha for wrestling or *pankration*. Likewise, he joins the beta with the beta and the others with the same letters in the same way" (*Hermotimus* 40). The number of heats depended upon the number of entries; odd runners would be attached to a heat rather than receive a bye (Gardiner 1912, 278). It is with heats in the running events, moreover, that the caution against moving the *grammê* makes the most sense. After several races, the *grammê* evidently became blurred and had to be redrawn. Where the line was placed did not matter for finals since all contestants began from the same point. But it was critical—if not in real terms, in psychological terms—that runners in all the heats start from the same line and run the same distance to avoid an athlete's qualifying for the final over a shorter course.

According to Philostratos' coaching manual, sprinters ideally had "light slender legs." Because "they move their legs with their hands for a quick run," they also must have had considerable upper-body strength, but this had to correspond to the strength of their other parts *(Gymnastic* 32). The heavy muscle of the boxer or wrestler is counterproductive in a runner who requires quick muscle (Wells, 17). Philostratos details the ideal runner's physical attributes:

> Runners in the *stadion*, the lightest of the events, are very good when symmetrical in build, yet better than these are those who, while not excessively tall, are taller than proportion would have them. Excessive height, like plants that have shot up too high, lacks sturdiness. They should be firmly built, since the beginning of running well is standing properly. The proportion of these elements is as follows: the legs should be equally balanced with the shoulders, the chest smaller than normal but ample for the organs, the knee quick and nimble, the lower leg straight, and hands larger than average. The muscles are in proportion, for beefy muscles are a dead weight for running *(Gymnastic* 33).

Lucian's Solon remarks how Greeks train their runners to be "light of foot for the most speed over a short course" *(Anacharsis* 27). To accomplish this, they had runners train in deep sand where the footing was unsteady. This method, requiring constant shifting of grip far beyond the requirements of an actual *stadion*, may have developed "fast muscle power as opposed to slow, heavy power" and stretched the muscles and reflexes beyond what was needed to run competitively and avoid injury (Wells, 17, 22).

Statius exemplifies the warm-up and preparations for the race that surely prefaced every *stadion*:

> The runners are stretching
> and warming up their swift strides in their usual ways
> and energizing their limbs in practiced disorder.
> Now they are squatting with knees bent, now slapping
> their oiled chests smartly, now lifting fiery
> legs and repeating short sprints that suddenly stop
> *(Thebaid* 6.587–592).

Even without his vignette, we must assume that Greek athletes warmed up before competing. The human body cannot go from stasis to full speed without risking muscle pulls and ruptured tendons.

The lot may have determined the order across the line, but there was no advantage in position in the straight dash to the end except perhaps for one created by the immediate conditions of the track. According to Atticist lexicographer Moeris (second century C.E.), the herald called for the athletes to stand at the *balbis* (*Attikistes*, in Bekker193.4,); he presumably called for the same when the *grammê* or its version in stone was used. The runners stood in a straight line "on their marks," that is, behind the *grammê* or behind the *balbis*. They set themselves by extending their arms and arranging their legs and feet in position for the run. For those athletes behind a *grammê*, what constituted "go," whether a shout or trumpet call, is not known. Those behind the *balbis* waited for the fall of the bar. Ploutos, the god of wealth, explains the speed with which riches flee a place by an image from the *stadion*: "As soon as the *hysplex* fell, I am already being declared the victor by the herald" (Lucian *Timon* 20). Ploutos, it may be surmised, was intent on the race, that is, on betaking himself (wealth) elsewhere. From the instant of release, the good runner focused only on a quick, straight dash to the finish:

> The good runner, as soon as the *hysplex* falls down, aims only at what lies ahead and concentrates upon the goal. He has his hope for victory in his feet and does not foul the runner beside him or concern himself with the contestants. But the poor and unathletic runner, despairing of all hope based on speed, turns to fouling. He looks only toward how he will hold up or hinder the runner so that, if he fails in this tactic, he will never be able to win (Lucian *Slander* 12).

How timeless Lucian sounds when compared with Margot Wells's instructions on starting the 200-meter sprint:

> When the starter says "on your marks" all athletes must walk forward and go down together. This is often where gamesmanship will occur with one athlete standing up or moving around a bit while the others go down. Do not let this upset you, because if others are thinking of delaying tactics, their minds are not 100 per cent on the race, and the only person they are putting off is themselves (58).

The *stadion* runner in full stride closely resembles the modern sprinter. A Panathenaic amphora, a two-handled jar that once contained oil from Athena's sacred olive trees, shows a profile on its reverse side of *stadion* runners in full stride moving from left to right (Illustration 4). Their arms are moving backwards and forwards, parallel to their bodies. Philostratos likened this motion of the arms to having wings as hands (*Gymnastic* 32). The reciprocating drive of the arms quickens the feet and causes the body to lean forward from the waist (Wells, 43–44). The runners have the high knee action that enables them to achieve the

Illustration 4. The victor pulls away from the field. Red-figure Panathenaic amphora, ca. 460 B.C.E. Courtesy of the Archaeological Museum of Bologna, Bologna, Italy.

Illustration 5. Footrace. Black-figure Panathenaic amphora, 530 B.C.E All rights reserved, The Metropolitan Museum of Art, New York, New York, U.S.A.

long stride essential to this event. The show a natural and winning technique, and the right leg covers the genitals. Vase painters often swept away this impediment to the viewer's pleasure by having the left arm move with the left leg (Illustration 5). This pose allowed the painter to show the runner's genitals as well as the front of his torso, but such artistry produced a physically impossible stride.

The most famous *stadion* of them all was run at the fifteenth Olympiad (720) when Orsippos of Megara lost his loincloth, persevered, and ran to victory. Pausanias visited his grave in the city of Megara where he may have seen Orsippos' epitaph, and had this to report:

> Near Koroibos is buried Orsippos who won the *stadion* at the Olympic Games by running naked when, at the time, athletes wore loincloths at the contests according to ancient custom. They also say that Orsippos, while a general, appropriated territory belonging to his neighbors. I believe that even at Olympia the loincloth was slipped off on purpose, since he realized that it is easier for a naked man to run than one wearing a loincloth (1.44.1).

The epitaph, found at Megara in 1769, is preserved in a late Roman or Byzantine copy "engraved on a block of stone which served to keep open the door of a hovel" (Frazer, 2:537). Simonides (ca. 556–468) is held to be the author (Hicks and Hill, 3–4); if so, he wrote it long after Orsippos' deed or from the story long told by Megarians. The epitaph speaks to the passerby in the Megarian dialect, pronouncing the name of the dead as Orripos:

> For militant Orripos, the Megarians, in obedience to a Delphic oracle,
>   set me up, a memorial seen clearly from afar.
> He freed the greatest boundaries for the fatherland,
>   when the enemy were appropriating much land,
> and was the first of Greeks in Olympia to be crowned
>   naked, when others wore loincloths in the *stadion*
> (in Hicks and Hill, 3–4).

The story of Orsippos is an etiology that explains the origin of athletic nudity. Orsippos begins the *stadion* at a time when athletes, consistent with the Homeric world (*Iliad* 23.710), wore a girdle or loincloth. Orsippos loses—or lets slip—his loincloth, manages not to fall down, and finishes the race *gymnos*, "naked," not "lightly-clad," as the squeamish have often rendered the Greek (Sturtevant; Mann). Thus the race ends in a new era when all athletes—runners and wrestlers and boxers—convinced of the advantages of nakedness by Orsippos' success, compete naked.

Athletics is a social phenomenon; it shares in, and is shaped by, the same economic, political, religious, and moral forces that shape society and its culture. The Greeks did not know much about their history before 650 and could not find out about it, because they lacked evidence and, before Herodotus, a time frame for events of the past two centuries (Finley 1975, 18–20). Consequently, they organized extant traditions, myths, and memoirs according to experiences of their own world. Earliest times for them consisted of the monumental acts of founding gods and heroes like Herakles, Perseus, and Theseus. The Megarians, it seems, created in Orsippos, who appears historical and may indeed have lost his loincloth, such a hero, an individual responsible for the innovation of athletic nudity. But by the time Orsippos ran in the nude, the naked male youth had become an accepted phenomenon. Otherwise, Orsippos would surely not have finished the race, being too preoccupied with replacing his loincloth and covering his shame.

Greeks knew that their men had not always exercised and competed naked. The boxers and wrestlers of Homer's day gird themselves for a match (*Iliad* 23.683, 710). Moreover, the shame and degradation that underlie Odysseus' threat to strip and flog Thersites naked (*Iliad* 2.261–264) derived from the meaning of human nakedness— shame, humiliation, poverty, and slavery—common among other Mediterranean peoples (Bonfante, 546–547). Throughout the eighth century, concomitant with the rise of the *polis*, Greeks were freeing themselves of the taboo on nakedness that other Mediterraneans continued to observe (Burn, 89). By the classical period, athletic nudity was pandemic among Greeks and universally shocking to foreigners. The Perizoma Group of vases showing older athletes wearing white loincloths were made for the Etruscan market and reflect Etruscan, not Greek, values (Webster 1972, 270–272, 292; Boardman 1974, Ill.219; Bonfante, 564).

The explanations of scholars seeking to define the origin of Greek nudity range from the practices of primitive hunters to conceal their scent from prey (Sansone, 107–114) to ancient beliefs in the protection the warrior's nudity afforded him and the fear it aroused in his enemies (Mouratidis) to the athlete's pride in his self-control before spectators (Arieti). A more promising approach, because rooted in social evidence for Greek culture, is that of Larissa Bonfante who traces the changes in cultural attitudes toward the naked young male and the transition from religious to civic values attributed to his nudity, that is to say, the transition from the nude male as manifestation of the initiate and of the god Apollo to the embodiment of the heroic warrior (543–558). Bonfante suggests that nudity, no longer denoting vulnerability, came to signal confidence and self-reliance in exposing oneself to danger, qualities manifested by the gods who "could be nude because they relied on themselves" (556). Whatever its origin, athletic nudity defined the Greeks as Greeks, as different from, and superior to, foreigners (Thucydides *Histories* 1.6.5) whose bodies, deprived of the sun, seemed pale and pasty, weak and womanly, in their eyes. Thus, "When Agesilaos' soldiers saw [the captured foreigners] white because they never stripped and fat and lazy from always being in wagons, they believed that the war would not be any different from fighting with women" (Xenophon *Agesilaus* 1.28).

Added to the Olympic program in the fourteenth Olympiad (724) (Pausanias 5.8.6), the *diaulos* consisted of two laps, each a *stadion* in length (Pollux *Onamasticon* 3.147, in Bethe, 1:200). In Olympia, runners left the starting line at the west end of the stadium, turned the *kamptêr* at the east end, moving from left to right, and dashed back to the finish. This view of the event is supported by Pausanias' comparison to the *diaulos* of letters written in boustrophedon on a cedar chest that he saw in the temple of Hera at Olympia: "From the end of the line, the second line turns back as runners do in the *diaulos*" (5.17.6). Writing in boustrophedon imitates how an ox plows a field; coming to the end of one furrow, it turns back to plow another beside the first. The out-and-back movement of the *diaulos* also informs the direful prescription of Clytemnestra in the *Agamemnon* (458) of Aeschylus (ca. 525–456):

> For a safe return to their homes,
> [the Greeks] must bend back the other limb of the *diaulos*
> (342–343).

Aeschylus' Greeks have completed the first lap by gaining possession of Troy. To return home, they must turn the bend by reverencing the gods and shrines of the conquered land (*Agamemnon* 338–340).

Because of Agamemnon's sacrifice of their daughter, Clytemnestra invokes disaster for the Greeks at the bend. Aeschylus probably had in mind collisions at the *kamptêr* in chariot races, but turning the *kamptêr* in the *diaulos* 180 degrees at a runner's speed might also result in tripping and fouling, especially if all runners turned the same post as is generally thought (Harris 1964, 71–73). Yet the sources say nothing of such disasters, a strange silence made stranger by the tales of crashes at the turning post in chariot races. But if, as Miller suggests, each runner had his own post and two lanes, one out and one back, which were marked by lime or gypsum spread on the track, he could turn the post into an empty lane without incident (1980, 164). Miller sees in

Eudoxos' gift of ten shields in 271 for the hoplite race (a *diaulos*) at
Delphi, recorded in an inscription (Inscription 419 in Dittenberger 1982,
1:657–658) a clue to alternate lanes in the *diaulos* (1980, 162). At the
time, the stadium at Delphi had *at least* seventeen lanes. If, as seems
proper for a gift, Eudoxos' ten shields were all that were required for
the race, ten hoplite runners or *diaulos* runners could have run in alternate
lanes. The image of runners moving out and back in the *diaulos* inspired
Euripides' image of Polydoros' corpse "being carried by the many *diauloi*
of the waves" (*Hecuba* 29). "To suppose a single post with a string of
runners rounding it is to rob Euripides of his vivid metaphor" (Miller
1980, 163).

In the absence of direct evidence, Miller's thesis remains conjectural,
but practical considerations favor it. H. A. Harris's objections to all
runners rounding one *kamptêr* or to each runner in adjoining lanes turning
around his own post vitiate either arrangement (1964, 71–73). Moreover,
had either been the case, the resulting calamities would have been a
rich source for poetic embellishment. A similar argument from silence
attenuates Broneer's suggestion that "the runner could grab his post
with his left hand and swing around with a minimum of loss of time and
momentum" (1973, 139). By contrast, the well-attested turning at the
kamptêr became equivalent to ending one's life. Hence, Euripides'
Hippolytus prays to Artemis: "So may I turn the post of life as I began"
(*Hippolytus* 87), and his Electra declares that no man is certain "that
he has outrun Justice, until he arrives / across the scratch-line and makes
the turn around the goal of life" (*Electra* 955–956). The *kamptêr* served
as both the turning post and goal. The idea of goal where the race
ended in victory or defeat was extended to the end of life.

The *dolichos* or long run was first held at the games of the fifteenth
Olympiad (580) (Pausanias 5.8.6). All runners ran around the same
posts, one at each end of the stadium. In the stadium at Nemea, the
kamptêr at the south end was set off the central axis and away from
the starting line as, presumably, was the one at the north end. This
placement allowed the runner to avoid tripping on the raised starting
line. He could approach the post as closely as possible and then, as his
momentum took him, swing wider to the left (Miller 1980, 159). The
number of laps varied from contest to contest within a range of seven
to twenty-four stades (Jüthner 1968, 108 n. 232).

Philostratos has these recommendations for the physique of the
runner in the *dolichos*:

> The one who will run the *dolichos* best should be strong in the
> shoulders and neck much as for the pentathlon. He should have light

Illustration 6. Runners in the *dolichos*. Black-figure Panathenaic amphora, 333 B.C.E. © The British Museum, London, England.

> slender legs just as the runners of the *stadion* . . ., since the latter move their legs with their hands for the quick run as if outfitted with wings as hands. *Dolichos* runners do this at the end, but the rest of the time, they act almost as if they are walking, holding up their hands out before them, for which reason they need stronger shoulders (*Gymnastic* 32).

Near the finish, the *dolichos* runner broke out in a "kick" like the sprint of the *stadion* and *diaulos* runners, but over the many laps he relied upon his stamina to keep him up with the leaders and put him in a position to sprint for victory. A Panathenaic amphora from 333 shows the stride of three *dolichos* runners (Illustration 6). They hold their bodies upright; their arms are bent at the elbow and held close to the body; their hands are held in a loosely clenched fist. Most of the race would be run as if the legs were carrying the upper body. Consequently, the *dolichos* runner developed strong legs but also needed considerable upper-body strength to hold his arms in place. Without it, his shoulders would begin to ache, and the race would fall into doubt.

The footraces were introduced traditionally in the order *stadion-diaulos-dolichos*, but, according to Pausanias, they were run in the order *dolichos-stadion-diaulos* when Polites of Keramus won all three in the 212th Olympiad (69 C.E.) (6.13.3). Philostratos discusses the races in the latter order (*Gymnastic* 4–6). Scholars have commonly attributed the priority of the *dolichos* to the organizers' desire to have this longer, less exciting race run in the early morning in order to make way for the thrilling sprints for which the spectators would gather in numbers. Hugh M. Lee offers the following explanation based on the layout of the stadium and the use of the *hysplex*. The *dolichos* did not need an exacting start, and its runners all turned the same posts, one at each end of the stadium. For the *stadion* at Olympia, the *hysplex* was set up for the start at the east end of the stadium and the finish in the west end. For the *diaulos*, it was moved to the west end for the start, and the poles on the east end served as *kampteres*. The *hysplex* was now positioned for the hoplite race, another *diaulos* and the last athletic event of the festival (1992, 108–109).

Pythian Games: Horse Racing

In the early spring of 1676, an adventurous young English gentleman, George Wheeler, arrived at the port of Itea as had before him countless visitors and pilgrims bound for Apollo's sanctuary at Delphi (Hoyle, 146). With Pausanias as his guide, Wheeler set out for the village of Castri where, he was told, there were many ancient ruins. It was the road that Pausanias himself had traversed and, in the time of first beginnings, the god Apollo himself. Wheeler recounts his approach: "We soon began to mount the Ridges of the Mountain *Parnassus*, by a very bad rough way, South-Eastwards, until we arrived, in four or five Hours time, at *Castri*; which we no sooner approached, but we concluded, that it was undoubtedly the Remainder of the famous city of Delphos" (in Hoyle, Ills. between pages 172 and 173). With the publication of Wheeler's *Journeys* (1682), Delphi began its own journey, as it were, to reclaim its place as a glory of the ancient world:

> Castri, or Delphos, is situate [*sic*] on the South side of the Mountain Parnassus, something inclining to the West; not on the top, nor at the foot of the Mountain; for it hath a great way to the Plains of Crissa below it, and much more to the Mountain above it. The high Cliffs in sight above it from the Town seem to end in two points; whence I judged it was call'd of old Biceps Parnassus: For it hath many more tops, and much higher than these, being a great Mountain: But these two tops seen from Delphos, hide all the rest. Between which the Water falls, in great abundance, after Rain or Snow, and hath worn them almost asunder. There is also a Fountain, with a very plentiful Source of Water, continually issuing out from among those Rocks,

> just under that Separation: which by the Marble Steps descending to
> it, and the Niches made in Rock for Statues above it, should be the
> Fountain Castalia, that so inspired the antient Poets (Wheeler, in
> Hoyle, 147).

Wheeler's "Biceps" or two-headed Parnassus denotes the horns of the
Phaedreiades, the Shining Ones, that focus the summer's light upon
Apollo's shrine. They tower menacingly over the god's temple clinging
to the mountain slope two thousand feet above the plain of Krisa, modern
Itea. Assaulted by earthquakes, rock falls, and landslides, Delphi defied
nature like Apollo himself. Brought finally to ruin by Christian piety, the
shrine later lost its name to that of a Norman castle that Turkish
conquerors of Greece destroyed.

Known originally as Pytho, Delphi was inhabited during the
Mycenaean period and abandoned after the collapse of the palace
system, not to be resettled until the early ninth century. Around 800, cult
activity recommenced at Delphi as witnessed by bronze offerings
(Morgan, 134). By the eighth century, Apollo, an Anatolian god, had
settled at the sanctuary, taking the name Apollo Pythios. Village and
sanctuary grew in importance throughout the eighth century. Unlike
Olympia, Delphi was never isolated from its neighbors. The village acted
as a point of exchange for pottery and other exports from Corinth in
trade routes along the Krisan plain. The sanctuary established an oracle
through which its priests served the interests of, and advised, an ever-
widening clientele of elite from emergent *poleis* and tribal communities.
In Apollo's name, they confirmed the policies that its petitioners had
developed, and foretold future events with cunning and convincing
ambiguity (Morgan, 154–157). In the seventh century, Apollo's shrine
received its first stone temple, and throughout this and the next century,
things sacred gradually replaced the houses and other buildings around
the sanctuary.

Delphi's prosperity as an economic center and its importance as an
independent sanctuary and political consultant brought about other
changes. In the early sixth century, the Delphians lost control over their
sanctuary through what later became known as the First Sacred War
(Forrest; Fine, 114–118). In the propaganda of the victors, the war was
fought to liberate the sanctuary from the impious interference of the
Kirrhans who were levying tolls upon pilgrims to Delphi. More likely, it
was undertaken "'for the possession of' not 'for the sake of ' Delphi"
(Forrest, 51). At the time, Kirrha was a flourishing commercial city
located on the Krisan plain. Its influence over Delphi and the oracle
angered its neighbors, most prominently, the tyrant Kleisthenes of Sikyon

and the Thessalians. The amphictyony or league of neighbors centered to the north of Delphi at the shrine of Demeter at Anthela and under Thessalian leadership attacked Kirrha with the aid of the Sikyonians and Athenians. The war dragged on through the 590s, but at the end of the decade, Kirrha was captured and razed, its inhabitants annihilated or scattered to oblivion, and the plain declared sacred to Apollo, never to be tilled. The Delphians maintained independence in the operation of the oracle, but management of the Temple of Apollo and its votives was assumed by the victors. Among their first acts, the Thessalian general Eurylochos inaugurated athletic competitions to celebrate the victory.

In accordance with their tradition, Delphians had long celebrated a musical contest every eight years from Apollo's arrival at their shrine. The contest consisted of a competition in singing a hymn in honor of Apollo with the singer accompanying himself on the *kithara*, a stringed instrument with two necks (Strabo *Geography* 9.3.10; Pausanias 10.7.2). Apollo is said to have founded the contest as funeral games for Python, the dragon who guarded the shrine and uttered prophecies (Clement of Alexandria *Exhortation* p. 29) and whom Apollo slew when he seized it (*Homeric Hymn to Apollo* 356–362). Chrysthemis of Crete won the first competition. The notable singers Orpheus and Musaios refused to be tested in competition. Homer and Hesiod were turned away, the former for his blindness and the latter for his inability to play the *kithara* (Pausanias 10.7.2–3). Such myths promote the games as ancient and worthy of respect.

On taking over Delphi, the Amphictyons celebrated the musical contest and contests in flute playing and singing to the flute. From the spoils of their victory, they also offered athletic contests including all those held at Olympia except the chariot race for four horses and added a *dolichos* and *diaulos* for boys, providing monetary rewards to all the victors (Pausanias 10.7.4–5). Although the Amphictyons imitated the Olympic program, their games were not isolympic. At their next games, they discontinued singing to the flute, because they thought its strains mournful and unpropitious and too much like music at funerals (Pausanias 10.7.5). The Amphictyons began awarding victors with a crown of laurel cut in the Tempe Valley and brought to Delphi by a boy whose parents were alive—a boy not touched by death—and who was accompanied by a flute player (Plutarch *Moralia* 1136A; Scholiast on *Pindar Pythian Odes,* hypothesis c, in Drachmann, 2:4). The value of laurel was bound up in myth. Apollo was once enamored of Daphne (laurel), daughter of the river god Peneios who flowed through the Tempe Valley (Pausanias 10.5.9). But Daphne spurned his attentions and fled, praying to be turned into a tree and so escape the god. Her wish was granted, and from then on, Apollo held the laurel dear (Ovid *Metamorphoses* 1.452–567).

Scholars agree upon the sequence of chrematic and stephanitic games and upon the date of the latter (582). They are divided, however, over the date of the first (cf. Miller, 1979 and Mosshammer, 1982). The earliest source, a marble slab found at Paros in the Cyclades and dating to 246, places them in 590 (Parian Marble 52–54, in Jacoby1980,12–13). Pausanias assigns them to 586, stating specifically, "For the first time, they put up prizes for athletes" (10.7.5). In question are both the inaugural date of the Pythian Games and the year that the First Sacred War ended. The problem, too complex to be analyzed here, holds more than historical interest in that it illustrates the methods and skills required to create a consistent narrative of the past from a broad diversity of conflicting sources.

Delphi, perched high on the slope of Mount Parnassus, was hardly an ideal setting for athletic contests and did not have a stadium until the mid-fifth century. Before then, the Amphictyons may have held the games on the future site of the stadium, a level plateau higher up the mountain slope, or on the Krisan plain at the foot of Mount Parnassus. Although many famous athletes won Pythian victories, including the wrestler Milo, the pentathlete Phaÿllos, both of Krotona, and the boxer Theagenes of Thasos, Delphi remained more renowned for its musical contests, since they had been established by the god in the time when the world was being made. The athletic games were set up by men who conceded their newness by not attempting a foundation myth. From the outset the chariot races conducted on the plain attracted attention among the elite of northern Greece whose wealth and status resided in horses (Gardiner 1910, 210–211). The chariot race added for the celebration of 582 (Pausanias 10.7.6) was won by the Kleisthenes who was instrumental in the league's victory in the Sacred War. At the forty-eighth Pythiad (398), the Amphictyons introduced a chariot race for two horses, and at the fifty-third (378), one for foals. The two-foal chariot race and the horseback race for foals were first held in 338 and 314, respectively, decades before their introduction into the Olympic program.

The most famous chariot race of the Pythian Games never happened. The race in which Orestes dies while maneuvering a post is twice a fiction, the invention of a character in Sophocles' tragedy *Electra* (ca. 418–410). Orestes has returned to Mycenae from the exile his mother, Clytemnestra, and her lover, Aegisthus, imposed after they murdered

his father, Agamemnon. Orestes' sister, Electra, had entrusted him as
an infant to a slave and now, years later, he returns with his friend,
Pylades, and the slave to have his vengeance and claim his kingdom.
Trusting in an oracle of Apollo that cautioned him away from violence
and toward stealth, Orestes instructs the slave in the opening scene:

> Announce this word, padding it with bulk:
> "Orestes has died from a fatal accident
> at the Pythian Games when he was thrown
> from his wheeled chariot. Let the plot be thus" (47–50).

The slave conjures an exciting tale (*mythos*) from Orestes' plot (*mythos*)
that suggests the thrills of a chariot race and its grip upon spectators.
But his tale does more than embellish a plot: it assaults the emotions of
Orestes' sister and mother with a ruthless awareness for the power of
words that has already begun with the redundant "fatal" and the adjective
"wheeled," an unnecessary detail in describing a chariot.

Clytemnestra stands before the statue of Apollo. Electra is to the
side with the women of Mycenae who comprise the chorus. Orestes
has told his slave to await, and act at, the right moment (39), and now
the slave enters. He is Orestes' *paidagôgos* whose function in the
society of Sophocles' audience was to escort the boy outside the house
and see to his safe return. At long last, he fulfills his role with a deceptive
speech whose first words allude to the lie:

> Orestes came to the pride (*proschema*) of Greece, its renowned
> contest for the Delphic Games.
> when he heard the herald's shrill sounds
> announcing the footrace, the first contest, he entered the lists,
> the radiant object of admiration for all present.
> He made the outcome equal to his appearance
> and left with the prize honored above everything.
> There is much to say but, to tell you in a few words,
> I never knew such a man nor deeds like to his.
> Know this only: whatever event the umpires announced,
>   <corrupt line>
> he carried off the victory in each one.
> Again and again was he cheered, and his name called out:
> "Orestes of Argos, son of Agamemnon
> who once gathered the renowned host of Greece" (681–695).

The *paidagôgos*'word *proschêma* connotes pride or ornament but also
pretext or pretense. The games are a guise, an unheroic—Sophocles'
audience would think womanlike—sham to manipulate Clytemnestra
and regain for Orestes his heroic status (Segal 1981, 282). Orestes

enters the *stadion*, the first contest in the play and, since the audience, familiar with the Pythian Games, would recognize any deviation in the order, probably the first athletic contest at the festival. He beams with health and vigor, stirring wonder in all who watch him. By winning the *stadion*, he proves that the nature he received from his father equals his admirable appearance. In the same vein, Philoctetes praises Neoptolemos, youthful son of Achilles: "Your nature is well-born, being from the well-born" (Sophocles *Philoctetes* 874). Other victories follow, perhaps enumerated in the unintelligible line 691. The *paidagôgos* contends never to have seen his like as he builds the picture of magnificence intended for Clytemnestra. This woman has lived in fear of the son who will return to slay her. She has just welcomed the news of his death (675). The *paidagôgos* now holds before her another image, that of a *kalos k'agathos*, a fine and brave young man who, by honoring Apollo with victory, showers glory upon his family and city. This is a son in whom any woman would feel pride, perhaps even a Clytemnestra momentarily forgetful of the past (Kells 138–139). The cheering spectators acknowledge his great worth. But prosperity belongs to the gods; among mortals, it is notoriously insecure, even dangerous. It deludes judgment and attracts the envious eye of a god. So it was, the *paidagôgos* reports, with Orestes: "Whenever one of the gods interferes, / not even the strong can escape" (696–697).

Sophocles places the chariot race early in the morning "on another day." Although the expression does not mean "on the next day," Sophocles follows the order of events at the Pythian festival. Of the first two days, the seventh of Boutakios (roughly August) was devoted to sacrifices, and the eighth, to a communal banquet that began at sunset and carried on to the next day when the musical contests were held. Athletic events occupied the tenth, and on the eleventh and last day, the chariot and horse races took place (Mommsen, 213–214; Fontenrose 1988, 127).

Ten competitors present themselves for the four-horse race:

> On another day, at the rising of the sun, when the race
> for swift-footed horses was held,
> Orestes entered the lists along with many charioteers.
> One was an Achaean; one from Sparta; two
> were Libyans, masters of yoked teams.
> And fifth among them was Orestes with
> Thessalian mares. The sixth came from Aetolia
> with chestnut mares. Seventh was a Magnesian,
> and eighth, with white horses, a man of Ainian stock.
> The ninth hailed from Athens built by the gods.
> A Boeotian filled out the field of ten (698–708).

All are Greeks, since only Greeks could compete in the games. The Achaean and Spartan are Peloponnesians, the Libyans, north Africans from Cyrenaica, the others, from northern Greece. Orestes, an Argive and Peloponnesian, drives horses from Thessaly whose oligarchies bred fine horses for display and defense and trained them on the best plains for horses in Greece. That he has such steeds underlines his wealth and high station despite exile, an implication that would not have been lost on an Athenian audience. Only the wealthiest of the wealthy Athenian families could afford race horses and chariots (Davies, 98–101).

From the start of the race, each man strives to break free by getting his wheels in front of those of the other chariots and then his horses' heads beyond those of the other teams. Drivers who are passing feel the breath of the pursuing horses on their backs; those who have been passed see their wheels mottled with foam from the passing team:

> Standing where the umpires in charge
> positioned their chariots according to the lot,
> at the brazen trumpet's signal, they were off.
> All cried out to their horses and shook
> the reins in their hands. The whole track was filled
> with the thunder of rattling chariots. Dust
> rose up. All were bunched together and spared nothing
> of the whip in order for one among them
> to outstrip the wheel hubs and snorting horses,
> for the horses were spitting foam everywhere across the drivers'
> backs and over the wheels, and their panting struck all (709–719).

Sophocles could rely on his audience's knowledge of chariot racing. His modern readers may get an idea about an ancient chariot race from the race enacted in *Ben Hur*, the 1959 movie directed by William Wyler. No matter that the race takes place in a Roman setting, the Circus of Antioch, it remains the most exciting and realistic chariot race on film, although the scythe-bearing wheels on the chariot of the Roman Messala, Ben Hur's former friend and now bitterest enemy, smack shamelessly of Hollywood hokum. Charlton Heston, the actor in the title role, trained for weeks at driving a chariot, becoming "a modestly competent charioteer" (186). In his autobiography, *In the Arena*, he describes the rush felt in the start of a race when four horses accelerate from a standing start to full speed in a heartbeat:

> I slapped them on the rumps with the reins, yelled (more of a falsetto scream, actually), and we thundered off. Chariot teams only have three speeds: walk, trot, and dead run. Once in high, you can't really

do much with four horses except steer; they're not programmed for slowing down (185).

Sophocles clues his audience to recall the funeral games for Patroclus by using a word for calling out to the horses that appears here (712) and in the *Iliad* (23.363) but nowhere else in tragedy. In Homer's chariot race, Antilochos received the inmost lane in the lot (23.353) as well as a lengthy lecture from his father, Nestor, in maneuvering the turn. Homer does not describe the turn, but Sophocles puts the maneuver in the forefront from the start, adding a premonition of disaster:

> Orestes, holding just off the edge of the pillar,
> kept bringing the edge of the axle near it. Letting loose the trace horse
> on the right, he reined in the horse near the pillar.
> So far everyone stood upright in his chariot (720–723).

A chariot was made of wood; its box, ample for two standing men, was ringed with rails and rested on an axle to which were fixed two wooden wheels. The inner horses were yoked to the chariot; beside them, the outer pair or trace horses ran free and were controlled by reins. A black-figure vase from the mid-sixth century shows the

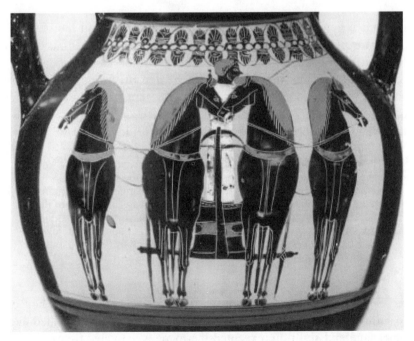

Illustration 7. Front view of a four-horse chariot. Black-figure amphora, ca. 540 B.C.E. Courtesy of the Staatliche Antikensammlungen und Glyptothek, Munich, Germany.

Illustration 8. Charioteer nearing turn. Black-figure Panathenaic amphora, ca. 420-400
B.C.E. © The British Museum, London, England.

difference between the *zygioi* or yoked middle pair and the outside
seiraphoroi or trace horses (Illustration 7). Because of the limits of the
technology and the conditions for racing, Heston can recapture the
experience in rounding the turn felt by the driver depicted on a
Panathenaic amphora held in the British Museum, his body tense with
anticipation and his eyes focused forward as the left trace horse nears
the pillar (Illustration 8), in terms that Nestor would recognize:

> The wheels on a Roman chariot can't be steered laterally to turn. You
> have to skid the chariot through by reining in the near horse, who
> runs diagonally to his left as a steadying counterweight, and whipping
> up the other three, particularly the off horse, always the fastest of the
> four, leading through the turn. The whole thirty yards or so of skidding
> turn throws up quite a lot of sand; you have to squint your eyes
> almost shut to keep the grit out so you can check traffic. The entire
> maneuver merits your full attention (185).

Sophocles passes over the results of the lot, relying on his audience
to surmise from Orestes' close turning of the pillars that he gained the
inner lane and skillfully executed the maneuver twelve times (Kells
143). Each time, he approached the pillar as close as possible and then

swung outward into the track before turning back into the inner lane (Kamerbeek,100). Nestor urges Antilochos to apply *mêtis*, ingenuity, in the race: "Come now, dear son, lay up in your mind ingenuity / of every sort so that the prizes may not flee out from before you" (*Iliad* 23.313–314) and praises ingenuity over brute force (23.315). But here brute force intervenes, it would seem, by divine will upon Orestes:

> Then the Ainian's hard-mouthed horses
> carried off his chariot by brute force as they were coming out
> of the turn on the sixth lap and already beginning the seventh
> and struck head-on with the chariot from Barca in Lybia.
> From one mishap one chariot smashed and fell upon
> another, and the whole plain of Krisa
> was filled with the shipwreck of chariots.
> The quick-witted driver from Athens saw what was happening
> and wrested his team toward the outside and, holding back
> on the reins, passed the storm of horses building in the middle
> (724–733).

As the Ainian is completing the turn around the pillar placed near the starting line, his horses, either no longer feeling the bit or biting it, seize control of the chariot. Euripides uses the same expression when the horses of Theseus' doomed son, Hippolytus, clutch the bit with their jaws and "carry it off by brute force" (*Hippolytus* 1224). The Ainian's horses bolt inward and to the left, crossing over the divide, and collide head-on with the Barcaean's team. Six drivers, barreling toward the turn, cannot get out of the way and collide with the first two, creating a huge pile-up in the middle of the leg of the track that leads into the turn. The Athenian, far enough back to assess the situation, deftly swerves his chariot toward the outer edge of the track and makes the turn. He is the eventual winner as Sophocles unobtrusively asserts the conceit of Athenian cleverness (Herodotus *Histories* 1.60.3).

Orestes has been hanging back:

> Driving last and keeping his horses behind
> was Orestes who put his trust in the finish.
> When he saw that only one rival was left,
> he hurled a piercing cry through his horses' ears
> and set forth in pursuit. They evened their chariots
> and were driving neck-and-neck, first one, then the other,
> thrusting his head out in front of the chariots.
> All the other laps the miserable youth
> had guided aright with his chariot upright.
> Then he made a mistake: he let out the left rein
> of the horse bending the turn and struck the edge of the pillar,
> breaking the axle hub down the middle.
> He slipped over the rails and was coiled and entangled

in the sharp reins. As he was falling to the plain,
his horses bolted into the middle of the course (734–748).

The *paidagôgos'* fictional Orestes exhibits characteristics of his real master, patience in waiting for the moment and trusting in the end: "What bother is it to me when, though dead in word, / I am rescued in deeds and carry off renown?" (59–60). Orestes is willing to risk the ill omen of declaring himself dead because of his confidence in the outcome of his plot. In the race, he jumps on the moment and quickly pulls even with the Athenian who lost ground while avoiding the pile-up. They race together, alternately taking and surrendering the lead over several laps. Orestes commands the inner lane, advantageous for its shorter distance but also more dangerous for being closer to the pillar. In the excitement, he lets up on the reins on the inner trace horse, and the horse pulls with more force. "The effect was to create an angular velocity, which brought the left wheel into collision with the goal" (Jebb, 109; see also 215–216). The chariot loses traction and slides into the pillar. With the left wheel shattered, Orestes is thrown over the rails of his chariot and into the reins where he becomes entangled. Meanwhile, as Nestor predicted of horses out of control in the turn (*Iliad* 23.319–321), Orestes' horses bolt into the middle of the track.

The spectators have accepted Orestes as their own and, like kinsmen, cry out in grief when they see that he is down:

When the spectators saw that he had fallen,
they broke into mourning for the youth,
that one who had accomplished such deeds met such misfortune,
now carried over the ground, now showing
his legs to the sky, until with difficulty
the charioteers brought the careening horses under control.
They freed him, so bloody that no friend or loved one
on seeing him would recognize his poor body.
They burned him immediately on a pyre,
and the men of Phokis who were chosen for this task
bring here in a small urn the wretched ashes
of that mighty corpse so that he may obtain burial in his fatherland.
Such is what I have for you, painful in the telling
and, for those of us who saw it,
the greatest of all misfortunes I have ever seen (749–763).

The victorious athlete Orestes dies young, but deprived of *ho kalos thanatos*, the beautiful death. He is not untouched and unchanged. Rather, the "sharp reins" lacerate the body as his horses drag him across the sand. Orestes is so disfigured that neither a friend nor kin (*philos*) could not recognize him. The *paidagogos* seeks to move Clytemnestra.

She is Orestes' *philê* and obligated to care for his body and ritually mourn his death, but she is neither his friend nor loved one. His tale elicits from her a *philê*'s anguished cry of grief: "Woe is me / if I am to save myself by my own misfortunes" (767–768), a sentiment soon to be replaced by the murderess's relief: "By this day, I am freed of fear / from both this one [Electra] and that one (783–784). The *paidagôgos* never names Orestes but refers to him as "that one." On Clytemnestra's lips, the words no longer evoke the victorious athlete.

In ancient horse races, the owner of the horse or chariot with horses—a king or a tyrant or a rich man—was declared the winner. A woman could enter a chariot and, if it won, be acclaimed victor, because horse racing was admired for its grandeur and, since the charioteers were slaves or hired men (Plato *Lysis* 208A), shame from defeat by a woman was not a factor in the competition. In 396, Kyniska [M 373, 381], daughter of the Lacedaemonian king Archidamos and sister of another, Agesilaos, won the four-horse chariot race at Olympia with

Olympiad	Year	Athlete	Moretti Number
58th	548	Evagoras	110
59th	544	Evagoras	113
60th	540	Evagoras	117
69th	504	Damaratos	157
73rd	484	Polypeithes	195
83rd	448	Arkesilaos	305
84th	444	Arkesilaos	311
85th	440	Polykles	315
87th	432	Lykonos	324
88th	428	Anaxandros	327
89th	424	Leon	332
90th	420	Lichas	339
96th	396	Kyniska	373
97th	392	Kyniska	381
98th	388	Xenarches	386

Table 2.

her own team (Pausanias 3.8.1, 6.1.6). Wealthy Lacedaemonians had been entering and winning the chariot races at Olympia for some time:

Other Spartiates must have been training teams and winning races in regional festivals as evinced by the inscription published by Damonon in which he records the forty-seven triumphs that his son and he won with the four-horse chariot and twenty-one with single horses at eight different festivals in Laconia and Messenia (*Inscriptiones Graecae* V.1.213). Such activities aligned Lacedaemonians with wealthy horsemen across Greece and flagrantly repudiated claims of equality among the Spartiates (Xenophon *Constitution of the Lacedaemonians* 10.7). Agesilaos apparently found all this threatening in the competition for prestige, since he countered by promoting the military uses of horses (Xenophon *Agesilaus* 9.6) for Lacedaemon's budding cavalry (Thucydides *Histories* 4.55.2). He also persuaded his sister to enter a team in order "to show the Greeks that victory was not a mark of excellence (*aretê*) but of wealth and expenditure" (Plutarch *Agislaos* 20.1). His plan was based on Greek prejudices that deemed anything that a woman could do as unworthy of a man, but it backfired. Gender aside, Kyniska was a Spartan aristocrat. When lured into the competition for *arete*, she emulated the values of her male counterparts by erecting statues of herself, her team and its driver in defiance of her brother who disdained such displays of personal accomplishment (Xenophon *Agislaus* 11.7; Plutarch *Agislaus* 2.4).

Kyniska's dedication at Olympia in honor of her victory shows that the driver was a man (Pausanias 6.1.6) whose status is clarified by the telling anecdote of the mare Aura (Pausanias 6.13.9). Aura threw her rider at the start, ran with the other horses, and turned the post in good order. On hearing the trumpet, she picked up her pace and outstripped the other horses to the finish. The Hellanodikai awarded her owner, Pheidolas, the victory and allowed him to erect a statue of his horse. It is, therefore, an irony of the evidence for the ancient world that the most famous of fifth-century free-standing bronze statues is that of the Delphi Charioteer held in the Delphi Museum. The Delphi Charioteer originally belonged to a tableau of a four-horse chariot and horses and stood in the chariot beside its owner and victor in the race, the Sicilian tyrant, Polyzalos of Gela (Boardman 1985, 52–53 and Ill. 34). Nearly six feet tall and without his left arm, he wears a tunic, belted at, and elongated below, the waist so that his upper body would be visible when seen from below. His head, bent slightly to the right, has a headband of silver inlay. Glass and stone form the eyes, and copperplate, the lips. Polyzalos' dedication was destroyed in the earthquake of 373 C.E. that took the sixth-century temple. Only the charioteer along with pieces of the horses, harnesses, chariot and, the inscribed stone base on which the tableau stood survived to be rescued in 1896 from the rubble behind the retaining wall north of the Temple of Apollo.

Isthmian Games

The Isthmus of Corinth, the saying goes, is "both beetle-browed and fraught with hollows" (Strabo *Geography* 8.6.23). Rough, rifted, and not very fertile, this low stretch of flatland, three and one-half miles wide, nonetheless caused men since Homeric times to bestow another byword upon Corinth, "wealthy" (*Iliad* 2.570). At every point of the compass, the Isthmus was strategically placed. It connected the Peloponnesus to the south with the mountainous Megarid and central Greece to the north. It separated the Gulf of Corinth and trade routes to Italy on the west from the Saronic Gulf and the ports of Asia on the east. "Corinth facilitated the exchanges of goods for those far removed from one another" (Strabo 8.6.20), and its elite profited from duties on imports and exports. Corinthians benefited from their isthmus in another way. Crowds of spectators flocked to their Isthmian Games, for travel by ship was readily available, and the shrine of Poseidon where the games were held lay on the main road from Athens and frequently hosted congresses and other meetings. More importantly, Corinth was a cosmopolitan city with lots of things to do besides watching games, and a sailors' port well known throughout Greece for its prostitutes. And so another saying, "Not for every man is the voyage to Corinth," hints at the separation of the sailor from his money, the business of its brothels (Strabo 8.6.20). The city described by the Roman historian Livy (59–17 C.E.) was no longer the Greek one but a Roman colony founded by Julius Caesar in 44, yet the Isthmus had its effect: "The Isthmian Games are always popular not only because of the zeal for games instilled in the Greek people who watch every sort of contest in skill, strength, and speed, but also because of the strategic location of the place" (*Ab Urbe Condita* 33.32.1–2).

Eusebius is the sole source for the foundation date of the Isthmian Games. For the third or fourth year of the forty-ninth Olympiad (584), Eusebius added the entry, "Isthmian Games after Melikertes," yielding a date traditionally set at 582 with the variations 581 and 580 (*Chronicles,* in Schoene, 2:94). The Corinthians held the games in the second and fourth year of an Olympiad during April, May or June before the new moon. Recognition of the Panhellenic status of their games, however, was slow in coming since they were administered by officials of one *polis*. Much later, in the 460s, Pindar could still use "Isthmus" as a synonym for Corinth (*Olympian Ode* 9.84). Corinthians retained their grip, with few interruptions, until their city was destroyed by the Romans in 146.

In the late eighth century, when visitors began to arrive at Olympia and Delphi, Poseidon's shrine by the road was a rural cult site for Corinthians. Religious activity carried on through the customary sacrifices, eating, and drinking, had been practiced there since Protogeometric times (Morgan, 213). But dedications like dress pins, bulls and horses in terra-cotta and bronze, tripods, and armor evidence only the presence of a cult to Poseidon and nothing about rivalries among the elite of several cities or the conspicuous consumption of wealth in dedications that occurred at Olympia. Those remains that relate to horses cannot testify exclusively to horse races, since Poseidon received votives as the god of horses (Gebhard 1992, 75). Moreover, the Corinthians themselves did not invest in the sanctuary but preferred to direct their funds outside their territory to Delphi, and inside it, to Perachora. Around 657 or 656, Kypselos overthrew the century-old oligarchy of the Bacchiads and established himself as tyrant with the support of the hoplites of the army (Fine, 109–114). Soon afterwards (ca. 650), he built the first monumental temple to Poseidon at the sanctuary. A political statement for and from the new ruler in the face of the city's Bacchiad temple, it remained in "splendid isolation" until the inauguration of the games (Morgan, 214).

The archaeological record excludes the presence of Panhellenic games or activity at the Isthmus before 582. The statement of the Roman Solinus (second century C.E.) that "in the forty-ninth Olympiad [584], the Corinthians restored to its pristine glory the spectacle interrupted by Kypselos" (*Collectanea Rerum Memorabilium* 7.14) is mistaken in that the games were not interrupted in 582 but rather inaugurated, probably in response to the recent death of Kypselos' son and successor, Periander. Another archaeological consideration rules out games before the traditional date: the lack of level ground for a stadium. The Earlier Stadium, its modern name, was built near the temple, the area on three sides of which was scored by channels worn in the ground by water flowing from the ridge to the south (Gebhard 1992, 75). Even in the classical period, when the Later Stadium, located 240 meters to the southwest of the temple, was in use, flat land was at a premium at the sanctuary. An obscene remark by a character in Aristophanes' *Peace* (421) prompted an ancient scholar to note:

> Those who wish to view the games obtain places [for their tents] beforehand. . . . Since the place is narrow, all are eager to get them in advance, since they do not find accommodations. . . . Since in Isthmia

it is not easy to light upon accommodations because of the want of room at the place, it is customary for those wishing to attend the festival to get tents (Scholiast to Aristophanes, *Peace* 879, in Dübner, 197–198).

Dio Chrysostom (ca. 40-ca. 112 C.E.) mentions that at the time of Diogenes the Cynic's visit some spectators, especially those who were poor or lacked lodging, left after hearing the philosopher's refutation of the athletes and their games (*Ninth Discourse* 22). Once the Corinthians had decided to offer games, however, they would have needed a stadium, a level track of six hundred ancient feet in length as well as a place for spectators. The date of the Earlier Stadium cannot be determined archaeologically because of the absence of datable pottery in the fill at the stadium site, but one near the time of the inaugural games is probable (Broneer 1973, 65). Elizabeth R. Gebhard, director of the University of Chicago excavations at Isthmia, describes the conditions confronting the builders:

> The continuous slope down to the east meant that from the time that it was first laid out a tremendous amount of terracing was required to create a level racetrack. The slope to the north, on the other hand, meant that the area along the northeast side of the track was below its surface. Thus, to provide a viewing area for the spectators, the Corinthians were required to bring in more fill along the northeast side (1987, 476).

Gebhard estimates that the Corinthians moved "at least 5000 cubic meters of soil" (1988, 85). Such effort and expense, unwarranted for local athletes at a rural shrine, support the view that athletic competitions were not held at Isthmia before 582.

With the games established, the poets of Corinth surely began circulating stories about the events leading to their creation. Of the two foundation myths associated with Isthmia, that of Sisyphus, founder and king of Corinth, goes back to Corinthian mythmakers. In the absence of Panhellenic athletics in honor of Poseidon before 582, it can be no older than the games themselves. The earliest evidence for the myth comes from the early fifth century. A fragment of an ode of Pindar: "They command Sisyphus, son of Aiolos, / to call forth a far-seen prize for the child, / Melikertes, who has perished," contains the essential elements (fr. 6.5 [1] in Snell, 2:3). The Nereids order Sisyphus to establish funeral games for the slain infant, Melikertes. Pausanias inserts what has proved to be the most complete version extant at that point in his narrative when he reaches the Molourian Rock on the Scironian road from Megara to Corinth:

Ino is said to have thrown herself from the Molourian Rock into the sea with her younger child, Melikertes. An elder child, Learchos, was already killed by their father, Athamas. One story has it that Athamas did this in a fit of madness. Another says that Athamas vented uncontrolled rage on Ino and her children, because he found out that the famine that befell the Orchomenians and the supposed death of Phryxos were not divine occurrences but had been engineered by the stepmother, Ino. Ino then fled to the sea and hurled herself and her child from the Molourian Rock. The boy was carried to the Isthmus of the Corinthians by a dolphin, as the story goes, and among other honors that were offered to Melikertes whose name was changed to Palaimon, they celebrated the games of the Isthmia for him (1.44.7–8).

The Scholiast continues the story:

> Some say that the Isthmian Games are in honor of Melikertes when, unburied, he came ashore at the Isthmus. Meanwhile, famine gripped the city of Corinth. The god said that there would be no other release from this evil than the obsequies and honors through funeral games for the unburied. After the Corinthians did this for a little while, they stopped, and the famine returned. The god then declared that the honor for the hero was to be given forever (Pindar *Isthmian Odes hypothesis* b, in Drachmann, 3:193).

More than other Mediterranean peoples, the Greeks imaged their world through myths about marriage and the family. The story of Athamas, complex with conflicting events, revolves around his three marriages and their six offspring (Gantz 176–180). Mythmakers varied the story not out of ignorance or neglect for the truth. Myths do not refer to a unique set of historical events but to other myths, in Athamas' case, myths about the dynamics of marriage, remarriage, and the stepmother. The impulse to make myths about the Isthmian Games, however, derives from the need to link them to another cultural institution, funeral games. Whatever the historicity of their belief, Greeks held that athletic competitions arose in connection with funeral games for a dead hero. The Olympic Games were said to be in honor of Pelops (Clement of Alexandria *Exhortation*, p. 29), the Pythian, for the dragon Python (Hyginus *Fabula* 140), and the Nemean, for the child Archemoros (*Fabula* 74). All Greeks were familiar with the games for Patroclus in Homer's *Iliad* 23, and the practice of holding games for a slain hero such as the Spartan general Brasidas, killed in battle against the Athenians in 422, continued into historical times (Thucydides *Histories* 5.11.1). But Melikertes is killed unjustly and prematurely, for which wrong he receives by way of compensation a cult offered to him as the chthonic deity under the name Palaimon. Sacrifices were conducted for Palaimon at night at his sacred place, perhaps a pit dug in the ground in earliest times, later a temple with statues of him, his mother Ino, transformed into the Nereid Leukothea, and Poseidon. Nearby also was an underground chamber where, it is said, Palaimon was hidden and where oaths were sworn (Pausanias 2.2.1). What more forbidding place for an athlete to swear his oath than a subterranean inner sanctum haunted by the god himself? (Burkert.1983, 197–198).

A second myth gives the founding of the contest to the Athenian hero Theseus:

> They say that Theseus established the Isthmian Games in honor of Sinis Prokrustes whom he slew when he killed the others, as Sophocles says of Theseus: "As I walked along the shore, I cleared the road of wild beasts" (Scholiast to Pindar *Isthmian Odes, hypothesis* b, in Drachmann, 3:192).

> Theseus acquired the Megarid by force, adding it to Attica, and erected a far-famed stele in the Isthmus. . . . Theseus was the first to found the games in rivalry with Herakles as he sought that through his efforts the Greeks celebrate the Isthmian Games for Poseidon as they do the Olympic Games for Zeus through the efforts of Herakles (Plutarch *Theseus* 25.5).

The myth is undoubtedly Athenian; Corinthians would hardly promote a foreigner as the founder of their games. Athenians frequented the competitions and enjoyed success, marvelous success, if the eight victories won by the clan of Timodemus were typical (Pindar *Nemean Ode* 2.21–22). A policy attributed to Solon rewarded victors at Olympia with five hundred drachmas but only a fifth of that amount to winners at Isthmia (Plutarch *Solon* 23.3). Competition was keener at the older and more prestigious Oympic Games, but the frequency of Athenian victories at the Isthmus may have detracted from their worth in honor as well as drachmas. On the other hand, a later Athenian law from ca. 425 awarded winners at any of the periodic games with the honor of meals at state expense for the rest of their lives (*Inscriptiones Graecae* 1^2 77).

Athenian mythmakers put Theseus' founding of the games in the context of his violent annexation of the Megarid on Attica's northwestern border. No less than the actions it portrays, the myth itself is an act of aggression, asserting a claim to the Corinthians' contest. Although the brash presumption, even hostility, is apparent, the time when a myth of this sort would be invented is open to speculation. Megara may provide a clue. In 460, the Megarians, allies of the Corinthians against the Athenians, fell into a dispute over their boundaries with the Corinthians

(Thucydides *Histories* 1.103.4), and the latter went to war, imperiling the alliance of Peloponnesian cities against the Athenian empire. The Athenians immediately capitalized on Megara's strategic position at the Isthmus and its port cities by erecting and manning walls that rendered the city nearly inexpugnable. Consequently, as Thucydides reports, "a bitter hatred first began to exist toward the Athenians" (*Histories* 1.103.4). Theseus the founder may have been malicious disinformation, another assault in the conflict building in the years before the Peloponnesian War, a conflict provoked by the Athenians' familiarity and possessiveness of the Isthmian Games compounded by their desire for more than an invitation.

The festival began with a sacrifice to Poseidon at the long altar in front of his temple (Xenophon *Hellenica* 4.5.1–2). Athletes were divided into three groups, men, youths, and boys. The athletic events copied those of Olympia with horse racing prominent. Nothing is said about a hippodrome, but after the construction of a theater northeast of the temple, musical contests were likely held, although no mention is made of them before the third century.

In his *Eighth and Ninth Discourses*, Dio Chrysostom, an orator and popular philosopher, imagines a visit to the Isthmian Games by Diogenes of Sinope who lived during the fourth century Exiled from his homeland on the southern shore of the Black Sea, Diogenes traveled to Athens where he befriended Antisthenes, a devoted follower of Socrates and, as it turned out, a formative influence on Diogenes' philosophy. Diogenes criticized society and its values, summoning everyone he met to a life of self-sufficiency and natural simplicity. He fancied himself "Diogenes the Dog," because "I fawn on those who give me things, bark at those who do not, and sink my teeth into scoundrels" (Diogenes Laertius *Lives of the Eminent Philosophers* 6.60). Plato thought him "a Socrates gone mad" (*Lives* 6.54). After Antisthenes' death, Diogenes the Cynic moved on to Corinth where he camped in a cypress grove. "He saw," Dio explains, "that many men gathered there because of the harbors and the ladies and because the city was situated, as it were, at the crossroads of Greece" (*Eighth Discourse* 5). He came as if he were a doctor able to cure the unwilling of their ignorance, dishonesty, and intemperance (*Eighth Discourse* 8). The time arrived for the Isthmian Games, and along with many others, Diogenes went down from Corinth but not for the usual reasons, not to watch the athletes and gourmandize (*Ninth Discourse* 1):

> It was his custom to observe men's interests and passions for which they left home and in what things they prided themselves. He offered

himself to any who wished to engage him in conversation. . . . At that time, you could hear around the temple of Poseidon many wretched sophists shouting and railing at one another and their so-called students engaged with one another in battles. Many writers were reading from their insipid works, and poets galore were singing their songs to the praises of many. Countless jugglers were showing off their antics, and soothsayers were interpreting signs and omens. Peddlers there were in no small numbers, trafficking in whatever they had to sell. Right off, men flocked to Diogenes, strangers, not Corinthians, who, after seeing him daily, did not think his company profitable. Each stranger spoke or listened to him briefly and left in fright before his refutations. . . . When someone inquired whether he came to see the contest, he replied, "No, to compete." The man laughed and asked him what opponents he would have. Diogenes, looking at him askance as he did everybody, said, "the most difficult and hardest to defeat. None of the Greeks can look them in the eye. They are not runners or wrestlers or jumpers or boxers or hurlers of javelins and discuses." "Who are they, then?" "Adversities," replied Diogenes, "strong and invincible. . . . The noble man considers these adversities to be his greatest opponents, and he is always ready to fight against them day and night, not for celery, like some goat, or ivy or pine, but for happiness and excellence, and does so all his life and not whenever Eleans or Corinthians or the amphictyony of Thessalians send out a proclamation" (*Eighth Discourse* 6–7, 9–10, 11–13, 15).

At first, the judges of the games generally ignored Diogenes. The respected and powerful, though sorely upset with him, passed him by in silence and with mean glances:

> But when he donned a crown of pine, the Corinthians sent their subordinates to order him to remove the crown and not to act against custom (or law). He asked them why it was against custom for him to wear a crown of pine and not for others. One subordinate said, "Diogenes, because you have not won a victory." "Many great opponents have I won against," he retorted, "not like these slaves who wrestle here and throw discuses and run but far more difficult ones, poverty, exile, and dishonor" (*Ninth Discourse* cf10–12).

For Diogenes, athletes excel at activities in which an animal can surpass them. The "fastest man of all the Greeks," winner of the *stadion*, cannot beat a rabbit or deer. Speed, he contends, is a coward's ploy (*Ninth Discourse* 14–18). He places a crown on the head of a horse who kicked another horse into flight, because "He won the victory in kicking" (*Ninth Discourse* 22). The human condition is defined in Greek mentality by its difference from the divine above and the bestial below. Athletics for Diogenes reduces humans to poor imitations of animals while uplifting animals to the human sphere. They divert men from the activities and values of excellence (*aretê*) that distinguish them from both gods and animals. But in Dio's discourses, Diogenes' voice is that of another philosopher, and both Dio and Diogenes were blowing in the wind of Greek love of competition and a good time.

Nemean Games

On his way from Corinth to Argos, Pausanias came to the small city of Kleonai (2.15.1). He visited its attractions, a shrine of Athena and the tomb of two Eleans killed by Herakles, and moved on down the road. Before him towered Mount Tretos and the choice of a vigorous climb by "a straight, toilsome path" or a roundabout route to the west "where the mountain is not so high, and runs up a gradually ascending gully" (Frazer 3.85). Locals still spoke of the cave of the Nemean lion that lived on a mountain called Tretos and was impenetrable. Herakles choked the lion to death, skinned him with his own claw, and wore the lion's skin as a trademark (Apollodorus, *Library* 2.5.1). Once over the mountain, Pausanias came into the valley of Nemea where the "height [333 meters above sea level] and the prevailing west winds off the mountains combine to keep the valley relatively cool during the summer months and damp and chill during the winter, when frosts, ice, and snow are common" (Miller 1990, 9). Near a sacred grove of cypresses, Zeus Nemaios had his sanctuary and temple. During the Roman Empire, the games were held at Argos, and the shrine at Nemea had fallen into disrepair. The temple Pausanias saw belonged to the fourth century (ca. 330); its roof had collapsed, and its cult statue had been removed. It replaced, and all but wiped out, every trace of an earlier temple built around 600, near the time of the inauguration of the games (Miller 1990, 130–132).

The archaeological record reveals little evidence for religious practice before the seventh century (Morgan 215). Soon after Zeus's shrine received its temple, the Kleonaians built a stadium close by and offered Panhellenic games for the first time in 573 at Nemea, an independent sanctuary about three miles away (Eusebius, *Chronicles*, in Schoene, 2:94). It has been suggested that the people of Kleonai had fallen under the suzerainty of Kleisthenes of Sikyon and founded the games to mark the return of their freedom (McGregor, 277–278). On the other hand, activity at Nemea coincides with building programs at Olympia and Delphi and with the institution of the Isthmian Games and may evince the rivalry among cities near the Isthmus of the sort that stimulated change and development elsewhere across Greece.

According to their foundation myth, the Nemean Games were occasioned by the death of the child Opheltes and first celebrated as funeral games in his honor by the leaders of the Argive king Adrastos' expedition against Thebes (Apollodorus *Library* 3.6.4; Hyginus *Fabula* 74). Lycurgus, king and priest of Nemea, entrusts the care of his son, Opheltes, to a nurse and slave, Hypsipyle, with instructions never to put him down until he learned to walk. A Delphic oracle declared that his son, if treated in this way, would grow up healthy. The Argives arrive at Nemea on their expedition to Thebes and, meeting Hypsipyle, ask her for water. Hypsipyle leaves the child behind in a patch of celery. While she is guiding the Argives to a spring, a serpent bites and kills the infant. The Argives slay the snake and institute funeral games for the boy, now named Archemoros, the Beginner of Doom. His death becomes a portent for the Argives, the first of many deaths that will accrue from the fighting at Thebes. Simonides catches the essence of the tale with "They wept the infant child of the violet-crowned mother as it breathed out its sweet spirit" (Athenaeus *The Deipnosophists* 9.396). The myth places the founding of the games in the remote times and probably was in place from the sixth century. Pindar (*Nemean Ode* 10.28) and his younger contemporary Bacchylides (*Ode* 9.1–24) knew it. Nonetheless, it offers no evidence that the Nemean Games were earlier than 573.

In the late fifth or early fourth century, the sanctuary at Nemea was nearly destroyed. No trace of the event remains in the written sources. The archaeological record indicates fire and armed violence as the means and humans as the culprits. The upper layer of debris includes large stone blocks, damaged but more or less whole. The lower layer contains broken and burned roof tiles, much carbon mixed in white clay of the kind used in paving east of the temple, melted bronze arrowheads, nails, and iron spear points (Miller 1978, 65, 82–83; 1980, 184–187). Miller explains: "The upper level may thus be interpreted as a deliberate, post-destruction dismantling of a building, while the lower level must represent the violent and fiery actual destruction of the building" (1980, 184). The victim of fire and battle could only have been the Temple of Zeus, a shocking barbarism perpetrated by Greeks upon Greeks but one that was in no way unique at the Panhellenic shrines.

At Olympia, the Eleans and their Achaean allies fought a pitched battle in the Altis in 364 against the Arcadians who had seized the sanctuary with two thousand Argives and four hundred Athenian cavalry (Xenophon *Hellenica* 7.4.28–31). The Arcadians were celebrating the contests of the 104th Olympiad (364) and completed the horse race and pentathlon when the Eleans entered the precinct under arms. Two sacred wars were fought over the oracle at Delphi. In 390, the Lacedaemonian general Agesilaos invaded the sanctuary at Isthmia while the Argives, who had taken control of the sanctuary from the Corinthians, were sacrificing to Poseidon in preparation for the competitions (Xenophon *Hellenica* 4.5.1–2). The Argives fled at his arrival, "but Agesilaos, though he saw them, did not go in pursuit but, pitching his tents in the sanctuary, sacrificed to the god and waited until the Corinthian exiles had conducted sacrifice to Poseidon and held the contest" (4.5.2). When he departed, the Argives returned and redid the games. Xenophon remarks that "in that year, in some of the contests, a man was defeated twice, and in others, the same men were proclaimed victors twice" (4.5.2). Two years later, Agesilaos invaded Argos by way of Nemea, even though the Argives insisted that the sacred truce for the games was in effect, and wreaked much destruction and terror in the countryside and city (4.7.2–3). About 235, Aratos of Sikyon, at war with Argos, secured Kleonai as an ally for the Achaean League and held the Nemean Games in Kleonai as the Kleonaians had the older and more fitting claim to them. The Argives held the games at Argos. The athletes were surely trapped in a dilemma between the prestige of a period game and Aratos' hatred of the tyranny at Argos, the city of his boyhood. Afterwards, the Achaeans treated as enemies and sold into slavery all athletes who were arrested in their territory after competing in Argos (Plutarch *Aratus* 28.4–6).

"At that time, the inviolability and assurance of personal safety extended to athletes were violated for the first time," Plutarch observes of the sacred truce proclaimed for the Nemean Games (*Aratus* 28.4). Agesilaos who transgressed such a truce at Isthmia respected the Nemean truce by consulting the oracles of Olympic Zeus and Pythian Apollo before moving on Nemea. He wished to be assured that the Argives, not he, were violating scruples by declaring the sacred truce that he contended they announced not because of the games but because they were about to be invaded. The gods sided with Agesilaos who had an army.

Argives, it should be noted, not Kleonaians, were conducting the Nemean Games when Agesilaos intruded upon the rituals. The fact is that the games were celebrated at Nemea less than a quarter of their nearly thousand years in existence (Miller 1992.83). Kleonaians controlled the games in Pindar's day, but by 388, probably as a consequence of the destruction of the temple and sanctuary, the Argives were in charge. In the face of the ruin of their facilities and their acceptance of Argive leadership in foreign affairs since at least ca. 460, the Kleonaians likely concurred with the shift (Miller 1982, 106–107). Afterwards, the sanctuary was abandoned during the first half of the fourth century.

No evidence of construction and almost no pottery shards belonging to this period have been found. A well discovered in the sanctuary shows material from the late fourth and early third centuries and, below it, a saltcellar from the last quarter of the fifth century but virtually nothing from the intervening period, ca. 410-ca. 340 (Miller 1978, 82–83). The games evidently had been moved to Argos. Fate had in store for the Nemean Games other such shifts whose direction depended upon the relative fortunes of the two *poleis*. In the 330s, for instance, the Macedonians returned the games to the Kleonaians while allowing the Argives to retain control over them. The Argives joined an alliance led by Athenians against the Macedonians, and the Macedonians chose to punish them by granting them the prestige of the games but not their benefits. Nearby Kleonai would be the source of lodging and supplies for visitors to the shrine until its fortunes changed with the death of Alexander (Miller 1982, 107).

Archaeologists have mapped the topography of Zeus's sanctuary, described the architecture of its buildings, and illuminated its history. A convenient summary of these studies may be found in *Nemea: A Guide to the Site and Museum* (Miller, 1990), but the few available literary sources have left little information about the games themselves. Contests were held every other year in August/September. The festival began with sacrifices to Zeus Nemaios at his altar which extended along the front of the temple. The games were officiated by ten Hellanodikai who wore dark clothes in memory of the sorrow over the death of the child (Scholiast on Pindar, *Nemean Odes*, hypothesis d, in Drachmann, 3:4). The Kleonaians' scheduling their games so as not to conflict with the Olympic Games and awarding victors with a crown of celery (hypothesis c, in Drachmann, 3:3) suggests that they offered a full panoply of Olympian athletic contests. Races with armor were especially prominent at Nemea (Philostratos *Gymnastics* 7). Athletes, divided into three classes, men, youths, and boys, came for the most part from Aegina, the Peloponnesus, Athens, and the islands. Equestrian events may have been limited to four-horse chariot races; the Scholiast specifically excludes the two-horse race and the horse race (on Pindar *Nemean Odes*, *hypothesis* b, in Drachmann, 3:2). Musical contests were added during the Hellenistic period (323–30). Thus, in the first centuries, the Nemean Games were strictly athletic and, in this regard, more like the games of Olympia than Delphi.

In the fullness of time, athletic contests proliferated wherever Greeks lived, but none aspired to Panhellenic status. Even the magnificent and wealthy Panathenaic, Games of All Athenians, were local, with some events not open to other Greeks. Local officials offered monetary prizes as inducements for athletes to come to their games. The crown of vegetation embodied an aristocratic ideal that itself was under increasing pressure from the monetary system and its values and from the transformation of the elite from landed nobility to an elite whose position and prestige were based increasingly on monetary wealth. The Panhellenic games belonged to an earlier day when the consciousness of Greeks as a unique and separate group among Mediterraneans was emerging. That spirit waned after the Persian Wars with the Athenian empire and with the tyranny and internecine bloodshed it inflicted that simultaneously polarized Greeks and atomized their cities as each scrambled for its own advantage and existence. The respect that moderns cherish in the Panhellenic ideal clearly was not always present, even for the period games. Sanctuaries were assaulted for military and political motives. The Nemean Games degenerated to a source of profit that cast a blind eye on Zeus and his sanctuary as well as on "the thrill of victory and the agony of defeat" that surpasses all things tangible and temporal.

Pindar's Epinician Odes

The name Pindar is heard frequently in any study of Greek athletics of the archaic and classical periods. It is inseparable from the periodic games, for he was their poet and the poet of those men and boys who were victorious at their contests. Little is known of his life, and although he often employs the first person, his references may relate to himself, the persona of the chorus, or a general observer, so that his poems tell little that can be confirmed. He was born in the village of Kynoscephalai near Thebes in Boeotia in 518 during the festival of Delphic Apollo (fr. 193, in Snell, 2:130). He came from an aristocratic family and first learned his craft from his uncle Skopelinos and from Apollodoros and Agathocles at Athens. During his lifetime, he traveled widely, visiting many cultural and political centers of Greece as the guest of kings, tyrants, and aristocrats. His first datable poem, *Pythian Ode Ten*, was written in 498 when he was twenty for a victor in boys' *diaulos*. The last poem that can be dated, *Pythian Ode Eight*, he wrote in 446 when he was seventy-two. At his death in 438, besides his victory odes, he left a large body of work that included songs to the gods, paeans, dithyrambs, processional hymns, songs for choruses for maidens and for dancing, dirges, and encomia. His epinicia or victory odes are divided into *Olympian, Pythian, Nemean,* and *Isthmian Odes*. These forty-five poems, composed for winners at the periodic games, alone have survived, because they were used as a school text by Roman masters in the second century of the common era.

The epinician ode was invented or refined by Simonides in the late sixth century and brought to its apogee by Pindar. It is a song in honor of (*epi-*) a victory (*nic-* from *nikê*) written to praise and commemorate the victor in an athletic contest, his family, and homeland. The ode was commissioned by the victor or, in the case of a boy, by his father or guardian, on behalf of the household and performed by a chorus of citizens under the poet's direction or by others following his instructions. Its primary function was to reintegrate the victor, segregated by his achievement, into his community by merging the interests of his household and community and allaying the envy of others toward him (Kurke, 6–7, 195–196).

In the autumn of 476, the citizens of Akragas, a Greek city on Sicily's southwestern coast, were celebrating the Theoxenia or Festival of Entertaining Gods. Castor and Polydeukes and their sister, Helen, had been invited to feast with mortals. During the festivities, all those gathered, children of gods and mortals, were treated with the performance of a victory ode by the famous Boeotian poet, Pindar. The tyrant of their city, Theron, had won the race for four horses at the last Olympic Games and commissioned the ode. Now they awaited the singing and dancing by a chorus of citizens who had been rehearsing these past weeks. They must have had some idea of what to expect, for it was to meet those expectations that Pindar created the kind of poem that is epinician. The ode the people of Akragas heard that day came to be known as *Olympian Ode 3*:

> Tyndareus' hospitable sons
> and lovely-haired Helen,
> I pray that I am pleasing
> when I praise renowned Akragas
> in raising a hymn of Olympic victory,
> finest product of Theron and his horses
> with weariless hooves. Thus the Muse somehow

stood beside me when I discovered
a sparkling new way of adapting the voice
of glorious revelry to the Dorian foot.
Since crowns yoked upon Theron's hair
exact from me this debt imposed by the gods,
that I blend in worthy ways the varied strains of the lyre
and the flute's scream and the order of words
for the son of Ainesidamos,
and Pisa also obliges me to celebrate, from whom
songs blessed by the gods come to men
upon whose brows the unerring man of Aetolia,
the Hellanodikes, fulfilling Herakles' ancient commands,
places the grey ornament of olive that once
from Istros' shady spring
the son of Amphitryon brought,
most beautiful memorial of contests at Olympia,

having persuaded with words the people
of the Hyperboreans, servants of Apollo.
With guileless intent he asked for the grove
of Zeus that receives all, a shady plant
open to men and a crown for achievement.
Already upon him, when his father's altars were hallowed,
the Moon at mid-month in her golden chariot
had lighted her full eye of the evening,
and he instituted the sacred trial of eminent contests
and the five-year festival as well
beside the hallowed banks of Alpheios.
But the land was not flourishing
with lush trees in the valleys of Cronus' descendant Pelops.
The garden, naked and without trees, seemed to Herakles
to succumb to the sun's piercing rays.
Then the impulse struck him to travel
into the Istrian land. There Leto's daughter, driver of horses,
had received him when he arrived from the ridges
and winding hollows of Arcadia.
At Eurystheus' commands, necessity
imposed by his father Zeus pressed him to fetch
the doe with the golden horns that once Taygeta
dedicated to Artemis Orthosia and inscribed as sacred to her.

While pursuing the doe, he also saw that land
beyond the breath of icy cold
Boreas. Transfixed, he stood in wonder of its trees.
Sweet desire overtook him
to plant them at the turning post of the racecourse
that is bent around twelve times. So now to this festival
Herakles arrives, with kindness and favor for the godlike
twin sons of Leda with the full and generous figure.
So to them he entrusted
the care of the contest, wondrous and watched,
for men's excellence at driving
swift chariots. And so, the spirit moves me

to say that to the Emmenidai
and to Theron has come glory granted by
those men skilled with horses, the sons of Tyndareus,
whom they among mortals honor with
countless feasts of hospitality,
observing the rites of the blessed gods with propitious thought.
If water is best, and gold
the most awesome of possessions,
Theron, arriving from home to the utmost
boundary by his own excellence, reaches
the pillars of Herakles. What is beyond
lies untrod by the skilled
and the unskilled. I will not pursue it. I would be a fool.

The poem consists of three stanzas. The first two are metrically identical in the Greek; the chorus moves in one direction for the first and the opposite for the second, turn and counter-turn, that is, strophe and antistrophe. The third, or epode, of a slightly different metrical pattern, the chorus sings while standing still. Pindar begins the ode on a typical note, "a striking, attention-demanding, opening" (Willcock 1995.12). He prays to the heroes, Castor, Polydeukes, and Helen, who was worshiped as a goddess at Rhodes, mother-city of Akragas, that they will be pleased with his praise of Akragas as he sings a song for an Olympic victory for Theron and his horses. Grandly and succinctly, Pindar sets forth the facts of his song, victor, city, and event. Since the chorus have been dancing as they were singing, the Akragans presumably saw for themselves the innovation in choreography he seems to be claiming. Pindar comments upon his craft, dance, music of the lyre and flute, and the lyrics, and, in doing so, slips in the last fact needed for the ode, the name of Theron's father, Ainesidamos. He later identifies Theron with his clan, the Emmenidai.

"Crowns yoked on Theron's hair" call to mind the olive that was placed upon Theron's head, and "yoked," the event. With Pisa, a synonym in the epinicia for Olympia, Pindar launches into the myth that often forms the center of an ode. The myth can come from the history of the honoree's city or family, from the games themselves, or from some other, not always apparent, association. It tells a story or illustrates a moral point or both as in *Olympia Ode Three*. The myths of Herakles' capture of the Arcadian hind and the founding of the Olympic Games and their crowns of ivy are told at length but interfolded and out of chronological order. D. S. Carne-Ross points out that Pindar begins at the end of the story and outlines the chronology that he uses: 1) Herakles brought the olive to Olympia from the land of the Hyperboreans to be the source of crowns for victors at his games; 2) While founding the games on an earlier occasion, he observed that the "garden naked and without trees" was overpowered by the sun's rays; 3) He went to the land of the Hyperboreans to fetch trees for shade; 4) He had been there before when, ordered by Eurystheus, he pursued the doe with golden horns; 5) At that time, he saw the trees and wanted them for his racecourse (54). Herakles makes two journeys to the land of the Hyperboreans, that is, to a paradise outside the realm of humankind. One he made under necessity to capture the doe, the other, to obtain trees for his garden. Perhaps as Carne-Ross suggests, "The garden, as it was to be, lay exposed to the full unshaded glare of divinity; that is what first marked it off as holy. . . . [But] [m]an cannot sustain the full presence of God; it must be tempered if he is to endure it." (57). The trees, then, moderate the sunlight and allow mortals to use the valley for their contests in honor of Zeus. References to "water is best" and gold characterize athletic success as comparable to water that in arid Greece is as precious as gold.

The myth also explains through Herakles' journeys how the olive came to be used for victory crowns. Theron's head was graced by its branches cut by a boy whose parents were still living from the Olive of Beautiful Crowns that grew opposite the back porch of the Temple of Zeus (Scholiast on Pindar *Olympian Ode* 3.60, in Drachmann, 1:122; Pausanias 5.15.3). It is suffused with the sacred, a holiness caused by, and identical with, its origin, a paradise lying beyond Boreas, its establishment at Olympia by Herakles, its cutting by a boy yet untouched by death, and its implementation by the Hellanodikes in accord with the founder's command. This contact with the time of first beginnings through the "crown for achievement" is what separates the victor from other men who can only enjoy comfort brought by "the shady plant." Theron's isolation, in turn, obliges Pindar to sing an ode of reintegration.

The poem ends quietly with a pithy, brief truism illustrated by a mythic allusion to the pillars of Herakles: to act beyond measure is a fool's business. Pindar takes full advantage of the elements—impressive opening, moralizing, myth, quiet close—of a typical ode, a form that offered manifold opportunities for variation (Willcock 1995.12–13).

Pindar says very little about an actual race or a boxing or wrestling match. He is not a sportswriter. He has much to say, however, about the qualities and attributes needed for victory. In *Isthmian Ode Three*, he brings them together in what may be read as a statement of his philosophy of victory. Melissos of Thebes won an earlier chariot race at the Isthmus and another at Nemea in 473. The ode, though celebrating the latter victory, is placed as the third of the *Isthmian Odes*:

If any man, fortunate in contests that confer glory
or in the power of wealth, yet reins in his heart hateful arrogance,
he deserves to be mingled in the praises of his citizens.
Zeus, great accomplishments follow
from you, and the happiness of those who revere you
lives longer. With hearts turned askance,
it does not abide, flourishing equally, for all time.
As a reward for famous deeds, we must hymn the good man
and exalt him with song's gentle charms as he celebrates his victory.
Melissos has as his lot twin prizes
to turn his heart to sweet
merriment. Amid the hollows of the Isthmus,
he received crowns, and in the low-lying valley
of the deep-chested lion, he acclaimed Thebes
by prevailing in the chariot race. He does not belie
the innate excellence of his kinsmen.
You know, surely, the ancient
glory of Kleonymos in chariots,
while from the mother's side, sharing wealth
with the sons of Labdakos, they tread in the toils of four-horse chariots.
Life with its revolving days exchanges this for that,
and that for this. At least sons of gods are unwounded.

Four things are needed for victory in Pindar's view: natural ability, hard work, wealth and the willingness to spend it, and divine favor (Willcock 1995, 15–16). All fell into place for Melissos. He lived up to "the innate excellence of his kinsmen" which he complemented by the toils of training and racing four-horse chariots. Glory came to him in the contest but also in the power of his wealth which he expended not only for the horses and chariot but also for the ode and its performance. Wealth for Pindar is not to be hoarded but consumed in securing the position, and aggrandizing the reputation, of the household among the other households in the community. All this has come the only way it could come, with the favor of Zeus. Those who revere him prosper throughout their lives, while the perverse of heart soon falter and fall. But the victor, Pindar warns, must not become blasé, cloyed by too much success. Any such feelings should be pressed deep in his heart, never to be made known. Life can always bring something else in place of present good fortune, as a descendant of Labdakos, father of Laïos and grandfather of Oedipus, surely knows. The ode ends quietly with a truism that leaves one thinking, because Herakles, Perseus, Theseus, and their like suffered despite their parentage.

By the end of the fifth century, the epinician ode was considered old-fashioned and passed away along with the particular form of aristocratic life it glorified and economic and social conditions that supported that life.

4.
The Heavy Events

The Eleans added wrestling to their athletic program in the eighteenth Olympiad (708), boxing in the twenty-third Olympiad (688), and *pankration* in the thirty-third (648) (Pausanias 5.8.7–8). Michael B. Poliakoff deems wrestling, boxing, and *pankration* "combat sports" because of the fighting. Ancient Greeks called them "the heavy events." Aristotle, restricting prepubescent children to "lighter exercises" to keep from hindering their growth, implies that the high level of exertion made them heavy (*Politics* 1338b 41–43). For Philostratos, they were heavy because they were the domain of men big in size and weight, as his idiosyncratic inclusion of the discus among them suggests (*Gymnastic* 3, in Kayser 262).

Theocritus (ca. 300–260) highlighted the nature of each in his description of Herakles' education:

> Every move the hip-twisting men of Argos
> use to throw one another, everything that boxers,
> formidable in their thongs, and every clever and useful trick
> pankratiasts have discovered by falling to the ground,
> all this Herakles learned at the feet of Harpalykos of Phanote,
> Hermes' son (24.111–116).

Wrestling required the most skill and cunning, boxing was the most brutal and dangerous, and *pankration*, the most exciting. The absence of weight classes in Greek athletics favored size and strength in these competitions. Stories of famous athletes emphasized these qualities. Lydamis, first victor in *pankration*, for instance, is said to have had sesquipedalian feet (Eusebius *Chronicles*, in Schoene, 1:198), and Milo of Kroton, one-time Olympic victor in boys' wrestling and five-time winner in men's, reputedly carried an ox in the procession at Olympia before cutting it up and eating it all, alone (Athenaeus *The Deipnosophists* 412F). On the other hand, by denying athletes any rest during the match, the absence of rounds and periods tempered the advantage of strength and size with the demand for endurance. The boxer who sought respite in a clinch could find himself being caned by the official (Plutarch *Moralia* 638E). As for Milo, upper-body strength lingers after the legs and lungs have begun to fade. Pausanias heard that he failed in his sixth attempt at the olive crown in men's wrestling when his opponent, Timasitheos, a fellow citizen of Kroton and younger man, refused to close and wore him down (6.14.5; Poliakoff 1987, 118). Perhaps Timasitheos realized Milo's prime had passed by watching him wrestle in Kroton and, unlike a foreigner, came to Olympia unawed, knowing how to handle him. But Milo's story has another version. His contemporary Simonides speaks of his attempt at a seventh victory with a happier ending:

> This is the beautiful statue of beautiful Milo who at Pisa
> conquered seven times and never fell to his knees
> (*Greek Anthology* 16.24, in Paton 5:173).

Simonides' Milo not only overcomes his opponent; he does so standing, without ever being in danger of a fall.

Athletes in the heavy events trained and competed on sand either at naturally occurring spots or in a pit dug in a *gymnasion*[1] or separate palaestra. Plutarch, swept up in speculations on the etymology of *palaistra*, denies that boxers practiced in palaestras (*Moralia* 638C-D) but elsewhere recognizes their presence in them (*Moralia* 825E). The athletes themselves loosened and fluffed the sand with a pick, the latter thus becoming an iconographic clue for the wrestler as well as for the pentathlete who also competed in a sand pit. On occasions for practice only, the pit was flooded for mud wrestling, an exercise intended to improve the athlete's strength and grip: "To pick up someone in the mud who is covered with sweat and oil and seriously trying to escape and break your grip—do not think this a small feat" (Lucian *Anacharsis* 28). Boxers needed only a flat space—their event did not take place in a ring—but wrestlers and pankratiasts required a soft surface to cushion falls and enable grappling on the ground, as the question to Drakontios concerning his proposed wrestling site reveals: "'How will they be able

---

1   The Greek *gymnasion* is to be distinguished from the modern gymnasium, which is often a room within a school where the well-meaning teach tumbling, rope-climbing, and other hellish exercises to the easily mortified. The Greek word applies to both the place and the physical exercises conducted there. To avoid associations with the gymnasium, a word derived from the Greek through Latin, the Greek spelling *gymnasion* (pl. *gymnasia*) is used.

to wrestle on so hard and overgrown an area?' he was asked. He replied, 'Whoever is thrown will hurt more'" (Xenophon *Anabasis* 4.8.26). Since the wrestler thrown to his back loses, Drakontios recommends not losing as the best way to wrestle among the brambles.

All athletes made generous use of olive oil, reputedly from the time Greeks began competing in the nude (Thucydides *Histories* 1.6.5). Athenians, who frequently boasted of their civilizing role in taming primeval savagery, claimed that stripping and anointing with oil were as old as their invention of the athletic contest itself (Aelian *Historical Miscellany* 3.38). Lucian sketches the preliminaries common for wrestling matches: "in the beginning, as soon as [the wrestlers] stripped . . . they anointed themselves generously and took turns rubbing each other down without hostility" (*Anacharsis* 1). Solon explains to Anacharsis:

> We slather the citizens' bodies with oil and soften them to create better skin tone. It is foolish, if we hold that leather softened by oil becomes harder to break and more durable, dead as it is, not to consider that the living body will not be better conditioned with the aid of olive oil (Lucian *Anacharsis* 24).

Wrestlers and pankratiasts gave one another a vigorous rubbing and sprinkled themselves with sand before beginning in order to insure a firm grip. An epigram for a six-time winner in "tortuous wrestling" implies that they used a different, perhaps finer, sand (*konis*) than the sand (*psammos*) in the pit (*Greek Anthology* 16.25, in Paton 5:173). On the other hand, the dishonest wrestler might dab grease on his neck or other strategic spot (Aristophanes *Knights* 490–491). Afterwards, they removed the oily and sweaty sand with a strigil, a sickle-like metal instrument (Swaddling, 28). All these preparations became more formal and elaborate with the development of the *gymnasion* and the palaestra as a separate wrestling facility and school.

Wrestling

Aeschylus cast the struggle for cosmic supremacy in the form of two contests:

> The one who was great before [Ouranos],
>   swelling with all-fighting daring,

will not be reckoned, since he existed in the past.
He who was born next [Cronus] has departed
      having thrice been thrown.
Anyone gladly screaming songs of victory for Zeus
will hit the mark of good sense completely (*Agamemnon* 168–175).

The expression "all-fighting [*pammachôi*] daring" indicates that Ouranos fights as a pankratiast against his son Cronus. With the full arsenal of the wrestler's and the boxer's panoply, the pankratiast was nearly unbounded by rules, a freedom that made him less a classic athlete and more like a brawler. Yet Ouranos loses to Cronus the wrestler whom his son Zeus throws three times. Zeus defeats the wrestler who overcame the pankratiast and emerges *triakter*, a term without a modern equivalent that may be translated "he who does the three [*tria*]," that is, he who throws his opponent's back to the sand three times. Zeus's triumph confirms not only his prowess as lord of the universe but also the widespread popularity of wrestling which assured Aeschylus that his audience would accept it as the deciding factor in the contest for heaven and earth.

Palaestra, daughter of Hermes, is said to have invented wrestling when she became of age in Arcadia, and "the earth rejoiced in her invention, since men will set aside the iron of war, and races will seem more pleasant than campaigns and men will compete in the nude" (Philostratos *Pictures in a Gallery* 2.32, in Kayser, 386). Some say that Theseus' trainer, Phorbas, discovered the art of wrestling, and that Theseus later taught it at Athens (Scholiast on *Nemean Ode* 5.89 a in Drachmann, 3: 98). Others contend that Theseus learned the rules from Athena (Scholiast on Pindar *Nemean Ode* 5.89, in Drachmann, 3: 98). Pausanias attributes its discovery to Theseus in his struggle against Kerkyon: "Before Theseus, men used only size and strength in wrestling" (Pausanias 1.39.3). Kerkyon "forced passers-by to wrestle with him and, while wrestling, killed them. Theseus, raising him into the air, threw him down, and killed him" (Scholiast on Plato, *Laws* 796 Kerkyon, in Greene, 328). From its foundation, the dichotomy between size/strength and skill, with the nod to the latter as the superior, characterizes wrestling, "the most technical and most cunning of the athletic events" (Plutarch *Moralia* 638D).

Since wrestlers often had to fight from their knees or on the ground, scholars postulated two kinds of wrestling, "upright," that is, wrestling proper, and "ground" wrestling "in which the struggle was continued on the ground till one or other of the combatants acknowledges defeat" (Gardiner 1910, 376). The distinction is false. Athletes drilled in ground wrestling to become proficient in fighting in this disadvantageous position, but there was only one kind of wrestling (Poliakoff 1986, 24). As Philostratos states, "wrestling . . . is upright, but it is necessary to roll" on the ground (*Gymnastic* 50, in Kayser, 289).

Orikadmos, who is no more than a name, formulated its rules (Aelian *Historical Miscellany* 11.1). Yet the very familiarity of wrestling has left no specifics about those rules. They must be reconstructed from allusions and clues scattered throughout literary sources. They allowed strangling and tripping but no striking, biting, seizing the genitals, or wrestling outside the sand pit. No rule prohibited attacks against an opponent's legs as in the modern Greco-Roman style of wrestling that bars moves below the hips and penalizes tripping. The deterrent to such attacks lay, rather, in the risk of being seized about the neck or at the waist (Poliakoff 1987, 44). Tydeus attempted to tackle the taller Agylleus' legs but failed to secure a grip because of his short arms. In reply: "Agylleus came down hard / from above and buried him under the huge mass / of his falling body" (Statius *Thebaid* 6.878–880).

A modern wrestler may win a match by decision, having accumulated more points than his opponent or by pinning his shoulders to the ground, a move than entails complete control over him for a specified length of time. The ancient wrestler did not enjoy the luxury of winning by points, but he did not need to pin his opponent. He earned a fall either by rendering an opponent immobile with a controlling grip or laying him out on his stomach (Poliakoff 1986, 9–10). It is this second method that defines the shameful defeat of the huge Agylleus. Tydeus hoists Agylleus into the air and then, releasing him suddenly and deliberately, twists him onto his side:

> Tydeus followed the falling Agylleus,
> and gripped his neck with his right arm and his groin with his feet.
> Thus encircled, Agylleus lost heart and struggled out of shame alone.
> Finally, his chest and stomach stretched out on the ground,
> he was laid flat. After a long time, he rose sadly,
> leaving behind the foul marks of his disgrace imprinted in the earth
> (Statius *Thebaid* 6.899–904).

Philo of Alexandria (first century C.E.) testifies to this manner of winning with his remark that in the games "a man could wrestle someone and stretch him out on his face" and not be prosecuted for hubris but obtain first place (*On Agriculture* 113). Theagenes apparently also defeats his opponent by forcing the Ethiopian giant's stomach flat to the ground:

> Theagenes moved up into his armpit and clung to his back. With
> some trouble, he reached his arms around the Ethiopian's broad middle.
> By vigorously and repeatedly hitting the Ethiopian's ankles with the
> heel of his foot, he upset his footing and forced him to his knee. Then
> he inserted his legs into the Ethiopian's groin and dislodged his wrists
> which he was using to keep up his chest. He drew his opponent's
> arms around to meet at the temples and, drawing them back over to
> his head and shoulders, forced his opponent's stomach to the ground
> (Heliodorus *Aethiopica* 10.32).

Sinking to the knee did not constitute a fall, but it did put the wrestler at
imminent risk of losing. In a wrestling metaphor, Herodotus comments
that defeat in a sea battle "sent Chios to its knee and, thus weakened, it
soon fell" (*Histories* 6.27.3).

The third way to secure a fall, and by far the most dramatic and
decisive, was to drive an opponent's shoulders or back to the sand.
Aeschylus' chorus in the *Suppliants* (ca. 463) point out the difficulty of
determining the will of Zeus, but they declare that whatever the god
decides "falls safely and not on its back" (91), which is to say, that the
plans of Zeus never suffer defeat. Aristophanes' chorus of horsemen
praise their fathers for carrying on after losing their fight by being thrown
to their backs:

> If they fell down on their shoulder in some fight,
> they would wipe off the sand and, denying they had fallen,
> begin the struggle anew (*Knights* 571–573).

In practice, however, it would seem unlikely that a wrestler thrown to
sand would hope to carry on, escaping the umpire's notice by rubbing
off the sand, had not the physician Galen (ca. 129–199 C.E.) lambasted
proponents of a rival school for resembling:

> the ignoramuses among the wrestlers who, dashed down by their
> opponents and lying on their backs, are so far from acknowledging
> the fall that they even lay hold of those who threw them by the neck
> and suppose in this that they are winning *(On the Natural Faculties,*
> in Kühn, 2:80).

The wrestler won a match by scoring three falls against his opponent.
Literary sources abound as evidence of this, including Milo's retort to
the jibes of spectators deprived of watching him wrestle for the lack of
an opponent:

> Milo the wrestler once was the only one to come to the sacred contest.
>   The judge called him to crown him on the spot.
> As he approached, he slipped and fell on his back. Some cried out:

"Do not crown him, if, being alone, he has a fall."
Milo stood up and shouted among them, "Are there not three?
I am laid out once. Let someone throw me the others" (*Greek Anthology* 11.316, in Paton, 4:217).

Three falls constitute victory in Orestes' struggle against the Erinyes, the avenging spirits of his mother, Clytemnestra. When he admits to killing Clytemnestra, the Erinyes exclaim in triumph: "Already one of the three falls" (Aeschylus *Eumenides* 589). The true lover and his beloved, when they regain their wings in death, have secured "one of the three truly Olympian-like falls" (Plato *Phaedrus* 256B). Seneca (first century C.E.) notes that "the wrestler who was thrice thrown has lost the palm" (*On Benefactions* 5.3), and Plato, that "Euthydemos was lighting into the young man as if to throw him down for a third fall" (*Euthydemos* 277D). Philostratos comments that "wrestlers compete in three preliminary contests, because that many falls are necessary" (*Gymnastic* 11, in Kayser, 266). Five preliminary bouts were allotted, since this number insures that a wrestler would become a *triaktêr*, the winner of three.

A victory won *aptôs*, without a fall, came sweet: "Kleitomachos did not get dust on his shoulders but, wrestling without falling, took the three struggles at the Isthmian Games" (*Greek Anthology* 9.588, in Paton, 3:329). Sweeter still was "the palm without dust" (Horace *Epistles* 1.1.51), the victory that came *akoniti*, without having to compete. Dorieus, son of the famous boxer Diagoras, took a Pythian crown this way (Pausanias 6.7.4), and Dromeus of Mantineia [M 202] won *pankration akoniti* for the first time ever at the seventy-fifth Olympiad (480) (6.11.4). The boast in *akoniti* lay in scaring off the competition. Its antithesis was winning *anephedros*, without a bye, that is, not sitting out a round. The *anephedros* athlete won the event after overcoming a rival in each preliminary. Aristomenes, victorious in boys' wrestling at Pytho in 446, went through four opponents:

You fell from on high
on four bodies, harboring evil intent,
and no happy homecoming was declared
in Pythia for them as it was for you.
. . . .
He who has gained a new success,
in his great prosperity,
takes flight in his hope
on soaring wings of manhood, with
his thoughts on more than wealth
(Pindar *Pythian Ode* 8.81–84, 88–92).

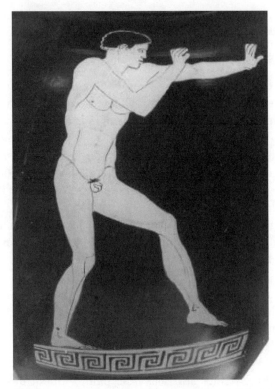

Illustration 9. Youthful wrestler. Red-figure amphora, ca. 450 B.C.E. Courtesy of the Staatliche Antikensammlungen und Glyptothek, Munich, Germany.

The passage recognizes the pitiless resolve that wrestling required as well as the intense joy that crushing rivals in the zero-sum game of Greek athletics showered upon the victor.

In wrestling, everything starts with the stance, the means for seizing control and avoiding its loss. The wrestlers began in an upright position either facing one another or standing side by side. A youthful wrestler on a red-figure amphora from the mid-fifth century stands ready to meet his opponent (Illustration 9). Although his left leg appears elevated, it must be on the ground for him to be stable. In a stance similar to his, Theagenes faces the Ethiopian:

> Theagenes stretched out his hands before him and planted his feet firmly. Bending his knees, he hunched his shoulders and back and leaned his neck slightly back, drawing in his whole body like a wasp's (Heliodorus *Aethiopica* 10.31).

His opponent comes out swinging, an obvious mark of barbarism in a wrestling match: "he threw his arm down on Theagenes' back like a crowbar" (*Aethiopica* 10.31). In the ensuing match, Theagenes illustrates the superiority of skill and guile over brawn:

> Theagenes, as a man who was in the *gymnasion* and a student of the oil since youth and trained to perfection in Hermes' competitive art, decided, after testing his opponent's strength, to give way at first and not to close in on his opponent's vast and rough bulk but to circumvent his rustic and savage strength with his own experience and skill. Right away he started wobbling from the blow [he received], pretending to be in more pain than he was. He offered the other side of his neck, exposed and unprotected, for another blow. When the Ethiopian reached out, Theagenes gave way before the blow and feigned a fall onto his face. Seeing this, the Ethiopian became emboldened and, throwing caution to the winds, was already advancing for the third blow. He raised his arm again and was on the verge of bringing it down when Theagenes suddenly crouched down and shot under the blow, avoiding the downward stroke. With his right arm, he gained control of his opponent's left and shoved him. The latter, carried along by the momentum of his arm when it encountered no resistance, was drawn to the ground (Heliodorus *Aethiopica* 10.31–32).

Lucian summarizes the maneuvers that ensued from the opening stance:

> Those who bend their heads, brow-to-brow, and wrestle learn how to fall safely and to get up easily, to push against an opponent, to tie him up in a clinch, to twist him, and to hoist him on high (*Anacharsis* 24).

And Nonnus (*floruit* fifth century C.E.) illustrates the opening maneuvers of a match between Aristaios and Aiakos:

> Both athletes
> began by clinching both hands at the double-yoked wrist,
> on this side and on that, and dragged one another in turn
> across the surface of the loose sand, their fingers interlocked
> in a tight grasp. One man would circle around,
> leading the whirling man with a hand leaning to one side,
> dragging and being dragged, for both were bound
> together by the hands. They curved their necks
> and strained with heads butted at the middle of the forehead,
> inclining to neither side and bowing to the ground. From their
> foreheads pressed against each other, sweat, harbinger of toil,
> began to flow (*Dionysiaca* 37.557–567).

The wrestlers tie up each other at the wrist. The control of the wrist or neck provides the avenues to more assertive moves. Each tries for control, but neither can overpower the other, so they exchange dominance in a struggle that, fought at the wrist, causes them to spin in circles over the sand. Then they bend their heads, pressing forehead against forehead, which forces them to nod their heads downward. The wrestlers drag and pull each other until Aristaios slips around Aiakos and, gaining a waist lock, heaves him off the ground by main strength. But wily Aiakos does not forget his cunning. In imitation of Homer but also in recognition of the shrewdness needed for wrestling, Nonnus emphasizes the wrestler's trickiness. Stealing behind his opponent's left knee with his foot, Aiakos knocks his leg out from under him. Carried by his own weight, Aristaios falls on his back, and Aiakos gains a fall (*Dionysiaca* 37.577–582).

Nothing counted when wrestlers fell together, as in Homer's match between Odysseus and Ajax (*Iliad* 23.706–737), but returning smartly to a standing position was crucial to avoid being overpowered from above. Clinching denotes the various holds on an opponent's arms, neck, or head, all of which secured leverage and control over him. The defensive wrestler attempted to free himself by breaking the grip or attacking another part of the aggressor's body. Galen's comment on a training exercise reflects that in a match where "one either grasps the other about the waist or is grasped himself with hands and fingers interlaced, [the instructor] would order the one being controlled to free himself or he would free himself [on his own] from the one controlling him" (*On Protecting One's Health,* in Kühn, 6:141–142). From a grip

Illustration 10. Theseus and Kerkyon wrestle. Attic psykter, ca. 510 B.C.E Courtesy of the Museo di Antichità, Turin, Italy.

on a wrist or arm, the aggressor could drag his opponent off balance, allowing him to slip behind the defensive man for a lift and throw (Poliakoff 1987, 34). A wine cooler in red-figure (ca. 500) shows Theseus with his arms locked around Kerkyon's neck and armpit (Illustration 10). Kerkyon is being pulled forward and is on the verge of losing his balance, prelude to a fall. The upright wrestler on a black-figure amphora from the late sixth century grips his opponent's elbows from the side and attempts to throw him over his hip to the ground (Poliakoff 1987, 38 Ill.26). But his adversary, although bent forward at the waist, has his legs, which are endowed with huge thighs, spread in a stance apparently too stable to be moved.

On an Attic amphora by the Andokides Painter, two pairs of wrestlers practice waist locks under the supervision of a trainer who stands on the left side of the scene, an iconographic clue that the athletes are wrestlers (Illustration 11)—a trainer on the right of the athletes indicates *pankration*. The offensive wrestler of the left pair, the one on the right, is attempting to slip around his opponent, a move, if successful, that would allow him to grip his opponent in a waist lock from behind. His opponent thwarts him by holding his wrist, preventing the hands from closing, and by trying to unbalance him with his arm and shoulder. The offensive wrestler of the pair on the right has locked his arm around his opponent's ribs, the move Aristaios executed, and has lifted him for a

Illustration 11. Wrestlers practice before a trainer. Attic amphora, ca. 525 B.C.E. Courtesy of the Bildarchiv Preußischer Kulturbesitz, Berlin, Germany.

throw. His opponent counters by trying to pry the offensive wrestler's arms apart and by inserting his right foot behind the left knee to hamper the lift and possibly dislodge the knee. The wrestler caught in a waist lock teeters on the edge of defeat.

In the match with Pallene, daughter of the Thracian king Sithon, Dionysus moves smoothly and quickly from a waist lock to a throw to the ground. The god came to King Sithon's court to avenge Pallene's many suitors slain by her father who desired her for himself. Sithon proposes a wrestling match for the maiden's hand (Nonnus *Dionysiaca* 48.90–103). As they grapple, Dionysus becomes increasingly enamored of the girl. Nonnus entwines an accurate description of wrestling moves with the erotic titillation of Dionysus' mounting passion for his opponent:

> Lovely Pallene, with a cunning tactic from wrestling,
> tried to pick up Dionysus with her woman's hands,
> but she did not raise him, so heavy was he. She grew tired
> and gave up on Dionysus' male limbs that remained unmoved.
> The god countered, seizing the lovely maiden
> about the waist with his arms and, lifting her as lightly as his wand,
> he turned her to the side and over his shoulder.
> Restraining his strength, he heaved the strong girl
> and laid her out on the ground unmoving (*Dionysiaca* 48.138–146).

Dionysus twists Pallene to the side, using his shoulder as a fulcrum to heave her over it and down to the pit. Pallene jumps up and fixes her feet a second time, but:

> With a swift, unbridled thrust of his knee,
> Dionysus seized control of Pallene's midriff, wanting
> to roll the maiden over the ground with a sideways heave.
> But he changed his grip and wound his hands around her ribs,
> and, bending his neck to the side, he shifted his fingers
> to the middle of her back, interlacing them, and formed
> the resolve to snatch an ankle or leg or knee.
> The god fell to the ground of his own accord,
> defeated by her empty strength. He kept holding the desired
> medicine for his passion, and he lay
> in the sweet dust, supporting on his stomach
> Eros' lovely burden. He did not shake off the girl
> but held her tight with a bond that charms the heart (48.152–164).

Dionysus puts his knee against Pallene's stomach and pulls her toward him. He could then have rotated as he fell back, throwing her onto her shoulders. Instead, he falls deliberately, grasping her to his stomach, evidently with his ulterior motive in mind: "Relish the pleasure of coupling with the god of the grape cluster as your lover and husband" (48.216).

Dionysus lets Pallene down gently, but the shoulder throw to the ground could be devastating for the defensive wrestler, as the look of

Illustration 12. Shoulder throw before an alarmed trainer or umpire. Attic cup, ca. 500 B.C.E. Courtesy of the Bibliothèque Nationale, Paris, France

alarm on the face of the umpire or trainer intimates on an Attic cup (Illustration 12). The movement begins with seizing the opponent's arm with both hands and ducking under his arms, pressing firmly against his body. The aggressor then twists his buttocks and, by pulling the arm down straight, shifts the defensive wrestler onto his back. Stooping to one knee facilitated the move that culminated in the trapped man's being thrown over his opponent's shoulder for a forceful fall.

The Eleans preferred wrestling to boxing and *pankration*:

> The Eleans consider wrestling to be tough and grievous, as the poets say, not only in the complexity of its grappling but also because the wrestlers have to compete three times in a preliminary, since that is the number of falls needed. The Eleans believe it appalling to grant the crown in *pankration* and boxing without an actual competition [*akoniti*]. . . . During a competition, the boxer receives and gives wounding blows and attacks his opponent's legs, but in training, he only shadow boxes. The pankratiast competes with every one of the many stratagems in his event, but he practices them one at a time.

> Wrestling, however, is the same whether in a preliminary or a final.
> Each offers a test of how many moves an athlete knows and can
> execute. . . . The Eleans crown the man most well trained on the basis
> of his training alone (Philostratos *Gymnastic* 11, in Kayser, 266).

Victory *akoniti* in boxing and *pankration* galled the Eleans because
those athletes did not train as hard as wrestlers during the training period
before the games. The wrestler competed every time with every move
he could muster and accomplish, offering the Eleans ample opportunity
to observe each athlete and put him through their trials. Accordingly,
rewarding the wrestler with the olive *akoniti* did not upset them, since
the training proved to be an elimination tournament.

Boxing

The earliest victors in boxing hailed from Ionia. Foremost among
them was Onomastos of Smyrna who won the first competition and
later wrote the rules of boxing (Pausanias 5.8.7; Philostratos *Gymnastic*
12, in Kayser, 267). To be precise, Onomastos more likely formulated
customs as rules, for the principles and methods of boxing had long
been established. The easy way that Achilles arranges the boxing match
at Patroclus' funeral shows as much. In that match, the boxers wear
ox-hide strips on their hands (*Iliad* 23.684), since it is a formal contest.
Bare fists were not a feature of Greek boxing, so that the bare-fisted
encounter between the beggar Iros and Odysseus disguised as a beggar
is a street fight (*Odyssey* 18.1–107). Though bigger than Odysseus,
Iros lacks strength and vigor (18.3–4). Odysseus is of medium height
and muscular, "evidently a typical middle-weight: ten years earlier he
had been one of the best runners and wrestlers in the Greek army, so
that he had possessed that quickness on which a middle-weight must
rely when pitted against a man heavier than himself" (Frost, 216). With
his left, Iros crashes down a chopping blow that Odysseus blocks with
his right shoulder while he counters with a right cross to Iros' head that
lands on the neck beneath the ear, the result of the difference in height.
With Iros' lead to the body instead of the head, Homer characterizes
him as a street bully, which Antinöos calls him (18.79), in a fight with an
experienced boxer

Of the heavy events, by far the roughest and most physically
damaging was boxing. Kleitomachos [M 584] who won the three events

on the same day at Pytho knew from experience the differences between them and appealed to the Hellanodikai at the 141st Olympiad (216) to announce the *pankration* before he received the wounds at boxing that would hamper his chances in *pankration* (Pausanias 6.15.3–5). According to tradition, the Lacedaemonians invented boxing to practice warding off and enduring blows to the head (Philostratos *Gymnastic* 9, in Kayser, 265). The myth gains credence from the fact that boxing was a violent combat whose foremost strategy was attacking the head. Centuries after the Lacedaemonians had abandoned boxing as too athletic, Artemidorus of Ephesus (second century C.E.) interpreted dreams on the basis of the injuries resulting from this head-hunting: "To box is harmful in every way. Boxing indicates harm and disgrace, for the face becomes disfigured, and blood is shed" (*Interpretation of Dreams* 1.61).

The Greeks developed the format for a boxing match early in their history (Illustration 13). As in any event at a Greek athletic festival, the winner in boxing was the best man on that day. There were no rounds, no ring, only the surrounding circle of spectators. Fights went on without formal interruptions, with pauses in the action coming with a knockdown

Illustration 13. Boxer signals defeat. Red-figure amphora, early fifth-century B.C.E. National Archaeological Museum, Athens, Greece.

or mutual exhaustion. At all times clinches were forbidden: "The judges do not let the boxers, who dearly want to, hold onto one another" (Plutarch *Moralia* 638E). Vases show the umpire whipping weary fighters who seek a rest in clinches (Poliakoff 1987, 81 Ill.83). A fight ended with a knockout or when one fighter signaled defeat by raising the index finger of his right hand. Plutarch explains the absence of Lacedaemonians from the heavy events by their repugnance for this stigma of defeat, noting that, to the contrary, "concerning athletic events, Lycurgus did not keep the citizens from competing in those events in which a hand was not raised" (*Lycurgus* 19.9).

The ready use of strips of cowhide by Homer's boxers indicates that they were common throughout the Greek world. During the sixth and fifth centuries, boxers exclusively used thin, supple strips of cowhide (Pausanias 8.40.3) which they brought to a fight gathered into a bundle. From the size and number of coils in the bundles depicted on a wine-cup held in the British Museum (Poliakoff 1987, 72 Ill.73), the strips may have been ten or twelve feet long. A standing boxer involved in wrapping his hand and often using his teeth to tighten the wrap was a favorite subject for painters as it was easily captured and uniquely representative (Yalouris 219, Ill.122). Individuals apparently had a preferred style of wrapping, since the vases show different coverings (Yalouris 219, Ill.122; 220, Ills.123 and 124), unless, of course, the variation belongs to the painters rather than the athletes. Philostratos describes a common mode:

> Ancient boxing was equipped in the following fashion: four of the fingers were put into a band and stuck out from this band only so far as to make a fist when they were clenched. The fingers were held together by a strip that went down the forearm as a support (*Gymnastic* 10, in Kayser, 265).

This system covered the two rows of knuckles closest to the wrist and left the fingers free to form a fist (Jüthner and Mehl, 1318). Sometimes, the thumb was wrapped, but it was always free. "As a rule the thong is wound several times round the four fingers and knuckles, passed diagonally across the palm and back of the hand, and wound around the wrist, the binding sometimes being carried some distance up the forearm" (Gardiner 1910, 406). Because painters depicted strips as a latticework of lines, the vases impart little perspective of their thickness, but a ten-foot strip of cowhide would have formed a "glove" of some size and hardness. Strips served to protect the boxer's wrist and fingers from being broken and kept his knuckles from swelling which would deaden the blows. Some believe that the strips were an offensive weapon (Frost, 214), but they could not have offered a compelling advantage, since not all boxers chose to cover their knuckles (Poliakoff 1987, 70). Nonetheless, blows from fists supported by layers of rawhide surely hurt and encouraged boxers to fight defensively.

However painful the traditional strips, their effect paled before the ones that boxers began using in the fourth century (Illustration 14). So damaging were these "sharp strips" that the old-style strips came to be known as "soft strips" in retrospect (Pausanias 8.40.3). The new strips

Illustration 14. Boxer wearing sharp thongs. Bronze statue, first century B.C.E. Museo Nationale Romano, Rome, Italy.

were fashioned around a sheepskin glove with holes cut for the fingers. The thumb remained free. The glove, secured to the arm by strips, ran up the lower arm, ending in a fleecy sheepskin band, apparently with the inner lining folded over. The telling innovation was a piece of leather attached to the glove that covered the fingers from the hand to the first row of knuckles. It stands out prominently on the hands of the Terme boxer, a bronze statue of a sitting boxer now in the National Museum at Rome. Poets represent the knuckle pad as "dry" (Apollonius Rhodius, *Argonautica* 2.53; Nonnus *Dionysiaca* 37.507) and as "hard as horn" (Quintus Smyrnaeus *Fall of Troy* 4.339). Philostratos describes it as made of leather and as "sharp, protruding from the hand" (*Gymnastic* 10, in Kayser, 265). Despite that description, he believed it was intended to mitigate a blow for its recipient, but the Terme boxer's scarred and battered face and cauliflower ears testify to the contrary.

Sharp strips became the standard by the first century when the Terme boxer was cast, and sometime afterward acquired the nickname "ants." The epigrammatist Lucillius (first century CE) writes graphically of a boxer's face:

> Your head's become a sieve, Apollophanes,
> or a moth-eaten edge of a papyrus.
> Actually, they're holes, crooked and straight holes, left by ants,
> like the musical notations of poets from Lydia and Phrygia.
> But have no fear. Box away. If you get hit up top,
> whatever holes you got, you'll have. You can't get more (*Greek Anthology* 11.78, in Paton 4:110).

Along the same lines of facial destruction is the joke by Hierokles (date uncertain), preserved in *Philogelos*, a collection of mirth from antiquity:

> A man from Kumae, seeing a boxer who had many wounds, asked him where he got them. And when he replied, "From the ant," the man said, "If that's the case, why sleep on the ground?" (72).

Both humorists expect their audience to know why strips resembled ants. Ants bite and sting, and the dry, hard leather pad across the boxer's knuckles produced a stinging cut on the face of the opponent. The metaphor may be undermined by the absence of any species of ant known from antiquity whose bite caused a wound large or deep enough to pockmark the skin (Scanlon 1982–1983, 34). Nevertheless, both the real and metaphorical ants dug up surfaces and bore holes in them. On the basis of the comparison of other things to ants, for example, reefs, warts, and sea rocks, Thomas F. Scanlon offers another explanation, namely, that the strips looked like ants:

> (1) the fist with a leather ring is significantly larger than the wrist, as the head of the common worker ant is conspicuously larger than its thorax, (2) the glove extending over the wrist and up the forearm and crossed by smaller straps resembles the shape of the ant's body having a thin thorax and visible segments on its abdomen (1982–1983, 38).

In any case, for the boxer, the strips resulted in a scarred and damaged face that, as the jokester would have it, not even "his mother would recognize":

> The Olympian, such as he is now, Augustus,
>   had once a nose, a chin, eyebrows, ears, and eyelids.
> Then he signed up as a boxer and lost them all
>   so that he lost his portion of his father's estate.
> His brother proffered a picture of him,
>   and he was judged a stranger—no resemblance (*Greek Anthology* 11.75, in Paton, 4:108).

A boxer could not win on points or rounds. He had to beat an opponent into submission or knock him out. The inevitable bloodletting explains, in part, the reason for introducing sharp strips. Unique in the games to boxing, bloody physical damage supplied more thrills and helped bring about the denouement, a not inconsequential factor in contests without rounds. Moreover, boxers by the third century were better conditioned and trained, and the strips offered them greater challenges, particularly in defensive fighting (Scanlon 1982–1983, 40). Greeks tolerated the violence and enjoyed gallows humor about the strips. Meanwhile, the boxer endured, for he was a boxer.

For all its violence, Greeks admired boxing as a contest, because skill was expected to triumph over brutality. This is the implication of Apollo's interest in the event. God of the civilized arts of healing, music, oracles, governance, and purification, Apollo boxed at Olympia, defeating Ares (Pausanias 5.7.10), held the title of Boxer at his shrine in Delphi (Plutarch *Moralia* 724C), and, from his role in Homer's boxing match (*Iliad* 23.660–661), appears to have been the patron god of boxing. The *periodonikês* Glaukos exemplified the ideal when he became by the end of his career the foremost exponent of hand movements and speed among his contemporaries (Pausanias 6.10.1–3). But his beginnings speak to the opposition between training and natural talent, between knowledge of the techniques of an event and the strength that indelibly marks boxing. A thunderous blow delivered by a neophyte can nullify years of training and experience for its recipient. When the father of Glaukos [M 134] saw his son fixing a plow with his hand instead of a hammer, he took him from their native Karystos in Euboea to Olympia to fight with his fists in the sixty-fifth Olympiad (520). Unversed in boxing, Glaukos was roughed up and cut by his opponents and nearly rendered unconscious in the fight against the last one. Then his father cried out, "Boy, the one from the plow." Glaukos snapped out of it and won by a violent blow (Pausanias 6.10.2)

In Philostratos' prescriptions, the ideal boxer has "long hands; strong forearms, upper arms, and shoulders; and a strong, long neck":

> He should support himself on firm, compact hips, for the forward thrust of the arms throws the body off balance unless it is held on firm hips. . . . The boxer should have straight lower legs in proportion with thighs that are separated and apart from each other. The boxer's body is better for offense if the thighs do not touch one another (*Gymnastic* 34, in Kayser 278–279).

Philostratos expresses his disdain for large calves in any athlete but especially in the boxer, as they slow the man down, allowing him to be easily caught. Philostratos' ideal brings to mind the ideal modern boxer exemplified by Max Baer, heavyweight champion of the world in 1934 and 1935: "He had massive shoulders, long and supple muscular arms, slim waist, strong legs, and a deadly right hand" (Fleischer and Andre, 123). No doubt Philostratos would have approved of Baer's legs—muscular, light, and slim. On the other hand, although granting that the "best stomach is one that does not protrude, since such boxers are light on their feet and well-winded," he finds some good in a large stomach. When a boxer draws his head back to avoid a blow, "such a stomach defends against blows to the face by getting in the way of an opponent's approach" (*Gymnastic* 34, in Kayser, 279; Harris 1964, 177).

Greek boxers concentrated on blows to the head and generally ignored the body. Body blows characterize inept boxers like Homer's Iros (*Odyssey* 18.95) and Theocritus' Amykos who "aimed his punches at the chest and below the neck, while the unbeaten Polydeukes kneaded Amykos' face with disfiguring blows" (22.109–111). That Polydeukes is said to be "unbeaten" underscores the primacy of hitting the head. That an unwritten and unannounced rule kept fighters from working the body, as Gardiner speculates (1910, 421), is unlikely; had boxers not commonly suffered body blows, Paul could not have contended that his preaching was tried and true because, like a boxer, he bruised his body (*First Corinthians* 9.26–27). The fate of Kreugas who was hit in the side before the judges at the Nemean Games about 400 suggests that Greek boxers avoided the body by choice:

> The Argives awarded Kreugas, the boxer from Epidamnos, the crown at the Nemean Games, although he was dead, because Damoxenos of Syracuse, his opponent in the match, transgressed the agreement between them. Evening was drawing near as they were boxing, and they agreed within the hearing of witnesses that, in turn, each one of them would allow the other a blow. . . . At the time, Kreugas discharged a blow at Damoxenos' head. Damoxenos ordered Kreugas to raise his arm, and after he raised it, he struck Kreugas with his fingers straight out beneath the ribs. Because of the points on his nails and the violence of the blow, he drove his hand inside and, gripping Kreugas' entrails, pulled them outside and broke them off. Kreugas died immediately, and the Argives expelled Damoxenos in as much as he had transgressed the arrangement and, instead of one blow, used many blows against his opponent. They gave Kreugas in death the victory and erected a statue of him in Argos. It was still standing in the sanctuary of Apollo the Wolf in my day (Pausanias 8.40.3–5).

Damoxenos was wearing soft strips that left his fingers uncovered (Pausanias 8.40.3). After absorbing a blow to the head, he has Kreugas elevate his arm, a move that reduces the muscular resistance on Kreugas' side. Then, with his fingers together, he drives them into Kreugas' body where the force of the blow, concentrated on a small area, penetrates to the internal organs. If Damoxenos were right-handed, he would have entered Kreugas' left side and damaged his spleen, or if left-handed, the liver (Brophy, 386). The blow kills Kreugas instantly. Robert H. Brophy III accepts the veracity of the account except for the sharp fingernails which would have cut Damoxenos' hands and hampered him in forming a fist and striking blows (382–384). Sharp nails are a rationalization to explain the power of the fingers to penetrate the body, whereas the power comes from extreme force concentrated in a small area (Brophy, 384). The Argives rule against Damoxenos, not for hitting Kreugas in the body, but for dealing several blows, apparently one from each finger, instead of one from the fist. Notably, Pausanias passes over the blow to the body without comment. Greek boxers, it seems, simply preferred the head as a more vulnerable target. Heavy blows to the body can wear down a fighter, causing his arms to feel heavy and forcing him to drop them to protect aching ribs, but, at the same time, whittling away at an opponent demands patience, courts disaster by opening opportunities for being hit, and appealed less because less heroic in Greek eyes.

How a boxer sets himself for contact, his stance, says much about the kind of fight that is being fought as well as about the skills and intentions of its participants. The modern boxer faces his opponent at an almost ninety-degree angle, offering him as little of his body as possible. His left arm is extended but not completely, and the forearm is raised, alert for attack or defense. The right hand is carried near the chest, and both elbows are tucked in near the body to protect against body blows. His stance follows from the need to protect his head and body and from the readiness to strike the head or body of his opponent.

The stance of the Greek boxers, illustrated on an early fifth-century red-figure drinking cup reveals a different objective, that of striking only the head (Illustration 15). In this illustration, the boxers are facing one another, turned to the right as in the modern stance. Their heads and bodies are upright. The left leg is thrust forward and slightly bent. The man on the left lifts his right foot on his toes; the other firmly plants his foot. Both fighters have their left arm fully extended, the closed fist hovering before the opponent's face. The right hand is bent back and raised to the level of the shoulder with the fist consequently near the right ear. The left hand guarded the head and kept the opponent at a distance; it did little to protect the body (Gardiner 1910, 420). The stance has led to the characterization of the Greek boxer as a one-armed fighter who punches only with his right and never realized the power of the left jab or straight left (Frost, 218, 223). The charge, however, is refuted by

Illustration 15. Boxers before a trainer or umpire. Attic red-figure kylix, ca. 490 B.C.E © The British Museum, London, England.

vase paintings showing the knockout blow delivered by a left (Illustration 12) and by the literary descriptions of matches that report boxers using both hands for defense and offense.

Theocritus provides the most informative account of a boxing match in his twenty-second idyll. The poem relates the fight between the well-known boxer (*Iliad* 3.237), Polydeukes, the son of Zeus, and Amykos, the king of the Bebrykes. As Theocritus narrates the story, Jason's ship in his pursuit of the Golden Fleece arrives at the land of the Bebrykes. Polydeukes, who is also identified as the son of Tyndareos, and his brother, Castor, wander away from the ship and come upon a peaceful scene fragrant with flowers and intersected by a stream of cool, clear water. They encounter a man whose name, Amykos, Theocritus tells his readers but keeps from Zeus's sons:

> There a man confident in his strength sat, getting some air,
> dreadful to look at, his ears disfigured by hard fists.
> His huge chest and broad back
> bulged with iron-hard flesh, like a colossus of pounded metal.
> The muscles on his thick arms below the shoulder
> stood out like rounded stones that a swollen river
> rolled along and polished with its great swirling eddies.
> And more, over his back and neck was suspended
> by its extremities the hide of a lion (22.44–52).

Polydeukes greets the man and inquires whether he might give them a drink of water. When Amykos refuses, he asks him what he would take. "Stick up your hands, and face me, a man, one-on-one." Polydeukes' question, "Boxing with fists or striking the legs with the feet, too?" distinguishes boxing, which did not allow kicking, from a style of fighting that sounds like *pankration*. Amykos specifies fists and challenges Polydeukes to use his scientific technique all he wishes (22.61–67). Theocritus alludes to the opposition, pandemic to boxing, between the power to give and endure punishment and clever work with educated hands and feet. It is the same opposition in *bia* and *mêtis* that infuses Homer's games in *Iliad* 23 as well as Greek culture itself.

Pythagoras arrived in Olympia in 588 from remote Ionia, dressed in purple and the long hair of youth, and with skill defeated one opponent after another in men's boxing (Diogenes Laertius *Lives of the Eminent Philosophers* 8.47). In American boxing, Gentleman Jim Corbett came to New Orleans from far-off California in 1892 to shred the Boston Strong Boy, John L. Sullivan, on 7 September. Sullivan won the last bare-knuckle championship bout in 75 rounds in 1889, but with gloves and under Queensbury rules, he suffered an ignominious defeat in ninety minutes. Skillful use of the body distinguishes boxing from a street brawl and gives it its claim to being an athletic activity, an assertion that flies in the face of what the Greeks called it, *pygmachia*, battle with the fists.

Polydeukes tries to elicit the man's name but receives only a boast: "You see him nearby. No girly, he will be called The Boxer" (22.69). The remark, of course, impugns Polydeukes' manhood and asserts his own victory. Apollonius Rhodius (third century), in his version of the encounter, reads sexual attractiveness in the softness of Polydeukes' immature beard and the glow of his young eyes: "Such was the son of Zeus, blooming still with soft down / and fresh with the sparkle of youth in his eyes" (*Argonautica* 2.43–44). Indeed, behind Amykos' spontaneous quip about not being a woman may lie the implied threat that he might turn his sexual appetites toward the defeated youth, the handsome son of Zeus. The two men agree that each will fight for possession of the other. The defeated man becomes a slave, a possession, a thing that the winner can use as he pleases. The Greeks abhorred behavior "in which one treats other people just as one pleases, with an arrogant confidence that one will escape paying any penalty for violating their rights and disobeying any law or moral rule accepted by society" (Dover, 34). They called it *hybris* and prosecuted it, even when practiced upon a slave, with a *graphê*, a written public prosecution before a jury on behalf of the community against the offending individual.

The fighters gather their companions, for while a fight can be a private affair in an alley, to be a boxing match, a fight must be witnessed. Its purpose is not, as with the street fight, to beat the other guy into a bloody pulp, but to win and have others see and appreciate the victory. That betting on a fight, inseparable from the modern professional fight game, has gone unrecorded in the sources probably reflects the sources more than the event. The fighters wrap their hands with strips, which Theocritus views as a means of strengthening their hands, and begin:

> After the pair strengthened their hands with the straps
> of ox-hide and wound the long strips around their arms,
> they came into the middle, breathing murder at one another.
> Then they struggled and maneuvered vigorously
> over which one would have the sun at his back.
> With your skill, Polydeukes, you surpassed that huge man,
> and full in the face did the sun's rays hit him (22.80–86).

The sun could well prove a factor in fights held under the open sky, especially in the summers when the period games were held. Maneuvering one's opponent so that the rays of a blazing sun fell upon his eyes would surely offer an advantage. Theocritus' boxers move around so much that their attitude toward the sun would be constantly shifting, and Polydeukes' skill is enhanced by his success in manipulating Amykos into a position where "the sun's rays hit him."

The epic poet Quintus Smyrnaeus (fourth century C.E.) illustrates the caution with which fighters began as they felt one another out:

> Quickly, Epeios and Agelaos raised their hands at one another,
> staring intently, and moving on the tips of their feet;
> they kept shifting knees from one knee to the other in short steps,
> for a long time avoiding the other's great power (*Fall of Troy* 4.345–348).

The preliminary jockeying suggested itself to one philosopher as an analogy for the concept of *epochê*, philosophical suspension of judgment (Cicero *Letters to Atticus* 13.21.3). The enraged Amykos foregoes the niceties, and charges Polydeukes, his fists aimed at the young man. He moves forward, throwing haymakers, as if he knows no other tactic. They appear to be long, slow, looping hooks from the side, that Polydeukes avoids. Polydeukes counters with a straight shot—the right is the usual power hand—to Amykos' chin, let loose when Amykos is off balance:

> Tyndareos' son landed a blow to the point of his chin
> as Amykos attacked. Amykos, aroused more than before,
> fought wildly. He bent his head to the ground
> and advanced. The Bebrykes were screaming. From the other side,
> the heroes kept on cheering strong Polydeukes
> in fear that the giant of a man might overwhelm
> him in the narrow place and defeat him.
> But the son of Zeus, shifting now this way, now that,
> cut him with both fists in rapid series and held off
> the onslaught of Amykos, mighty as he was (22.88–97).

When Amykos' heavily muscled arm crosses over his chest, his body has no choice but to follow its arch, putting him off balance and exposing his head. Brought up sharply by stinging leather on his face, Amykos attacks with his head to the ground. Taking his eyes off his opponent, he forfeits his body in an effort to bully Polydeukes into a tight spot in the terrain. At the games, the arena was flat and open, but this one beside a stream has some configuration that presents the danger of being "caught in a corner." Polydeukes responds by moving right and left and by peppering Amykos with punches from different angles. The straightforward boxer can defend himself only from the front and is open to blows from the sides. Polydeukes mangles Amykos' face and mouth with cutting blows. None stops his opponent, but their cumulative effect renders him groggy. He pauses to clear his head and spit out the welling blood.

Theocritus' older contemporary Apollonius, called Rhodius because of his retirement in Rhodes, relates a fight between Amykos and Polydeukes in his *Argonautica*, an epic about Jason's voyage to Colchis in search of the Golden Fleece and his return to Greece. It was famous in antiquity for Apollonios' depiction of the awakening of love in Medea, daughter of Aeêtes, king of Colchis, and her efforts, often brutal and savage, to aid Jason. As befits an epic, Apollonios creates a more elaborate scene of boasts, challenge, and preparation. He then begins the fight ominously: "Amykos' henchmen, the fools, did not know / that in his evil lot they had bound those strips for the last time" (2.65–66):

> When they were fitted with the rawhide, Amykos and Polydeukes
> stood apart, and at once they raised their heavy hands before
> their faces and bore their might against one another in battle.
> There the lord of the Bebrykes, as a wild wave
> from the sea rises to a crest against a swift ship, and the ship,
> thanks to the skill of its shrewd helmsman, barely
> escapes being carried into the wall of the flood,
> so Amykos pressed the son of Tyndareos, forcing him into flight and
> affording him no rest. But Polydeukes, ever free of cuts because of
> his skill, slipped his foe's advances and quickly sized up
> the rough fighting of his fists, where his power was invincible
> and where inferior. He stood close and exchanged blows unceasingly.
> As when shipwrights draw the ships' timbers close
> and pound them with sharp nails
> and one heavy sound resounds on another
> in abundance, so their cheeks and jaws
> rang from both sides. They ground their teeth
> constantly and did not leave off hitting in earnest
> until they completely lost their breath and were subdued (2.65–85).

The wave simile characterizes the fight not only as a confrontation between *bia* and *mêtis* but as a clash between the forces of nature and the devices of culture as a towering sea threatens to overwhelm a swift ship that is rescued by its wise helmsman at the last moment. Amykos' onslaught is like a storm, dangerous, overpowering, but unruly, not guided by skill or intelligence. He attacks, driving Polydeukes back by a barrage of punches that hit only air. Polydeukes bobs and weaves, backing up and, at the same time, sizing up, his opponent. Perhaps realizing he can take Amykos, he stops and goes head-to-head with him in an exchange of blows that resound off the cheeks and jaws of both men like the powerful blows that drive nails into ships' timbers. Neither boxer could in reality have sustained so many blows to the head with "the strips / of rawhide, hard and exceedingly dry—kneading the cheeks of men with their blood" that Amykos uses to make dough of a man's flesh and blood (*Argonautica* 2.52–53, 59). Disfiguring an opponent with kneading blows, corrupting the civilizing art of the breadmaker into savagery, is what boxers do, as the image used by Theocritus for Polydeukes (22.11: "the unbeaten Polydeukes kneaded Amykos' face with disfiguring blows") and Apollonius for Amykos affirms (*Argonautica* 2.59).

Theocritus continues his account as Amykos endures even greater punishment:

> As his face swelled, his eyes began to close.
> Lord Polydeukes confused him by feinting
> from every direction. When he saw that Amykos was helpless,
> he hit him with a punch to the nose below the brow
> and laid his forehead bare to the bone. Amykos
> went down on his back, laid out flat on the thick leaves (22.101–106).

More serious problems develop as his face swells around his eyes, closing them off and narrowing his vision to a blurry slit. Compounding his difficulties, Polydeukes refuses to stand still but dances about in front of him, faking with rights and lefts. "The art of misdirection is one of the fundamental arts of boxing. It's simply the ancient art of hitting where they aren't watching" (Fitzgerald, 65). Amykos cannot watch or even see his opponent very clearly. He is helpless, and Polydeukes unloads to the bridge of his nose, splitting the thin flesh and cutting him to the bone. The stunning punch puts Amykos down on the leaves. Amykos scrambles to his feet, the blood now flowing into his eyes and down his cheeks. Facial wounds bleed profusely. He is a crude fighter, with few skills, who shows his colors by going for the body:

> They were striking with the hard strips, intent on killing one another.
> But the chief of the Bebrykes aimed his punches at the chest
> and below the neck, while the unbeaten Polydeukes
> kneaded Amykos' face with disfiguring blows.
> As Amykos sweated, his flesh began to shrink, and from a big man,
> he was rapidly becoming a small one. But as his effort was increasing,
> his opponent grew stronger and healthier looking.
> How did the son of Zeus destroy that bully?
> Speak, goddess, for you know. I am but an interpreter for others
> and will say what you wish in a way that pleases you.
> And then Amykos, focusing on one big shot,
> seized Polydeukes' left hand with his left
> and leaned to the side as he lunged forward and came in
> with his right, bringing his huge fist up from his right side.
> Had it landed, he would have hurt the king of the Spartans,

> but Polydeukes ducked and, at the same time, stepped in,
> countering with a closed fist, a straight shot from the shoulder to just
> below Amykos' left temple, splitting it open. Deep red flowed profusely
> from the cut. Polydeukes landed a left to his mouth, and his teeth
> rattled. With quickly repeating blows, he ravaged his face
> until his cheeks were smashed. Then Amykos
> lay on the ground, dazed senseless and, giving up the fight,
> raised both hands, since he was near death (22.109–130).

That Amykos can seize Polydeukes' left hand with his left indicates that Polydeukes has his left outstretched to guard his head when he is not jabbing and hooking with it; Amykos, leaning to the side, draws Polydeukes' left hand and arm across his body to the right, a move that exposes the left side of Polydeukes' head. As Amykos is pulling his opponent's arm out of the way, he begins a right from his hip, aimed at the left side of Polydeukes' head. Had the blow landed, Theocritus says, "he would have hurt the king of the Spartans"—indeed, he would have knocked him cold. To land the blow, Amykos shifts his weight onto his left foot to swing with his right. A power blow, it has to cross from his right hip, covering an upwards and transverse distance, but power blows, unlike straight jabs, are slow. Polydeukes moves his head to the right, following Amykos' force in pulling him to his right. Amykos is off balance, his right has missed, and his left hand is far removed from his face. He is wide open. Polydeukes steps toward him and with a solid right thrown from the shoulder with his body behind it smashes Amykos on the left side of his head, splitting the skin. His left hand freed and Amykos reeling in its direction, Polydeukes lands a left to the mouth that rattles Amykos' teeth. Punches in combination follow, and Amykos, pulverized, paralyzed, and prostrate on the leaves, near death, raises his hands in defeat. Having proven that Amykos, despite his boast, will never be called a boxer, Polydeukes then shows that he is in no way like his opponent as he exhibits no *hybris* and exacts nothing unseemly from him but only the promise that "he never again willingly cause trouble to strangers" (22.134).

Apollonios ends his version of the fight between Amykos and Polydeukes in imitation of Homer:

> Again they charged at one another like bulls
> fighting in a rage over a grazing heifer.
> Then Amykos, raising himself up on his toes,
> like someone sacrificing an ox, stretched up to his full height
> and swung his heavy fist down at him, but Polydeukes evaded its
> rush, slipping his head to the side, and took a glancing blow from
> Amykos' arm on his shoulder. He drew near, stealing his knee past

Amykos', and countered, striking him above the ear and shattering
the bones. Amykos fell to his knees in pain. The Minyan heroes
cried out for joy. And Amykos' spirit poured out in full (2.88–97).

Amykos raises himself on tiptoe, a maneuver to surmount Polydeukes'
guard but a dead giveaway of a chopping blow, a blow outlawed in
modern boxing. He resembles the sacrificer who lifts himself as high as
he can above his victim in order to get the most force behind the blow.
Polydeukes sees it coming and, unlike the animal victim, avoids the
blow, taking it on the shoulder. He then slips his knee past Amykos'
knee and, getting in close, explodes a right hook to the ear, shattering
the bones. Odysseus splinters Iros' bones with a similar blow, and
although Iros is alive when Odysseus leaves him, the scene of Odysseus'
dragging him from the door of his house (*Odyssey* 18.101) recalls the
familiar scene of a fallen comrade being dragged from the fray (e.g.,
Iliad 13.383). In this way, Apollonius' Amykos dies the death
foreshadowed by Homer's Iros.

Pankration

According to Bacchylides (13.44–66), *pankration* was founded to
commemorate Herakles' struggle against the lion of Nemea, whose
hide, impenetrable by weapons, forced Herakles to strangle the animal
to death (Apollodorus *Library* 2.5.1). Others claim that Theseus invented
pankration "when he was in the labyrinth matching strength with the
Minotaur, since he did not have a knife" (Scholiast on Pindar *Nemean
Ode* 5.89, in Drachmann, 3: 98). Aristotle attributed its discovery to
Leukaros of Akarnania (Scholiast on Pindar *Nemean Ode* 3.27, in
Drachmann, 3:46). Quintus Smyrnaeus portrays Ajax as a pankratiast
in his desire to contend "with hands and feet" (*Fall of Troy* 4.479–
480), anachronistically, since Homer does not include *pankration* among
the competitions held during Patroclus' funeral. It is a relatively late
event, added to the Olympic program in the thirty-third Olympiad (648)
where it was won by Lygdamis of Syracuse, a big man, reputedly the
size of Herakles (Pausanias 5.8.8). The Eleans did not sanction boys'
pankration until the 145th Olympiad (200) (Philostratos *Gymnastic*
13, in Kayser, 268).

Pankration, "all-power" or "all-victory," unites the striking of boxing
and the locks, throws, take downs, and escapes of wrestling with its

own particular features, kicking and falling to the ground. *Pankration* is, as Plutarch says, "a mixture of boxing and wrestling" (*Moralia* 638D), and as Philostratos says, "a concoction from imperfect wrestling and imperfect boxing" (*Gymnastic* 11, in Kayser, 266), and then some. "Perfect competitors for the *pankration* are those who are more suitable for wrestling than boxers and more suitable for boxing than wrestlers" (Philostratos *Gymnastic* 36, in Kayser, 281). On the other hand, pankratiasts did not need the size of the wrestler or boxer to be successful. One athlete, for example, whose father called him *Halter* or Jumping Weight, because he was small, used the tactic of seizing his opponent's heel and not letting go until he submitted (Philostratos *Heroic* 52–54 in Kayser, 146). The jumping weight, a stone that jumpers held in propelling themselves through the air, suggests that Halter was compact, strong, and lively.

Ambrose (ca.339–397 C.E.), bishop of Milan, describes *pankration* as a free-for-all:

> Other athletes mix murder and throwing of dust with entwining the limbs and every kind of hitting. These are pankratiasts, because they are permitted all struggles and fights against one another (*Commentary to Psalm* 36.55).

Ambrose exaggerates, but barely. Strangling was allowed in *pankration* as it was in wrestling. Excluded specifically at Olympia were biting and gouging of eyes, mouth, and other tender spots (Philostratos *Pictures in a Gallery* 2.6, in Kayser, 348; Aristophanes *Birds* 438–443). Among the Lacedaemonians who were always in training for war, both tactics were permitted (*Pictures in a Gallery* 2.6, in Kayser, 348). A red-figure cup (circa 490) confirms not only the illegality of gouging but also pankratiasts' disregard of the rules at the cost of a good caning (Illustration 16). Foul play was such a part of the *pankration* that it nicknamed practitioners of the event:

> When Demonax saw many athletes fighting dirty and biting against the rules instead of engaging in the *pankration*, he said: "With reason, the fans of today's athletes call them 'lions'" (Lucian *Life of Demonax* 49).

The Stoic philosopher Epictetus (ca. 55–135 C.E.) warned those wanting to compete in *pankration* at Olympia about the treatment they could expect in the contest:

Illustration 16. A forbidden act in *pankration*. Attic cup 480 B.C.E. Attributed to the Foundry Painter. Vase E 78. © The British Museum, London, England.

> You must match gouging with your opponent; sometimes dislocate your hand, sprain your ankle, eat a lot of dust, and be caned. After all this, you can lose (*Discourses* 3.15.4–5).

A match began with both competitors on their feet. Their fingers were slightly bent and their hands outstretched (Galen *On the Movements of the Muscles,* in Kühn, 4:395), ready to be clenched in a fist or widened for an open-handed blow leading to a snatch. They focused with an intensity that inspired Aulus Gellius (ca. 130–180 C.E.) to recommend similar concentration to men of public affairs:

> The life of men who spend their time in the midst of affairs and who want to be of use to themselves and their people brings problems and dangers suddenly, continually, and nearly every day. To be on guard against them and to evade them, such men must always be alert and focused like those athletes called pankratiasts. Just as these athletes, when summoned to the match, take up a position with their arms held high and stretch forth and protect their head and face by presenting their hands to their opponent like a rampart, and all their limbs, before the battle has begun, are on guard to avoid blows, the spirit and mind of the prudent man ought to be focused (*Attic Nights* 13.28).

The athletes needed also to guard against their fingers' being seized and dislocated, a tactic perfected by *pankration*'s Sostratos of Sikyon [M 420, 425, 433], who acquired the appellation Akrochersites or Fingers, because he "would seize his opponent's fingers and, bending them, not let go until he saw his man acknowledging defeat" (Pausanias 6.4.1).

The contenders could expect to fight from the ground. The fall, dreaded by the wrestler, did not concern the pankratiast, since he did not lose by getting sand on his back. He could attack his opponent's legs without hesitation over suffering the reprisal unleashed on Tydeus or choose to fight from the ground, deliberately falling because the move opened other ways of fighting. "Pankratiasts have the technique of falling on their backs, which is not safe for the wrestler, and moves by which a man may win by falling" (Philostratos *Pictures in a Gallery* 2.6, in Kayser, 348). Pindar praises Melissos, victorious at the Isthmus, for his cunning in fighting from his back: "he is the fox that falls onto her back and awaits the swoop of the eagle" (*Isthmian Ode* 4.65–66). Ground fighting at some point lost favor in competitions, if an inscription setting the rules for an athletic festival in the Greek city of Misthia in Pisidia in southern Asia Minor is indicative of more than local preference: "pankratiasts are not to use dust for sprinkling or wrestling falls but are to compete upright" (Gardiner 1929, 210).

Pankratiasts were free to strike with their hands and feet (Quintilian *Education of an Orator* 2.8.13). Kicking distinguishes theirs from the other heavy events, and consequently, winning athletes were praised for their big feet (Illustration 17):

> Glukon, renown of Asian Pergamum,
> thunderbolt of the *pankration*, he of the broad foot,
> the new Atlas, and those unconquered hands of his
> are gone (*Greek Anthology* 7.692 in Paton, 2: 367).

Reliance on kicking, however, exposed pankratiasts to effortless ridicule: "Should you tell me, 'I kick a great kick,' I will say to you, 'You boast of an accomplishment that belongs to a jackass'" (Epictetus *Discourses* 3.14.14).

Hitting with fists separated the pankratiast from the wrestler both in competition and in vase painting. A father lectures his son on the value of a good punch:

> Now listen to me.
> When I was a spectator at Olympia,
> Ephoudion fought with Askondas nobly,
> although he was an old man. Then the older guy
> popped the younger one with his fist and knocked him down.
> And so watch it, buster, that you don't get a black eye
> (Aristophanes *Wasps* 1381–1386).

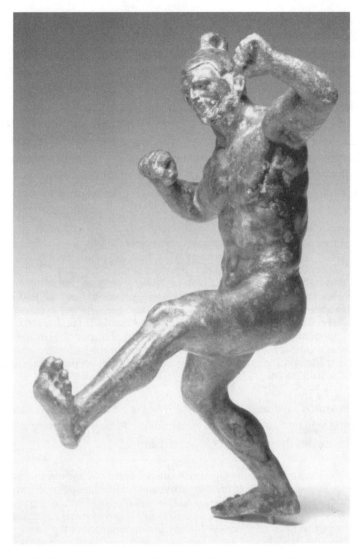

Illustration 17. Roman bronze statuette, first century C.E. Copyright Réunion des Musées Nationaux / Art Resource, NY.

Occasionally, a competitor wore boxing strips, support for his wrist and fingers that curtailed flexibility in grabbing an opponent. For such an athlete, the advantage gained by hitting an opponent outweighed that of the wrestler's skills (Poliakoff 1987, 56). The match continued until one athlete was incapable of continuing or signaled submission by raising his index finger. As in wrestling, the Lacedaemonians refused to compete in *pankration* at the Panhellenic festivals to save themselves the shame of announcing their own defeat and exposing themselves to slanders of cowardice (Philostratos *Gymnastic* 9, in Kayser, 265).

Pankratiasts "who strike, choke, break, and sometimes kill," Dio Chrysostomos expounds, are like boys who "play with trying to put out a fire with their tongues. . . . If you really attack a fire, you put it out. But if you attack it cautiously and fearfully, you get really burned" (*Eighth Discourse* 19). Boys who play with fire get hurt as do pankratiasts who play with death. The most famous death—and the sole recorded death—in *pankration* is that of Arrachion or Arrichion [M 102] of Phigalia. Both Pausanias and Philostratos give an account of his final match:

> Arrachion won two Olympic victories before the fifty-fourth Olympiad [564], and another came his way in the fifty-fourth because of the fairness of the Hellanodikai and Arrachion's own courage. When he was fighting for the wild olive against the last remaining competitor, whoever that was, his opponent gripped Arrachion first and held him in a scissors hold with his legs. At the same time, he was pressing on Arrachion's throat with his hands. Arrachion dislocated his opponent's toe but expired from the choking. The one choking him at that moment acknowledged defeat because of the pain from his toe. The Eleans proclaimed and crowned Arrachion's corpse as the victor (Pausanias 8.40.1–2).

Philostratos' account is a description of a painting that he sees while touring a picture gallery with a young friend. Acting as the wise instructor, he explicates the portrait for his companion:

> You have arrived at the Olympic Games themselves and the noblest of the events in Olympia, men's *pankration*. Arrichion is being crowned, although he died in victory, and the Hellanodikes here is crowning him. . . . For now, let us look at Arrichion's deed before it is over, for he seems to have conquered not only his opponents but the Greeks in the audience. In any case, they are leaping up from their seats and shouting. Some are waving their hands or cloaks, and others are jumping into the air. Others are pounding their neighbors on the back in joy. The spectators are seeing something so amazing that they cannot contain themselves. Who is so unfeeling that he doesn't cry out at the athlete? This accomplishment of his is greater even than his great deed of winning twice before at Olympia, for this victory came at the price of his life, and he is being escorted to the Land of the Blessed with the dust still on him. Do not think that victory happened by accident. No, he figured out very cleverly the move leading to victory. . . . Arrichion's opponent, having already grasped him around the waist, has decided to kill him. He inserted his forearm on Arrichion's throat, blocking his breathing. He then fit his legs around Arrichion's groin and passed the ends of his feet through [Arrichion's legs] and

pressed one against the bend of each knee. Because of the stranglehold, Arrichion's opponent got ahead of him as the drowsiness of death was creeping over his senses from this point. But his opponent, in relaxing the pressure of his legs, did not get ahead of Arrichion's stratagem. Arrichion kicked back the sole of his [right] foot. His right side was threatened as his bent leg was left dangling. Arrichion gripped his opponent with his groin so that he no longer resisted. Then throwing his weight to his left, he locked the end of his opponent's foot in the bend of his knee and, with a violent wrenching outward, he did not allow the anklebone to remain with the ankle. His spirit, departing his body, acted listlessly but gave him the strength for what he aimed to do.

The strangler is painted in the picture to look like a corpse. He is acknowledging defeat by his hand. Arrichion is painted in the way victors always are. His blood is in flower, and his sweat is still fresh. He is smiling just as the living when they have become aware of victory (*Pictures in a Gallery* 2.6 in Kayser, 347–349).

Arrichion's anonymous opponent in the finals of the fifty-fourth Olympiad seizes control of him and the match by executing a *klimakismos* or ladder grip. In terms of the name, he makes a *klimax* or ladder out of Arrichion by climbing up his back. Anacharsis describes the maneuver in a sarcasm about the enemy's fear of the Greeks' wrestling moves: "The enemy runs away in fear that you [Greeks] will leap around behind them so as to get on their backs and wind your legs around their stomachs and, slipping an arm beneath their helmets, throttle them" (Lucian *Anacharsis* 31). Arrichion's opponent somehow gets behind him or spins him around and jumps up on his back. He winds his legs around Arrichion's groin, inserting his feet between Arrichion's legs and hooking his toes in the bend of Arrichion's knees. "The pressure that this grip causes on the mid-section of the opponent [that is, Arrichion] is quite painful; the pressure on his knees forces him to sink down" (Brophy, 378). Simultaneously, Arrichion's opponent cuts off his breathing by an arm pushed against his throat. At this point the opponent is in command, but, apparently losing concentration or wearying himself, he relaxes his legs. Arrichion, feeling the easing of tension, snaps his legs together, gripping his opponent's legs and feet and neutralizing his resistance. He then shifts his weight to his left foot and starts to fall sideways, his nearly unconscious body adding dead weight. At the same time, he kicks violently backward with his right leg. Arrichion's opponent's foot is still locked behind the knee, and when Arrichion's knee moves back and up against his thigh, the opponent's foot is pulled apart so ankle bone and foot do not remain together. That is, Arrichion dislocates his opponent's ankle as he dies (Harris 1964, 108; Brophy, 379). In agony, his opponent signals his submission, and Olympic officials confer the crown upon Arrichion's corpse.

The Greeks believed that Arrichion was on the verge of expiring from suffocation when he snatched victory with alert thinking. Philostratos emphasizes how Arrichion's opponent beat him out in the matter of the grip but failed to do so in strategy. Brophy, however, points out that suffocation causes the loss of consciousness before death (380). With a clue in Eusebius' notation for the fifty-fourth Olympiad—"Arelion (*sic*) of Phigalia, winning in his second (*sic*) *pankration*, died after suffering decapitation (his skull having been broken)" (*Chronicles*, in Schoene, 1:201)—that hints at "the true medical reason for his death," Brophy concludes that Arrichion probably broke his own neck:

> Anatomically, Arrichion's head should have led or accompanied the leftward thrust of his body as he kicked up and back with his right foot, but his opponent was holding it immobilized. The snap of his fall or leap sideways, while his opponent still retained his strangle hold, caused the same effect as death by hanging: the fracture of the dens of the axis bone, severing the vertebrae from there down (381).

When Arrichion moved to his left, his head, held tight by his opponent's arms, could not follow. In the heat of competition, with his focus on victory, Arrichion killed himself.

Philostratos sets forth the meaning that Arrichion had for later generations of Greeks: "This accomplishment of his is greater even than his great deed of winning twice before at Olympia, for this victory came at the price of his life, and he is being escorted to the Land of the Blessed with the dust still on him" (*Pictures in a Gallery* 2.6, in Kayser, 348). Arrichion died the death that the Greeks most admired, for his was *ho kalos thanatos*, the beautiful death met at the peak of his fighting skills and in the flower of his youth (Vernant, 1991).

5.

Athletics in Athens

Tombs discovered under the classical agora dating to the Mycenaean, Protogeometric, and Geometric periods suggest that the early agora was a burial ground and that aristocratic families across Attica conducted games there for their dead in which they awarded others of the elite with prizes for victory in athletic contests (Thompson 1961, 231). Conferring prestige and honor in the form of a tripod palliated the exchange of property and solidified bonds of friendship and mutual obligation. In this milieu, athletics benefited a wealthy landed elite and helped elevate them above others. This situation did not change significantly in the seventh century. Festivals for a divinity or a hero were held, developing perhaps out of funeral games that included athletic contests among their rituals. Congregations for these celebrations comprised a wider range of citizens than private funerals among the clans, but athletics remained the province of aristocrats. The association between athletics, particularly equestrian races, and the agora continued throughout the classical period.

In 696, Athenians gained their first Olympic champion, Pantakles [M 25], winner in the *stadion* at the twenty-first Olympiad. Pantakles repeated in the *stadion* and added the *diaulos* to his victories in the next Olympiad (Eusebius *Chronicles,* in Schoene, 1:195). Other victors followed: Eurybates [M 36] in *stadion* (672), Stomas [M 54] in *stadion* (644), Phrynon [M 58] in *pankration* (636), and Akmeon [M 81] in the chariot race (592). Nothing is known about Eurybates and Stomas, but all were probably aristocrats (Kyle 1987, 20). Their accomplishments indicate an environment at Athens and in Attica conducive to athletics as does the failed attempt of Kylon [M 56] to become tyrant over the Athenians in 632. Aristocrat and winner in the *diaulos* in 640, he counted upon his status as an Olympic victor to rally the people behind his coup d'état (Herodotus *Histories* 5.71). However mistakenly Kylon interpreted the significance of his victory for his political ambitions, interest in athletics and outstanding athletes was evidently spreading among Athenians.

In the sixth century, the Athenians embarked on their own path when the emphasis veered, subtly at first, "from typically Panhellenic, aristocratic Greek athletics toward the *polis*-oriented, civically operated, and distinctively Athenian athletics of the Panathenaea" (Kyle 1987,15). Not that Athenians or their legislator and reformer, Solon, archon in 594/593, knew that a revolution was underway when, as part of his program, he rewarded by law the victor in an Olympic event with five hundred drachmas and an Isthmian victory with one hundred (Plutarch *Solon* 23.3). Solon's program of reforms had sweeping, lasting, and hardly anticipated effects upon the future of Athenian society, preparing the foundation for the democracy of the fifth century. Solon set out to remedy the immediate political and economic differences that were rending the social fabric (Fine, 192–208). His law on victors, like his reforms, was intended to diminish aristocratic privilege and curtail its disruption of the community. By confining funerals to the house, for example, and restricting processions to the early morning, Solon marginalized elite funerals. Granting a financial reward for victory at Panhellenic games placed the victor's accomplishment under the aegis of the *polis* with the victor becoming a hero of the community and promoting the glory of all Athenians instead of that of only his family (Kyle 1987, 22). Thus, the athlete's triumph turned into a source of communal pride and honor that the community recognized by a cash prize that no family could stake.

Athenians had long celebrated the Panathenaea or Festival of Athena each year on her birthday, the twenty-eighth of Hekatombaion (roughly July) (Burkert 1985, 232). They gathered, forming a procession, brought a new dress for Athena's wooden statue, and escorted victims to the goddess's altar on the Acropolis where they performed the sacrifices (Parke, 33). A feast and merry-making ensued in the agora. Tribes competed in a beauty contest for men, a torch-race, and the traditional steps of the pyrrhic dance performed in armor (Davison, 25–26). Equestrian and musical contests were probably also held.

Eusebius' *Chronicles* records under the third and fourth years (566/565) of the fifty-third Olympiad (568) "an athletic competition that they call Panathenaea" (in Schoene, 2:95). Eusebius' date of 566 for this innovation is accepted, albeit reluctantly, because his is the sole chronological evidence for the addition to the Panathenaea of athletic competitions open to all Greeks (Kyle 1987, 25–28). Donald G. Kyle views these changes in the light of the political situation of the 560s:

> With the successful Olympic model at hand, with a native tradition of funeral games, and even perhaps with a fear of the negative political potential of aristocratic athleticism, the political powers at Athens—perhaps urged by Solon or Pisistratus—recast a traditional festival to include games and an extended format every fourth year. The idea of patriotism and decreased factionalism would appeal to perceptive leading citizens, and the opportunity to compete and observe at home would appeal to all (1987, 29).

The Athenians followed the Olympic model in holding contests every four years. The quadrennial festival, more elaborate with the games and with increasing opulence as the city flourished in the fifth century, became known as the Great Panathenaea and the others, the Little Panathenaea. Nothing excludes an Olympic athletic program similar to that of the mid-sixth century from the first Panathenaea, but only the running events are known. The games were administered by a board of eight *Hieropoioi*, Doers of Sacred Things, and after 421, by *Athlothetai*, Administrators of the Games. Monies were allocated, spent, and accounted for in managing the Great Panathenaea on the same footing as other four-year festivals. However, diverging from the practice of the period games, Athenians awarded prizes to competitors placing second and sometimes even lower. In a more striking departure, they established the tradition of giving valuable prizes, large amphoras filled with olive oil, for the athletic and equestrian events (Illustration 18). The oil was gathered from Athena's sacred trees scattered throughout Attica and, upon being sold, could realize considerable sums of drachmas.

Throughout their history, the games of the Great Panathenaea redounded to the glory of Athenians as their festival became a showcase for their magnificent city (Parke, 33–50). They drew Greece's best athletes and musicians and allowed Athenians to watch excellent competitions. Yet the Panathenaic Games remained a local *chrematitês*, an ineradicable stigma that mired them forever in the second echelon of athletic festivals.

Illustration 18. Striding Athena. Black-figure Panathenaic amphora, ca. 480–470 B.C.E. Vase C.959.53. Hood Museum of Art, Darthmouth College, Hanover, New Hampshire; gift of Mr. and Mrs. Ray Winfield Smith, Class of 1918.

Panathenaic Games

Touch a Panathenaic amphora, and you connect with a victor who once handled it and took pride in it as a symbol of his *aretê*. He accepted the divinity of Athena depicted on the obverse or chief side of the vase and was the best on her birthday in the event shown on the reverse. Many victors surely sold the oil and amphoras before going home. What would the winner in men's *stadion*, the new owner of one hundred amphoras, do with over a thousand gallons of olive oil? Athenians encouraged victors in the Panathenaea to take prizes home with them, since they allowed victors, and only victors, to export olive oil duty-free (Young 1984, 126). Theaios, son of Ulias, conveyed his amphoras filled with oil back home to Argos:

> In fire-roasted earth, the fruit of the olive came to Hera's valiant host
> in the jars'decorated enclosures (Pindar *Nemean Ode* 10.35–36).

Men like Ulias' son cherished their Panathenaic amphoras and took them to the grave. Vases have been found across the Mediterranean as far as the Black Sea. Every one of them embodies a link with a victor, for every one was made for, and came from, the games at Athens.

Shortly before a Great Panathenaea, olive oil and amphoras merged when the treasurers on the Acropolis measured out the oil for the administrators of the games (Aristotle *Constitution of the Athenians* 60.3). The oil had been accumulating on the Acropolis under the protection of the treasurers who received it as it arrived from the archon charged with its collection from the sacred trees, three half pints from each trunk. The demos regarded very seriously the welfare of its sacred trees. Athenians believed that the trees were descended from the olive Athena planted in the reign of Cecrops, the time of first beginnings (Apollodorus *The Library* 3.14.1). Anyone convicted before the Areopagus of cutting one down or excavating its stump was punished with death (Aristotle *Constitution of the Athenians* 60.2) or self-imposed exile (Lysias *On the Olive-Stump* 3). In the late fourth century, however, the *polis* suspended the trials without repealing the law and levied oil as a tax on owners of estates. Long-held religious scruples may be ignored but are best not openly defied, in defiance of the goddess's displeasure toward family and city.

The archon shared responsibility with the council for letting out contracts for the amphoras to the potters in the Kerameikos or Potters' Quarter (Aristotle *Constitution of the Athenians* 60). They threw, painted, and fired more than 1,400 for a festival (Johnston, 125). Each prize amphora cost a drachma, a day's wage for a skilled workman, and contained one *metrêtês* or about twelve *choes* (about 10.4 gallons of oil) (Edwards, 335 note 55; Neils, 39). At 24.5 to 27.5 inches, Panathenaic amphoras were one-third taller than standard Athenian amphoras. They had narrow necks that were stoppered with a lid and embraced by two handles, a reminder of their origin in transport jars. The shape changed somewhat in the course of their five-hundred-year history but remained recognizable as Panathenaic.

The decorations on the obverse of a Panathenaic prize amphora became canonical about 540 with a vase by the painter Exekias (Neils, 30, 31 Fig. 20). A helmeted Athena strides to the left, brandishing a shield on her left arm and a spear in her right hand. Her rear foot, the left, is slightly raised, an innovation from earlier vases like the Burgon, the earliest extant Panathenaic vase, that show both feet on the ground (Neils, 30 Fig. 19). Subsequent artists, perhaps to convey liveliness, continue the motif until the heel is fully elevated (Illustration 18). Flanking the goddess are two Doric columns, each topped by a rooster. The scene is generally thought to represent a cult statue of Athena on the Acropolis that played a part in the ceremonies. The cocks may allude to "the spirit of competition" (Boardman 1974, 167), and the columns, to Zeus. In this case, the scene depicts the Athenians' patron warrior goddess, Athena Polias, who watches over their *polis* with the aid of her father, Zeus Polieus (Neils, 36–38). The inscription that validates the vase as a Panathenaic prize amphora runs without word division parallel to one of the columns: ΤѠΝ ΑΘΗΝΗΘΕΝ ΑΘΛѠΝ. The vase speaks, identifying itself as one "from the games at Athens." A better, if more awkward, translation, "from the games from Athens,"

Illustration 19. Inscription. Detail of C.959.53, Hood Museum of Art, Dartmouth College, Hanover, New Hampshire; gift of Mr. and Mrs. Ray Winfield Smith, Class of 1918.

respects the Greek mentality by giving equal value to the event and the city (Illustration 19).

The reverse of a Panathenaic amphora was exempt from the restraints that convention imposed upon the obverse. This difference does not imply an opposition between the sacred and the profane, as the games themselves were celebrated in honor of Athena. The reverse panel, smaller than that enclosing Athena, depicts the athletic or equestrian event for which the vase was awarded. Painters indulged their creativity in representing the event realistically and with contemporary techniques developed in red-figure. They portrayed equipment and auxiliary figures such as trainers and umpires. Thirty-six percent of the earliest amphoras show the footraces, and another third of the extant sixth- and fifth-century vases depict an equestrian event (Neils, 34–35). The Burgon amphora shows a two-horse race (Neils, 93 Fig. 59), but the four-horse race is more common (Illustration 20). Rarest among extant vases are scenes from the pentathlon. Not until the mid-fourth century is the figure of the Panathenaic *apobatês* (dismounter) depicted. His name suggests that an athlete, armed with full armor or a hoplite shield and helmet (Reed, 308), jumped from a speeding chariot, ran, and, in cooperation with the charioteer, leapt back into it before the end of the race (Neils, 90 Fig. 56).

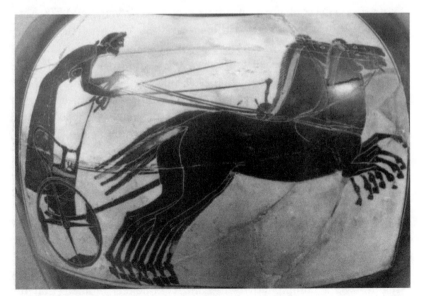

Illustration 20. Racing chariot. Black-figure Panathenaic amphora, ca. 500 B.C.E The Art Museum, Princeton University. Bequest of Mrs. Allan Marquand. Photo credit: Bruce M. White.

A fragmentary inscription supplies the fullest picture of the games in the fourth century (Dittenberger 1982, no. 1055; Miller 1991, 79–83). The program reflects changes, if indeed there were changes, introduced after the restoration of the democracy in 403 and by Pericles' earlier decree (446) concerning musical contests. Of this decree, Plutarch states in his treatment of Pericles' building program:

> The *Odeion*, with many seats and peristyles inside and a roof outside sloping from a single point, is made, they say, in imitation of the king's tent. Pericles was the overseer (*Pericles* 13.9). . . . Pericles, seeking distinction, for the first time had a decree passed that a contest in music be held at the Panathenaea, and he himself, the appointed administrator of the games, arranged the order in which the competitors were to play the *aulos* or sing or play the kithara. At that time and henceforth, they watched the musical contests in the *Odeion* (*Pericles* 13.11).

What Plutarch meant by "for the first time," remains uncertain, since ceramic evidence leaves no doubt that musical contests were part of the Panathenaea before Pericles' time (Davison, 33–36). But Pericles affected the games in some fashion, given the flourish of vases in the 440s depicting musical contests and musicians. He may have restored them after a hiatus (Davison, 36) or restructured and fixed them by law (Shapiro, 57). On the other hand, he probably did not build the *Odeion* or Music Hall, a large, nearly square edifice abutting the theater of Dionysus on the southern slope of the Acropolis (Wycherley 1978, 215–216). The Roman architect and military engineer Vitruvius (first century B. C.E.–first century C.E.) reports that Themistocles roofed off the area where contests were held "with masts and yardarms from the Persian spoils" acquired in the Greek victory at Salamis in September 480 (*On Architecture* 5.9.1). This nose-thumbing gesture befits the period after the defeat of Xerxes, the Persian king. More than likely, Pericles restored the *Odeion* and returned the contests to their proper venue (Davison, 34–35).

Inscriptio Graeca II^2 2311, once displayed in a prominent place, the agora or the Acropolis, announced to all, citizens and visitors, the prizes for the various contests. The information, in lapidary style, is succinct, formulaic, and declarative. The "for" of the translation below of lines 1–23 is expressed in Greek by a word ending, not a separate word, and "a" is used here where Greek lacks the indefinite article. A "kithara singer" sang and played the kithara himself, while an "*aulos* singer" was accompanied by the *aulos*. Brackets indicate that the enclosed material has been restored, and ellipsis points represent missing information:

. . .	[FOR RHAPSODES]
. . .	[FOR FIRST] A [C]ROWN
. . .	[FOR SE]COND
. . .	[FOR T]HIRD
	FOR KITHARA SINGERS
	FOR FIRST A CROWN WORTH
1000	OF GOLD BRANCH [AND]
500	OF SILVER
1200	FOR SECOND
600	FOR THIRD
400	FOR FOURTH
300	FOR FIFTH
	FOR MEN AULOS SINGERS
300	FOR FIRST THIS A CROWN
100	FOR SECOND
	FOR MEN KITHARA PLAYERS
500	FOR FIRST THIS
	A CROWN WORTH 300
. . . 200	FOR SECOND
100	FOR THIRD
	FOR AULOS PLAYERS
. . . 100	FOR FIRST THIS A CROWN
. . .	[FOR SECO]ND

Lines referring to rhapsodes have been conjectured, because these stitchers of songs are known from literary sources to have been part of the Panathenaea from earliest times.

Rhapsodes recited professionally the works of poets, especially Homer but also Hesiod, Archilochus, and others (Athenaeus *The Deipnosophists* 620C–D). Hipparchos, Peisistratos' younger son, is said to have "brought the epics of Homer to this land [Attica] and compelled the rhapsodes at the Panathenaea to relate them in order, taking up the cue" one from the other ([Plato][1] *Hipparchus* 228B). The text in which his story is told allows that Hipparchos introduced competitions for rhapsodes or, preferably, that he reorganized existing competitions and compelled the rhapsodes to strict recitation of the Homeric epics (Davidson, 39). Rhapsodes are attested at the Panathenaea for the

---

1 The brackets indicate that this work is attributed to Plato, but the author is considered unknown.

fifth (Plato *Ion* 530B) and fourth centuries (Lycurgus *Against Leocrates* 102). A Panathenaic-shaped amphora, dating to about 520, implies their presence at the festival not long after its inception. The vase shows a rhapsode standing on a dais and holding a crooked staff, sign of his craft (Neils, 74 Fig. 50). Before him stands a man who is listening, and behind, one who, from his forked cane, appears to be an umpire (Shapiro, 74).

Athenians could have put up gold and silver prizes from earliest times to attract top-echelon professionals and to make the journey worthwhile even for the fifth-place winner. Unlike oil, money is portable and convenient. The awards show that singers who accompanied themselves on the kithara were the stars, and *aulos* players, the bottom billing. David C. Young calculates on the basis of the drachma valued at $80.00 (U.S.1980) that the winner in singing to the kithara carried off the untaxed equivalent of $84,750, and fifth place, $16,950 (1985.125). Singers to the *aulos*, a clarinet- or oboe-like instrument consisting of a reed inserted into a cylindrical pipe pierced with holes, were required, as stated in an inscription mentioned by Plutarch, to sing elegiac verse set to music (*Moralia* 1134A). These were not the funeral dirges that so depressed the Amphictyons that they discontinued them for the Pythian Games (Pausanias 10.7.4–5). The singers sang to the accompaniment of an *aulos* long narratives, upwards of two thousand lines, on mythological and historical subjects (Bowie, 27–34). That contests in singing to the *aulos* and kithara playing were designated for men has led to the inference that similar contests were held for boys. All the contests are illustrated on Panathenaic amphoras of the sixth and early fifth centuries.

Lines 24–68 of II^2 2311 declare prizes in athletic and equestrian events. Prizes were offered in *stadion*, pentathlon, wrestling, boxing, and *pankration*, in three categories, boys, beardless youths, and men. The lists for men have been lost, but the one for boys is nearly complete (lines 24–38):

[FOR BOY WINNING STA]DION

50   AMPHORAS OF OLIVE OIL

10   FOR SECOND PLACE

FOR BOY WINNING PENTATHLON

30   AMPHORAS OF [OLIVE O]IL

6   FOR SECOND PLACE

FOR WINNING BOY WRESTLER

30   AMPHORAS OF OLIVE OIL

6	FOR SECOND PLACE
	FOR WINNING BOY BOXER
30	AMPHORAS OF OLIVE OIL
6	FOR SECOND PLACE
	FOR BOY WINNING *PANKRATION*
40	AMPHORAS OF OLIVE OIL
8	FOR SECOND PLACE

Prizes were given to first and second place in the proportion of five to one. The *stadion* was the premier event. First place among the beardless youths garnered sixty amphoras in *stadion* and forty in the other events. Prizes for men are known to be twice those of boys (Young 1985, 128 n. 19), to wit, one hundred amphoras for first prize in *stadion* and sixty for first in the other events. Equestrian contests (lines 54–69) included chariot races for two colts for which forty amphoras were awarded for first place and eight for second and races for mature horses that gave one hundred forty amphoras to the winner and forty to second place. Prizes for warriors offered sixteen amphoras for first place in a horse race and four for second, thirty for first place in a two-horse chariot race and six for second, four for first place in a processional chariot race and one for second, and five for first place in throwing a javelin from horseback and one for second. That the prizes were amphoras of olive oil rather than drachmas (as in tribal events) suggests that these events were open to all comers (Kyle, 1987.38).

Young has devised a conservative methodology for converting the value of the amphora prizes into equivalents in wages for a skilled workman in the year 400 (1985, 115–127). He takes twelve drachmas per amphora as "the *lowest* usable" figure for the cost of olive oil in the period. The value of the hundred amphoras for first place in men's *stadion* is twelve hundred drachmas at a minimum. With one drachma as the wage of a skilled craftsman for a day's work, the victor in the *stadion* won the equivalent in wages of 1,200 days' work by a stonemason, that is, 3.29 years of continuous employment. Even at the wage fifty years later, 1.417 drachmas a day, the sprinter has won the counterpart of 847 days' wages or 2.3 years of continuous employment. (That craftsmen did not get work 365 days a year must be factored into the worth of one hundred amphoras of olive oil.) As to the purchasing power of the *stadion* runner's prize, Young suggests:

> For example, he could buy six or seven *medium*-priced slaves (people!); or a flock of about 100 sheep. Or he could purchase outright two or three houses in Athens or elsewhere in Attica; for the full 1,200

drachmas, he could apparently buy a rather fancy house in the city
(1985, 127).

Greek athletes, we know, were not amateurs. They did not compete
for the love of the game or for the sake of participating. They strove to
win with winning the exclusive goal and sole objective. The number of
athletes who enjoyed great success was limited by the zero-sum process,
but those who won profited immensely from their victories. They could,
in fact, earn a princely living from the direct prize money extended by
local festivals and the rewards for a Panhellenic victory requited by
proud home cities. This situation raises the question: were all athletes
from the nobility, or did the rewards of athletics encourage and support
upward mobility in society? Could an athlete's later public prominence
be the result of his victories rather than of his noble origin with his
victories as added distinctions? Young explores this issue with the fervent
belief that athletes began from non-noble origins (1985,158–162).

Many Olympic victors, among them, Polymester of Miletus [M 79],
Glaukos of Karystos [M 134], and Milo of Kroton [M 115, 122, 126,
129, 133, 139], first won as boys. Young proposes a mechanism that
would allow boys of families of moderate means to become wealthy
through athletics. Since training was not as much a factor in boys'
events as in men's, a boy could win on natural ability, coming from
nowhere to win a local prize that would provide the means to train, hire
a coach to improve his skills, and travel to other festivals. Once he won
a victory in a periodic or Panathenaic contest, the boy would be in a
position to launch his career.

The evidence regarding the social standing of athletes, unfortunately,
is ambiguous. A case in point is that of Phaÿllos of Kroton who
commanded a warship at Salamis (Young 1985, 160–161). Did he do so
because he was an aristocrat, the common assumption, or, as Young
asks, because he could afford to outfit a trireme from wealth won in
pentathlon and *stadion*? To take another example, the boxer Glaukos
of Karystos [M 134] was slain while acting as governor of Kamarina in
Sicily; his punching power had been discovered when he fixed a plow
with his hand on his father's farm. Demylos worked the land himself,
yet he had the resources to leave the farm and take his son to Olympia,
perhaps even remaining there for the month of training (Pausanias
6.10.1–3; Young 1985, 162). Was Glaukos the son of a farmer or a
landed noble?

Opportunities lay open for non-noble athletes, but whether they
could overcome the social inertia that kept them in their place to excel
at elite games is questionable. After examining the social status of

Athenian victors from the sixth to the late fourth centuries, Kyle notes that the change in the social background of athletes took the form of a shift "from an élitism of *birth* to an élitism of *wealth*" (1987, 123). Those in the earliest period came from the landed aristocracy that pursued breeding and racing horses. Athletes in the fifth century belonged to less noble origins, but their families were wealthy and of the upper class, while those of the fourth century belonged to rich families whose affluence did not reside in land. "Given the natural physical inequalities of men and the fact that physical potential was a prerequisite, athletic success tended to favor the few who had the leisure, finances and inclination to train and travel" (Kyle 1987, 122). Young's up-and-coming boy is a possibility, but that boy required not only athletic ability, proper diet, and access to athletic facilities but exceptional initiative to break out of the mold of social classism. Children of poor farmers had little chance to become athletes.

The inscription (lines 70–79) ends with events in which members of the ten Athenian tribes competed with enthusiasm, no doubt, both for the honor and for the drachmas. After all, they had interrupted their lives for months in training for this day when they were competitors rather than spectators of an athletic prowess few could emulate. Fellow tribesmen surely enjoyed their victory and the bragging rights it granted before the Eponymoi, the statues of the eponymous heroes of the ten tribes that stood in the agora from at least 421 (Aristophanes *Peace* 1183; Wycherley 1978, 52–53). Here, under the statue of the tribe's hero, were posted announcements for men called to military service and other notices among which probably was the call for tryouts for the various events of the Panathenaea.

The pyrrhic dance, the first event, was invented by Athena in celebration of the Olympian gods' victory over the Titans and embellished her birthday with a reminder of the triumphal day of her father, Zeus. Males, armed with shield and spear, performed by moving in rhythm to the sound of an *aulos*, a movement that imitated the defensive and offensive maneuvers used to avoid and throw blows and missiles (Plato *Laws* 815A). The contest was paid for by a *leitourgia*, an assessment for a public function imposed upon, or assumed by, wealthy citizens, foremost among whom were the Hellanodikai in charge of the games. It cost one patron eight hundred drachmas (Lysias *Defense Against a Charge of Taking Bribes* 1). Another patron memorialized his victory with an inscription and a votive base that depicts eight nude dancers with shields and himself, fully clothed, watching from the left (Neils, 95 Fig. 61). In separate contests, teams of boys, beardless youths, and

Illustration 21. Torch race. Red-figure bell krater, ca. 430–420 B.C.E. In the manner of the Pelius Painter. Courtesy of the Arthur M. Sackler Museum, Harvard University Art Museums, Bequest of David M. Robinson. Photo credit: Michael Nedzweski.

men competed, with the prizes, a hundred drachmas and a bull, going to each winning team. Its members probably divided the drachmas and, after sacrificing the bull, celebrated with a feast.

Teams of tribesmen competed in strength and size in a beauty contest for men, the *euandria*. According to the inscription, the winning team received a hundred drachmas and a bull, although Aristotle says that winners received shields (*Constitution of the Athenians* 60.4).

A torch race, funded by a *leitourgia* for which the holder was rewarded with the title of *gymnasiarchos* or superintendent of the *gymnasion* (Demosthenes *Against Leptines* 21), brought fire to the altar for the sacrifices honoring Athena along the Panathenaic Way which Athenians also called the *dromos* or racecourse (Illustration 21). Square holes for starting posts, dating to the mid-fifth century, have been found in the road at the northwest corner of the agora (Shear). The race was run from the altar of Eros in the Academy outside the Dipylon Gate, through the Kerameikos and into the agora from the northwest, across the agora toward the southeast, and, finally, up the steep north slope of the Acropolis. Since Peisistratos founded Eros' altar, he is often credited with inaugurating the race at the Panathenaea (Plutarch *Solon* 1.7; Parke, 45), but he may have made his new altar the start for an existing torch race that began at the altar of Prometheus in the Academy (Pausanias 1.30.2). In any case, torch races were an ancient feature of Athenian festivals as shown by their administration under the king archon, the magistrate who assumed the religious functions of the Mycenaean king (Aristotle *Constitution of the Athenians* 57.1). They were run by individuals or in relays such as Pausanias describes in the race at the Festival of Prometheus:

> They run from the altar of Prometheus toward the city, carrying burning torches. The contest is to keep the torch burning during the race. If the torch of the first runner is extinguished, he has no victory, but victory lies with the second. If his no longer burns, the third is the one triumphant. If everyone's torch is extinguished, no one is left to be victor (1.30.2).

Runners who performed badly in the race could encounter "the blows of the Kerameikos" (Scholiast on Aristophanes *Frogs* 1093, in Dübner, 305). Aristophanes' Aeschylus, dead and in the underworld, complains that Euripides has corrupted the old morality and that "no one today can carry a torch / because of the lack of exercise" (*Frogs* 1087–1088). Dionysus picks up the thought with an example:

> No way they can, by Zeus. I laughed
> at the Panathenaea 'til I shriveled
> when a slow fellow was running, stooped over,
> pale, fat, and left behind
> and doing poorly. Then the folks from the Kerameikos
> at the gates began whacking him
> on his belly, ribs, flanks, and butt.
> As he was being hit with the flat of their hands,
> he farted,
> blew out his torch and absconded (*Frogs* 1089–1098).

The winning tribe received one hundred drachmas and a bull, while the victorious torchbearer was awarded thirty drachmas and a *hydria*, a water vessel. Thus, the first man to renew the fire on Athena's altar by running received a vessel used daily by women who, by walking, carried water, mortal and natural enemy of fire, to their houses from a public fountain. Men speed fire to the city/women walk water to the house— a typical Greek antithesis.

The inscription provides the earliest evidence for a contest of ships at the Panathenaea. The regatta was probably held at the Peiraeus, Athens' major harbor, and consisted of a race south and west around the promontory to the harbor of Mounychia. Three hundred drachmas rewarded the winning crew and two hundred more went for a feast.

Second place seems to have received two hundred drachmas and two
bulls, although the writing is too faint for certainty.

The Panathenaic Games were a local festival celebrated in the
streets and marketplace of the Athenians. The games were organized
and financed through the administration of the *polis* and served its
interests. They unified the community by honoring its goddess Athena
and helped to curb the disruptive effect of aristocratic influence. They
entertained citizens with the best athletes that money could attract and
drew visitors into the city from all over the Mediterranean to watch and
spend money.

The *Gymnasion* and its Culture

By the time in his travels that he arrived at Panopeus in Phokia,
Pausanias had visited many *gymnasia*. Males everywhere across
Greece found suitable areas for their physical exercises, so essential
were athletics to their lives. When Pausanias discovered that Panopeus
did not have a *gymnasion*, he questioned its status as a *polis* (10.4.1).
How could these Phokians call themselves Greeks and not have a
gymnasion? In his day, a *gymnasion* might be an elaborate structure
with covered and open running tracks, rooms for undressing and applying
oil and dust, heated and cold baths, lecture halls, and libraries. The
gymnasion of the sixth century, however, was not a building but an
open area for stripping naked and exercising. Its spaces furnished the
room needed for running and throwing, its trees shaded the sun, and a
river or spring supplied water for bathing.

The individuality of each *gymnasion* brought about by its setting in
the landscape, associations with age-old cults, and the interests of its
users complicates the study of the *gymnasion*. At Athens, the remains
of major *gymnasia* lie buried beneath the modern city, and literary
evidence about them is less than direct. Questions abound. What was a
gymnasion, and what distinguished a *gymnasion* from a palaistra?
Where were the major *gymnasia* located in Athens? Only the Academy
has been identified with certainty. How were they administered? How
did the role of wrestling instructor or *paidotribês* differ from that of the
trainer or *gymnastês*? How did the culture of the *gymnasion* begin? In
athletics or military training of the city's soldiers or in the physical
education of its youth? Solutions remain tentative because of silence

probably imposed by familiarity with the subject, fragmentary evidence, and imprecision among the ancient secondary sources.

The etymology of *gymnasion* underlines its inseparability from nudity; in *gymnasia*, boys, youths, and men exercised *gymnoi*, that is, naked. A *gymnasion* was an athletic facility, and that part of a *gymnasion* where the wrestlers had their *skamma* was the palaestra, a term derived from *palê* or wrestling. But palaestras sprang up across Athens during the fifth century in the form of separate, mostly privately owned, schools ([Xenophon] *Constitution of the Athenians* 2.10). Because the Athenians did not always specifically distinguish between *gymnnasion* and palaestra, the differences between them became blurred in antiquity and, consequently, for modern scholars. That *gymnasia* were open to the public is implied by the law concerning thefts perpetrated in them (Demosthenes *Against Timocrates* 114) and by those legislating the conduct of wrestling instructors and their operations (Aeschines *Against Timarchus* 9–10). The Old Oligarch, the name given to the author of an antidemocratic treatise on governance handed down among the works of Xenophon, takes for granted that palaestras are private, and *gymnasia*, public, and sarcastically attacks the demos for its aristocratic pretensions:

> Some of the wealthy have for their private use *gymnasia*, baths, and dressing rooms, but the demos itself constructs many palaestras, dressing rooms, and baths for its private use (*Constitution of the Athenians* 2.10).

Besides private palaestras, the wealthy could afford private *gymnasia*— so be it—but in its effrontery, the demos has reversed the order of things by building public palaestras in addition to its public *gymnasia* (Glass 162).

Stephen L. Glass sees in Vitruvius' description of the Greek palaestra another way to distinguish between the institutions (163–165). Vitruvius details the layout of his ideal palaestra in terms of peristyles and wide recesses or *exedrai*:

> In palaestras, square or rectangular peristyles are to be made so that they have a perimeter for walking that is two stades in length, a distance that the Greeks call a *diaulos*. Of these peristyles, three are to consist of a single colonnade, while the fourth, the one facing south, is to be a double colonnade so that, when the windy storms come, the rain cannot reach the inner part. Spacious recesses are to be arranged off the three porches that contain seats on which philosophers, teachers of rhetoric, and others who delight in studies may sit and discuss. In the double porch, however, are to be located the following units. The room for youths lies in the middle (this recess is the largest and has seats) and is one-third longer than it is wide. To

its right is the punching-bag hall, and then next, the dusting room. Leading from the dusting room at the corner of the colonnade is the cold bath, which the Greeks call a *loutron*. To the left of the room for youths is the oiling room and near the oiling room is the cold room and from the cold room the way leads into the furnace room in the corner of the porch. Beside the furnace room, inside and in a straight line from the cold room, is situated a vaulted sweating room, twice as long as it is wide, which has in the angle of the colonnade on one side a sweating room in the Laconian style built in the manner described above [that is, domed and circular] and in the corner opposite is the warm bath (*On Architecture* 5.11.1–2).

A description of bathing facilities with Latin names and Roman origins follows. When Vitrivius moves outside the palaestra, he speaks of colonnades, walkways, running tracks, and groves of trees, the sorts of things found in Athenian *gymnasia* (*On Architecture* 5.11.3). Glass concludes that Vitruvius distinguishes between the palaestra, a building with rooms, and the outside grounds that constitute the *gymnasion* proper. "Structurally, then, a palaestra with facilities for running is a gymnasium" whose open spaces also served discus and javelin throwers (165). Whereas a palaestra could exist without a *gymnasion*, the reverse was not possible, since the athletes needed facilities to prepare and recover from exercise.

Athenians of the classical period had three major *gymnasia*, the Academy, Lyceum, and Kynosarges, all of which they believed belonged to a time before Solon, but no physical remains can be positively identified before the mid-fourth century. Literary sources date their appearance to the mid-sixth century, soon after the founding of the periodic games as well as other athletic festivals. The new athletic movement naturally generated the need for places to exercise and train. A poem attributed to Theognis who lived in the mid-sixth century is the earliest, but not unequivocal, testimony to a *gymnasion*:

> Blissful is he who, aroused with passion, *gymnazetai* and, going home, sleeps with a beautiful boy all day (*Elegies* 1335–1336, in Edmonds, 1931.1.394).

Theognis' happy man *gymnazetai*, but whether he "trains in a *gymnasion*" or "engages in exercises naked" cannot be ascertained. Yet he returns home from somewhere, so that "one is entitled to ask from where, if not from some area which had been set aside for such activity, however formally designed such an area might have been" (Glass, 159–160). Demosthenes expects his audience of jurors to agree that the law establishing death as the penalty for stealing from the

Academy, Lyceum, or Kynosarges was Solonian (*Against Timocrates* 114), but the date for the law is too early (Delorme 36–37). The orator, lacking the historian's chronological scruples, often graced a law with Solon's name to lend it, and his reasons for referring to it, solemnity and authority. Other evidence, however, points to a later date during the sixth century. Hipparchos is said to have built a wall around the Academy which later became proverbial for an expensive job (*Suda*. in Adler 4:567). Charmos, the lover of Peisistratos or his son Hippias, set up a statue to Eros "near the Academy" (Athenaeus, *The Deipnosophists* 60D) or "before the entrance to the Academy" (Pausanias 1.30.1). The inscription on the statue suggests that by the time of Hippias' death in 510, the Academy was recognized as a *gymnasion*, perhaps the first in Athens:

> Clever-devising Eros, Charmos set up this altar for you
> in the shady boundaries of a *gymnasion* (Athenaeus
> *The Deipnosophists* 609D).

Jean Delorme contends that the *gymnasia* were established to promote the readiness of the citizenry for military service. For Delorme, the hoplite revolution brought about the creation of *gymnasia*, first, as a program of exercises and then, as places for exercising (24–25). Men needed to be prepared and trained in the movements and mentality of the hoplite phalanx without such obligations dominating their lives as they did among the men of Sparta. A gymnastic education was developed that could quickly be assimilated to the demands of the formation. Fundamental to Delorme's thesis (19–20) is the elegy of Theognis which, while allowing the existence of exercising naked or of a *gymnasion* in the mid-sixth century, does not support his educational program. Evidence for a military presence in the *gymnasion* points rather to its use as a convenient and suitable location for military parades and reviews and for mustering soldiers before a campaign. The old men of Aristophanes' chorus in *Peace*, for instance, complain that "we are worn to a frazzle from wandering to the Lyceum and from the Lyceum with spear and shield" (355–356). The Scholiast explains:

> Before military expeditions, men took up arms in the Lyceum because
> it was near the city and offered a review of men more prepared for
> war (on Aristophanes *Peace* 353, in Dübner, 182).

The cavalry took advantage of the *gymnasion*'s open spaces to conduct maneuvers and reviews (Xenophon *On the Cavalry Commander* 3.1,

6; 14). Apparently, the purpose was to show off their skills, since Xenophon recommends training the cavalry in sandy and other terrains where wars were fought (*Memorabilia* 3.3.6). On the other hand, the rise of the *gymnasion* may be associated with the conversion to hoplite warfare for the same reason that led to the rise of athletics itself—the need for displays of personal *aretê*. Athletics, competitions, and Panhellenic festivals gave an outlet for the need to compete in the game of winning honor and dispensing shame, opportunities diminished in hoplite warfare. The *gymnasion* at Athens, in turn, provided facilities for practice and training for the Panathenaic Games as well as for exercise and camaraderie.

"[O]ne can think of [the old *gymnasia*] as distributed around the outer periphery [of Athens], to the northwest, east, and south, and associated each with one of the Athenian rivers" (Wycherley 1978, 230). Only the location of the Academy is known. Situated to the north of the city, about a mile and a half from the agora (Delmore, 38) and three quarters of a mile from the Dipylon Gate (Cicero *de Finibus* 5.1.1), it lay near the Kephisos River. To its northwest stood Kolonos Hippios, Hill of the Horse, where Oedipus first appeared in Attica (Sophocles *Oedipus at Colonus* 53–61). Serendipitous digging by an electric company yielded the northern boundary of the Academy when it uncovered at the corner of Haimon and Tripolis Streets a stele of Pentelic marble about thirty-three inches high. Still set where Athenians of the sixth century had placed it, an inscription ran vertically up the "side of the stone facing anyone coming from Athens to the Academy: ΗJΟΡΟΣ ΤΗΣ ΗΕΚΑΔΕΜΙΑΣ, 'Boundary of the Hekademeia'" (Alexandris, 107).

Open spaces dedicated to a divinity tended to become places for mortals to have fun, exercise, and train. The area still known in the sixth century as the Hekademeia took its name from the hero Hekademos. It was said of Hekademos that when Castor and Pollux came to Athens in search of their sister, Helen, Hekademos alone of the Athenians told them her whereabouts. In return, the brothers honored Hekademos, and whenever their descendants, the Lacedaemonians, invaded Attica, they kept away from the Academy (Plutarch *Theseus* 32.2–4). Gratitude to Hekademos, however, did not preclude the Lacedaemonian king Pausanias from quartering his invading army in the Academy during the siege of Athens in 405 (Xenophon *Hellenica* 12.2.8).

Eventually, the Academy held the altars and cults of Athena, Prometheus, Hermes, Herakles, and the Muses (Athenaeus *The Deiphosophistae* 13.561D–E). Prometheus' altar and its fires provided the starting point for the torch race of the Panathenaea (Pausanias 1.30.2). A shrine for the Muses was founded by Plato sometime during the fifth century (Diogenes Laertius *Lives of the Eminent Philosophers* 4.1.1). Inside the Academy stood a sacred olive believed to be the second that Athena sent her Athenians (Pausanias 1.30.2), while around the Academy stood others of her sacred trees which supplied oil for her festival (Scholiast to Aristophanes *Clouds* 105, in Dübner, 123). And before the entrance, still standing in Pausanias' time, was Charmos' claim to glory, the altar for Eros (1.30.1).

The encircling wall attributed to Hipparchos perhaps served to hide the Academy's initial unattractiveness. In the years following the Persian wars, Cimon, prominent statesman and general famed for his generosity, "converted [the Academy] from a waterless and dusty place to an irrigated grove adorned with open running tracks and shady walking areas" (Plutarch *Cimon* 13.7). It thus became a more useful place. Aristophanes' golden age of Athenian youth testifies to its groves of trees penetrated by running courses:

> Glistening with oil and blooming with health, you'll pass time in
> *gymnasia* far from the course ribaldry they practice these days in the
>   agora,
> far from being dragged into to court over some picayune lawsuit.
> No, you'll go down to the Academy and race under the sacred olives,
> garlanded with green reeds and joined by a modest companion,
> smelling of the yew, leisure, and the white poplar,
> delighting in the season of spring, when the plane tree whispers to
>   the elm (*Clouds* 1002–1008).

Sacred groves continued to grace the confines of the Academy long after Aristophanes' death around 385. In 87–86, the Roman general Sulla, in his rapacious lust for timber for his siege machines against the city, cut the trees of its "most densely wooded suburb" (Plutarch *Sulla* 12.4). Still, the Roman poet Horace (65–8) "sought truth among the forests of the Academy" (*Epistles* 2.2.45). Pliny (23–79 C.E.) remarks that the trees of one avenue in the Academy were famous for their height *(Natural History* 12.9). Much later but before the urban sprawl of the twentieth century, John Mahaffy could say in the late nineteenth century:

> I have wandered many hours in these delightful woods, listening to
> the nightingales, which sing all day in the deep shade and solitude,
> as it were in a prolonged twilight, and hearing the plane-tree whispering
> to the elm, as Aristophanes has it, and seeing the white poplar show
> its silvery leaves in the breeze, and wondering whether the huge old

olive stems . . . could be the actual sacred trees, the o , under which
the youths of Athens ran their races (1913, 132–133).

In 423 when Aristophanes produced his *Clouds* with its vignette of
young life in the Academy, he had to have known that no such dichotomy
with the agora existed. Socrates, that corrupting influence in the agora
(Aristophanes *Frogs* 1491), was to be found in the Academy (Aelian
Historical Miscellany 9.29), while ever since returning from Italy and
Sicily in 387, Plato taught philosophy from his school there (Diogenes
Laertius *Lives of the Eminent Philosophers* 3. 5, 7). Despite the
Academy's reputation as an unhealthy place and despite his doctor's
advice, Plato refused to move to the Lyceum: "I would not move even
to the summit of [Mount] Athos for a longer life" (Aelian *Historical
Miscellany* 9.10). Instead, Plato or Annikeris of Cyrene, on his behalf
(Diogenes Laertius, 3.20), purchased a garden (Plutarch *Moralia* 603B)
in nearby Colonus for three thousand drachmas. Plato formed a *thiasos,*
a company dedicated to the cult of a deity, in this case, the Muses. As
tutelary deities of education, the Muses commonly had shrines in schools
throughout the city (Aeschines *Against Timarchos* 10). Plato set up a
shrine to them in the Academy in which Speusippus, Plato's successor,
added statues of the Graces (Diogenes Laertius, 4.1.1). A prominent
feature of the religious life of Plato's *thiasos* was the common meals.
Conducted according to rules (Athenaeus *The Deipnosophists* 5.186B),
they directed his guests' appetites. The guests came to appreciate the
stimulating conversation and how the simple food preserved their bodies
from debilitating hangovers and dyspepsia (Plutarch *Moralia* 686 B-C).
Plato did not deliver public speeches (Chernis, 10) but engaged his
students in dialectic. Among the subjects he entertained were
mathematics, an essential tool for pursuing the Good, and political theory.
Botany may also have been taught. The comic poet Epikrates (early
fourth century) depicts Plato teaching classification to boys in the
gymnasion:

> I was at the Panathenaea and saw
> a herd of youths
> in the *gymnasion* of the Academy.
> I heard strange words, not to be repeated.
> They were laying down definitions about nature
> and marking off the life of living things,
> the nature of trees and kinds of vegetables
> and, among their subjects, the pumpkin—
> they were inquiring into what kind of a thing it is (fr. 11, in Edmonds
> 1959, 355–356).

After Plato's death at eighty-two in 347, Speusippos and thenXenocrates continued to maintain the school and the presence of philosophers in the Academy (Plutarch *Moralia* 603B). Plato was buried not far from his beloved Academy where his tomb still stood for Pausanias to see (1.30.3).

On the eastern side of Athens, outside the Gates of Diochares (Strabo *Geography* 9.1.19) but near the city wall (Scholiast to Aristophanes *Peace* 353, in Dübner, 182; Suda s.v. *Lykeion,* in Alder, 4.294), stood the Lyceum, a sanctuary of Apollo Lykeios, that is, Apollo the Wolf or Slayer of Wolves (Lucian *Anacharsis* 7). Nothing is known of the cult during the classical period, but Apollo as a wolf-god probably belongs to the earliest stratum of Greek religion (Farnell, 112). The grounds of the Lyceum extended far enough to accommodate military maneuvers by infantry (Aristophanes *Peace* 355–356) and cavalry (Xenophon *On the Cavalry Commander* 3.1). They held a *gymnasion* but, in the absence of evidence, no temple of the god. The sanctuary contained trees, some of them large, and was watered by channels (Theophrastus *Inquiry into Plants* 1.7.1), perhaps from the Eradonos or Ilissos River or, if sufficiently expansive, both (Strabo 9.1.19, 24).

Literary and epigraphic sources leave open the exact location of the Lyceum (Lynch, 16–29; Kyle 1987, 77–79). The proximity of the Ilissos River and the sources of the Eridanos River point to the neighborhood near the foot of the south or southwest slope of Mount Lykabettos (Strabo *Geography* 9.1.19). Recently a site has been suggested that lies more to the south and near the north bank of the Ilissos River (Athens News Agency: News in English, 97–01–14). That the Lyceum abutted, or nearly abutted, the walls of the city is supported by Plato's depiction of Socrates leaving the Academy for the Lyceum "by the road that runs along the wall outside the city" (*Lysis* 203A). As Wycherley points out, "Such a position ["right beneath the wall itself'] would suit Sokrates' general habits too—he constantly frequented the Lyceum but he seldom went far outside the city" (1978, 228). This location and open spaces made it strategic for Thrasyllos to marshal Athenians nearby in 410 when they repulsed the Spartan incursion on the city from Dekeleia to the northeast (Xenophon *Hellenica* 1.1.33).

The sources give three founders for the Lyceum. The fourth-century historian Theopompos cites Peisistratos, and Philochoros (ca. 340-ca. 261), best of the historians of Attica, credits Pericles (Harpocration on *Lykeion,* in Keaney, 167). Their claims are not necessarily contradictory. Peisistratos could have established athletic grounds and limited facilities that, after their destruction by the Persians, Pericles included in his program of restoration (Delorme, 43). The reputed third founder, the Athenian Lycurgus, could not have established the Lyceum, but he probably planted trees and built a palaestra ([Plutarch] *Moralia* 841D, 843F, 852C). It was before this palaestra that he set up a stele marking publicly the record of his achievements ([Plutarch] *Moralia* 843F).

In 335, Aristotle rented buildings (foreigners were barred from owning property) and took up practicing philosophy in the Lyceum where he remained for thirteen years (Diogenes Laertius *Lives of the Eminent Philosophers* 5.1.10). He believed in the lecture rather than Plato's discussion as the better way to reach his listeners. He spoke while strolling back and forth in a covered porch or *peripatos* with his students in tow, a habit from which they and his school came to be known as the Peripatetics. He treated subtle topics with select students in the morning, and in the evening, rhetoric and argumentation directed toward politics with an open audience (Aulus Gellius *Attic Nights* 20.5). Upwards of two thousand could attend the evening sessions (Diogenes Laertius *Lives of the Eminent Philosophers* 5.2.37). The space needed added to the burden that his activities placed upon the *gymnasion*. He collected manuscripts and maps, founded a library (Athenaeus *The Deipnosophists* 5.214D), and undertook research into a wide variety of topics, notably, constitutions, that is, forms of government, of 158 cities. Inquiry into Plants, a treatise written by Theophrastus, Aristotle's pupil, collaborator, and successor, observes that "the plane tree in the Lyceum beside the water channel, while it was still young, sent out its roots a distance of thirty-three cubits [ca. 50 feet]" (1.7.1), a detail that surely derives from Aristotle's interest in, and support of, botany.

The third major *gymnasion,* Kynosarges, lay to the south of the city, "not far from the gate," and near the Ilissos River (Diogenes Laertius *Lives of the Eminent Philosophers* 6.1.13). It was sacred to Herakles and sheltered his altar and those of his goddess wife, Hebe, his mortal mother, Alcmena, and his companion in many of his labors, Iolaos (Pausanias 1.19.3). As with much regarding Kynosarges, the date of its foundation cannot be determined. It held a *gymnasion* and shrine of Herakles in 490, since the Athenians camped in both after their victory at Marathon against the Persians in late summer of that year. A story in Plutarch's *Life of Themistocles*, if true, would push the date for athletic facilities in Kynosarges back into the late sixth century. Plutarch reports that Themistocles persuaded illegitimate sons of Athenian fathers and foreign mothers to enroll in Kynosarges, "a *gymnasion* of Herakles outside the gates, since Herakles was not legitimate among the gods but imputed with bastardy because his mother was a mortal" (1.3).

Themistocles' mother was not an Athenian, but he was considered a citizen, since sons of an Athenian father and foreign mother were not disenfranchised until Pericles' law of 451. The story of Kynosarges bastards was known in the fourth century (Demosthenes *Against Aristocrates* 231) and better suits that time than the early period of a more open definition of citizenship (Delorme, 45–46). On the other hand, the youths could have congregated at the hero's shrine in the *gymnasion*, perhaps forming themselves into a religious guild devoted to Herakles (Humphreys, 92).

Gymnasia in the Hellenistic and Roman periods were centers for organized athletic and formal educational programs (Wycherley 1978, 231–235). Throughout the classical period, the great *gymnasia* at Athens remained much simpler athletic grounds. Next to nothing is known about how they were administered in the classical period. The gymnasiarchs of the torch race were tribal officials who organized the race and trained the runners. No source attributes a wider role to them in managing the *gymnasion*. Slaves were forbidden to exercise (Aeschines *Against Timarchus* 138). Foreign sophists were admitted (Plato *Euthydemus* 271C) and probably metics, aliens who resided among the Athenians and paid a tax for the privilege. Athletes shared in the embellishments the shrine offered, in particular, the stoa or open row of columns paralleled by a wall and roofed for escaping the heat and sun. The *gymnasion* in the Academy was a walled-in area enclosing a running track and palaestra. In the lack of evidence, athletic activity at Kynosarges may reasonably be assumed but cannot be demonstrated. A building graced the *gymnasion* in the Lyceum. It had an *apodytêrion* or undressing room (Plato *Euthydemus* 272E), pillars (303B), an indoor covered track (273A), an outdoor track (Xenophon *On the Cavalry Commander* 3.6), and baths where Socrates stopped for refreshment after a famous night passed in conversation about Eros (Plato *Symposium* 223D).

Plato gives a glimpse into the dynamics of a palaestra in the opening scene of his *Lysis*:

> I was on my way from the Academy straight to the Lyceum by the road that runs along the wall outside the city. When I reached the little gate by the spring of Panops, I happened upon Hippothales, son of Hieronymos, and Ktesippos from the district of Paianiea and other young men standing around with them. Seeing me approach, Hippothales called out, "Socrates, where are you going, and where are you coming from?"
> "From the Academy," I replied, "I'm going straight to the Lyceum."
> "Come here," he said, "straight to us. Won't you let yourself be sidetracked? It's worth your while."
> "Where to," I asked, "and to whom?"

"Come here," he said, pointing me to a recess opposite the wall and an open door. "We spend our time here along with many other beauties."

"What is this place, and what do you do here?"

"It's a palaestra," he answered, "a brand new one. We spend a lot of time in conversations that we would gladly share with you."

"That sounds good," I said, "Who is teaching here?"

"A friend of yours," he replied, "and an admirer, Mikkos."

"By Zeus, nothing shallow there but a capable sophist."

"Do you want to come along and see those inside?"

"First, I'd welcome hearing the terms for going in there, and who the beauty is?"

"One seems beautiful to one, and another to another, Socrates."

"Who seems beautiful to you, Hippothales? Tell me this."

He blushed at being asked. And I said, "My boy, Hippothales, son of Hieronymos, you need not tell me any longer whether you desire someone or not. I know that you do not just desire someone but that you are already far gone in your desire. I'm not of much use at most things, but a god somehow has granted me the ability to recognize immediately the one who desires and the one who is desired."

When he heard this, Hippothales blushed even more. "How amusing," Ktesippos remarked, "you're blushing, Hippothales, and shrink from telling Socrates a name. But if he spends even a moment with you, he'll be worn out from listening to you prattle constantly. Our ears, Socrates, have been deafened, stuffed with Lysis. And if he has a drink or two, it's easy for us to wake up from sleep thinking we are hearing the name Lysis. What he has to say in great detail, bad as it is, is nothing compared to when he tries to deluge us with his poems and writings. Worse still are the times he sings about his beloved in an astonishing voice that we have to put up with hearing. Now when you put the question to him, he blushes."

"This Lysis is someone new, I take it. I heard his name, but didn't recognize it" (203A-204E).

The palaestra was new, too new for Socrates, a devotee of athletic establishments (Plato *Euthyphro* 2A), to have learned of it. Both details, its recent construction and Socrates' ignorance, suggest a thriving demand for athletic facilities in the fifth century. Only the palaestras of Taureas in the sanctuary of Basile outside the city to the south (Plato *Charmides* 153A), of Sibyritos (Plutarch *Alcibiades* 3.1), and of Hippokrates ([Plutarch] *Moralia* 837E) are known. The palaestra at which Socrates stops lay near the fountain of Panops outside the walls in the north (Judeich, 415). Its surrounding walls, broken by a single door facing the city walls, disguised its identity and muffled the sounds of those within. Boys and youths, as becomes clear, the sons of wealthy men (Plato *Lysis* 207C), were celebrating the Hermaia, a festival of Hermes held in the palaestra and regulated by public law (Aeschines *Against Timarchus* 10). Contrary to custom, they intermingled with one another for the occasion (Plato *Lysis* 206D). Hermes, who was often portrayed as a youth, and Eros along with the hero Herakles received worship in *gymnasia* and palaestras throughout Greece. Youths, like the virgins of the Heraia, were marginal figures, yet to be integrated into their adult roles as hoplites and fathers. During this liminal period in their lives, they enjoyed the protection of both gods whose nature it was to break barriers and transgress boundaries and a hero who was not himself fully civilized.

Socrates describes the scene in the palaestra:

> On entering, we found that the boys had conducted the sacrifices, and matters concerning the victims were about complete. They were playing dice, everyone dressed up. Some were playing odds and evens with many dice, picking them from little baskets. Many others were sporting outside in the courtyard. Others stood around, watching them. Among them was Lysis, crowned with a garland. He stood out from among the boys and youths, for he was not merely beautiful but possessed the beauty and gentility of the noble born (Plato *Lysis* 206E-207A).

Socrates and his companions probably sat in the *apodytêrion* where the athletes undressed for their exercises, as it was furnished with seats. Delorme concludes from the description that "The palaestra, then, comprises two parts essential to the interior of the enclosing walls: a courtyard and a large common room arranged as a common hall with *exedra*, facing the door of the entrance" (60). This accords with the pattern of the palaestra described by Vitruvius.

Gymnasia and palaestras were places for conditioning and learning and not for competition, at least not in organized contests. The open spaces and running tracks of the *gymnasion* beckoned those who favored the races and throwing events. The palaestras appealed to wrestlers of all levels of skill from the neophyte boy to the hard-edged competitor in the periodic and other games. The palaestra was usually a privately owned school, often independent of a *gymnasion* and under the management of a *paidotribês*. The latter's name hints that he once applied oil to the boys in his charge, but during the classical period, he instructed them in the basic skills of wrestling. Fathers, the wealthiest in particular, sent their sons to the *paidotribês* from an early age and prolonged their education until very late in their youth (Plato *Protagoras* 326C). Plato's Protagoras states their reasons and the goals they hoped to obtain from such expenditures:

> They send boys to the school of the *paidotribês* in order that, by having better bodies, the boys may have and serve a better mind and not be compelled, because of the poor condition of their bodies, to

act cowardly either in wars or in other circumstances (*Protagoras* 326ʙ).

According to Aeschines (ca. 397–ca. 322), the treatment boys received at the palaestra was regulated by law, because "the lawgiver believed that well-reared boys, on becoming men, would be useful for the city" (*Against Timarchus* 11). The lawgiver also prescribed when the palaestras opened and closed for the day and the numbers of boys in attendance, so that the *paidotribês* would not be alone with a student (*Against Timarchus* 10).

The young trained and strengthened their bodies, and their elders exercised and conditioned themselves in the palaestra and *gymnasion*. Vases show the trainer closely watching his charge practicing the jump (Yalouris, 184 Ill. 87), for example, or wrestling (Illustration 10). Boys and youths learned basic wrestling skills under the supervision of a *paidotribês*. The *gymnastês* or trainer coached athletes who were preparing for competitions in the festivals and supervised their diets and physical well-being (Galen *On Protecting One's Health*, in Kühn, 6:143, 153–157). The ages of their respective pupils, in fact, help distinguish between the *paidotribês* and the *gymnastês* in vase paintings. During the fifth century, *gymnastai* tended to be former athletes whose knowledge came from experience. Pindar praises the trainer Melesias in *Olympian Ode 8* (460) for his expertise acquired through participation at the highest level of competition:

> Among all men nothing will be equally pleasing.
> But if with my song I venture to extol
> the glory Melesias won from beardless youths,
> let not envy cast at me a rough stone.
> I will speak in equal portion
> of his victory at Nemea
> and then of his victory from the fight
> in men's *pankration*. But to instruct is easier
> for him who knows, and not to learn beforehand is senseless,
> for scatterbrained are the minds of the untried.
> Melesias could say further
> than others what way will advance a man who strives
> to win a most desired reputation from the holy contests (53–63).

Melesias was the greatest of Greek wrestlers in his prime and founded a wrestling family that included his two grandsons (Wade-Gery 1932, 208–210). He moved in the circle of aristocrats with connections throughout Greece and probably knew Pindar who also praises him in *Nemean Odes 4* (95–96) and *6* (65–66). In the latter, he calls him "a charioteer of hands and strength." Melesias could guide his students in the skills of his craft, develop them physically, and drive them to take the best advantage of their assets. Pindar refers to the trainer's profession in terms that anticipate Philostratos'.

By the time Philostratos was writing in the third century of the common era, distinction between the *paidotribês* and the *gymnastês* had long been in place. While the *gymnastês* was able to teach the material of the *paidotribês*—wrestling tricks, openings, attacks, and escapes—he specialized in tuning his athlete's body for optimal performance and, in this, intrudes upon the sphere of the doctor (Philostratos *Gymnastic* 14, in Kayser, 268–269). The profession of the trainer was just coming into vogue during Plato's time in the fourth century (*Gorgias* 452B). Plato fluctuates semantically in identifying the experts responsible for physical conditioning and athletic training, naming the medical doctor, the *paidotribês*, and, with a neutral term, an *epistatês* or supervisor, but his insistence on expertise is clear:

> When a man is training seriously, does he pay heed to the praises, censures, and opinions of every man or of that one man alone who is his physician or *paidotribês*? . . . He must act, train, eat, and drink in accordance with the way that seems best to one man, his supervisor who has expert knowledge, rather than to all the others (*Crito* 47B).

Trainers worked closely with their students. A red-figure amphora (ca. 525) shows two pairs of wrestlers practicing before a resplendently attired youthful trainer who holds a pomander to his nose, protection, it would seem, against the smell of sweat issuing from his grapplers (Illustration 10). A cloak hung on a hook and, below it, an amphora presumably containing oil show that they are inside a palaestra. Boys and youths practiced the basic skills from setups assigned by the *paidotribês*; men practiced in accord with instructions by their trainer. A papyrus fragment from an instructional handbook, published in the second century of the common era, offers a tantalizing glimpse of this world (*Oxyrhynchus Papyrus* 3.466, in Poliakoff 1986, 161–162). The fragment is very mutilated, often little more than a list of words. In a better preserved section, two wrestlers (A and B) are practicing moves together and wrestling out of situations created at the command of the instructor who is speaking:

> You (A) throw your foot forward. You (B) take hold around him. You (A) step forward, and try to bend him backwards. You (B), facing him, try to bend back, and throw yourself into him, planting your foot (28–30).

Drills like this were repeated until the athletes by sheer rote absorbed the moves and could execute them automatically at the appropriate moments.

In 388 when Plato founded his school of philosophy in the Academy, he was not innovating but capitalizing on available students. Aristotle later (ca. 335) chose the Lyceum for the same reason and because the Platonists were ensconced in the older shrine (Lynch, 68–75). *Gymnasia* attracted boys and youths in search of places to test one another in speed, strength, and endurance, and to take in, and be part of, the social scene. The centrality in the palaestra of the room for youths underlines the importance the athletic facility played in the traditional education of Athenian youth. Through interacting and associating with their elders, young men could learn the moral and social behavior expected of an adult male. The young males, in turn, made the *gymnasia* magnets for older men who came to watch their games, engage them in conversation, seduce them, and/or, if they were sophists, teach them rhetoric, philosophy, astronomy, and other subjects for a fee.

One notable denizen of the agora and athletic haunts of fifth-century Athens was Socrates, who is known only through the writings and statues (Richter, 1:109–119) of others. The Platonic Socrates looked for young men but settled for anyone who would converse with him. He began with an innocent question, or so it seemed, like "What is virtue?" When his respondent answered by giving him examples of virtuous deeds, Socrates would say that he had not requested a list of deeds but a statement of what virtue is, that is, a definition. Such talk was strange to men educated by the wisdom of the poets and brought up by associating with others and imitating their behavior. They soon became frustrated by Socrates' cross-examination and refutation of beliefs they had accepted as true and their inability to defend them. They stormed off, angry at Socrates for his temerity. But young men watched Socrates and emulated his treatment of their elders as best they could. The Athenians, however, did not have to rely on Plato. They could see what was happening for themselves, came to fear it, and, in 399, accusing him of corrupting the youth, executed Socrates for impiety toward his citizen's oath.

Daily in the *gymnasion* or palaestra, naked youthful male bodies were on display. Older youths like Hippothales and adult men, attracted to the youths, sought to engage them in the complex dalliance of lover and beloved. The lover offered the youth gifts and initiation into the ways of men and asked in return his sexual compliance. The onus was on the boy to tread lightly. He could not seem to be too eager or to enjoy the physical intimacy that everyone shunned mentioning in public. It was a self-serving fiction of this exchange that the boy neither became aroused nor enjoyed the advances made to him. His position as the object of the man's dominance placed him precariously in the role of a woman, and to seek actively the passive role further tarnished him with the stigma of the prostitute (Dover 81–109). The boy risked his right as a citizen to address assembled citizens, to hold public office, and to serve on juries, and opened himself to prosecution and exile later in life should he try to exercise these rights. The *gymnasion*, then, was a place for turning youths into men but possibly into social outcasts. In practice, however, the *kinaidos* or womanly man belonged less to real life than to rivalries and vilification of opponents in public life (Winkler, 46–54).

The culture of the *gymnasion* espoused a program of physical exercise, music, and poetry, intended, as Protagoras affirmed, to form supple bodies and alert minds. In the process it inevitably inculcated the Greek male's sense of life as a competition against enemies of his city, household, and self. John J. Winkler locates the underlying premise of this ideology in the belief that "male life is warfare, that masculinity is a duty and a hard-won achievement, and that the temptation to desert one's side is very great" (50). Cooperative learning under the supervision of a *paidotribês* contradicted the drive to win honor. So strong was this imperative that the Greeks did not want to concede honor, because they felt that in doing so, something of their own was lost. "It is not pleasant for men to honor someone else, for they believe that they themselves are being deprived of something" (*Anonymous Iamblici,* in Diels and Kranz, 2:400). These values for which the *gymnasion* was a seminary help define male life as warfare. That they frequently burst forth explains, and is confirmed by, the switch that the *paidotribês* liberally applied to the bodies of the unruly.

Although difficult to demonstrate, the presumption that not every boy or man embraced the athleticism of the *gymnasion* seems reasonable. A red-figure kylix (ca. 520) shows what Gardiner considered "an altercation between a fat and a lean youth" (Illustration 22). The scene is set outside in the courtyard of a *gymnasion.* A chair laden with clothes is an iconographic device for separating the above pair on the left from two athletes on the right, one of whom is tightening the thong of a javelin and the other warming up to throw the discus. Three of the four are slim and in proportion; the fourth has a protruding stomach, round and fully packed. There can be no doubt that the painter and his presumed audience esteemed slimness. The time spent in the *gymnasion*

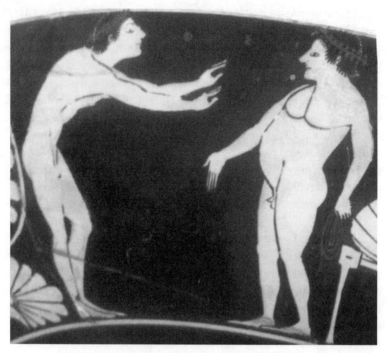

Illustration 22. The proposition. Attic red-figure kylix, ca. 520 B.C.E. © The British Museum, London, England.

Illustration 23. The proposition. Black-figure two-handled cup, ca. 520 B.C.E © Museum of Fine Arts, Boston.

for the deviant boy could not have been pleasant. But he does not seem to appreciate his deviancy. He is not arguing with the lean boy; he is attempting to seduce him. He holds out his right hand, palm upturned, fingers spread, toward the other boy's genitals. He gestures with the opening move of the lover to his beloved (Dover, 94–95; Illustration 23). The fat boy presumes to play the adult lover to the slim boy, casting the latter in the role of passive receptor of his phallus. The brazenness of the move is impressive, the rejection, surely devastating. Everyone wanted to play the games of the *gymnasion*, but some were excluded. Others excluded themselves.

On entering the *gymnasion* for the first time, the boy confronted daunting expectations of his achievements, expectations that had no regard for his individuality. The lives of ancient Greeks were determined in many ways by their gender roles, but their personalities did not disappear. The ideology of the *gymnasion*, however, assumed that the boy's nature conformed to the dictates of society. But what of the boy or man whose nature was not disposed to standing out from the throng? Who preferred another life to that of athletic or public distinction? Such estrangement from the dominant ideology of his culture could be overwhelming, encouraging him "to desert [his] side." Winkler's expression recalls similar obligations laid down by the British public school of the Victorian era according to whose ideology athletic prowess foreshadowed outstanding service to the empire. Aeschines justifies his resentment of men who live a life of prostitution by his concern for the city:

> What citizen did not feel indignation at Kephisodoros, called Molon's son, for having ruined his most striking beauty by utterly foul habits? Or Menesitheos, the cook's son? Or many others whom I am willing to forget? For I do not wish to go through each of them mean-spiritedly, name by name, but I would pray rather to be at a loss for such men in my speech because of my good will toward the city (*Against Timarchus* 158–159).

Such men, whether to satisfy sexual desire or to escape the demands of masculinity, deserted the *polis* by forfeiting the opportunity to attain honor in its service.

Xenophon's Socrates chides Charmides for his refusal to serve the city by first getting him to admit the cowardice of the would-be winning athlete who refuses to compete:

> On seeing Glaukon's son, Charmides, a respectable man, more capable by far than those engaged at the time in public affairs but one who

eschewed putting himself forward and managing the city's business,
Socrates addressed him with a question: "Tell me, Charmides, if
someone was capable of winning at the crown contests and,
consequently, capable of being honored himself and of making his
fatherland more renowned in Greece but did not wish to compete,
what sort of person would you think that man to be?" "Clearly, he is
soft and cowardly," Charmides replied (*Memorabilia* 3.7.1).

Charmides accepts the canon that a man of talent strives to compete
and win honor, and not to do so is to unman oneself from hard to soft,
brave to cowardly. Socrates, however, is not talking to Charmides about
athletics but about his removal of himself from the contests of political
life. Charmides confesses that he fears the ridicule of the assembly:
"To speak with someone in private and to enter the contests among the
mass are not the same thing" (3.7.4). It seems he has looked within to
his nature and, although responding in general terms, is speaking of
himself: "Shame and fear, do you not see, are innate to men and, by far,
more so in crowds than in private dealings?" (3.7.5). Socrates presses
by asking Charmides why he is not afraid to address the most thoughtful
and powerful men, but he shrinks in fear from speaking before "the
fullers or cobblers or carpenters or smithies or farmers or merchants or
those in the marketplace who rush about and worry about selling for
more what they bought for less, the men who make up the assembly"
(3.7.5–6). "Why do you think what you are doing is any different from
someone who is better than trained men but fears those without training?"
(3.7.7). Socrates advises Charmides:

> My good man, do not be ignorant of yourself and make the mistake
> that the many make, for the many set out to inquire about the affairs
> of the city and do not turn to examining themselves. Do not despair,
> but strive to turn your attention to yourself. Do not neglect the affairs
> of the city if in any way it is possible for it to be better through your
> intervention. With its affairs prospering, not only will other citizens
> but also your friends and you yourself profit greatly (3.7.9).

His advice suggests that the man who knows himself knows his
responsibility to the city. For his part, Charmides expects Socrates to
see that men are differently disposed by their natures. He is a man
whose intelligence and abilities shine in private, as athletic ability—
Xenophon's analogy allows the conclusion—shines in public. Their
conversation assumes an excellent athlete, but other males, irrespective
of their talents, must have neglected athletics for reasons independent
of ability. On the other hand, the argument that athletics, a pastime in
which nearly every Greek male engaged, had no value for war, may

have fed off the resentments of men who fought bravely in the phalanx despite their athletic mediocrity.

The Critics

Criticism of athletics and athleticism grew hand-in-hand with their rising popularity. As early as the seventh century, the Spartan general and elegaic poet, Tyrtaios, trumpeted the inferiority of the finest athlete to the soldier who could stand in formation and kill the enemy (fragment 12.1–14, in Edmonds 1931, 1:75). Xenophanes (ca. 570–ca. 475) of Colophon in Ionia spent all but twenty-five years of his long life in exile. He wandered the Greek world and, like Odysseus, "saw the cities of men and came to know their minds" (Homer *Odyssey* 1.3). Possessed of a wider perspective than most, he became a sage and singer of his own songs which observed and commented upon the ways of men. He knew his own worth and found, like many philosophers to follow, that it far exceeded the athlete's:

> If a man wins a victory with swiftness of foot
> > or in pentathlon where the precinct of Zeus
> lies beside the streams of Pisa in Olympia, or in wrestling
> > or engaging even in painful pugilistics,
> or in the dread contest that they call *pankration*,
> > and would be glorious for his townsmen to look upon
> and would win prominent pride of place in the contests,
> > and would receive bread from the public larder
> of the city and a gift that would be a treasure for him,
> > if even with horses he would obtain all these things,
> he would not be as worthy as I. Better than strength
> > of men and horses is my wisdom.
> Those opinions are ill-considered. It is not right
> > to prefer strength to my good wisdom.
> Even if a man good at boxing be among the people,
> > even if a man good at pentathlon or wrestling,
> even if in swiftness of foot, which is held in pride of place in
> > whatever deeds of men's strength belong to the contest,
> not for that reason would the city have better laws.
> > Small joy would it be for the city
> if an athlete wins beside the banks of Pisa,
> > for this does not fatten the storerooms of the city (Athenaeus
> *The Deipnosophists* 413F–414C).

The intelligentsia continued to contend that the contribution of their wisdom far outshone the achievements attained with the smell of sweat. The earliest extant Athenian condemnation of athletics comes from Euripides who, according to Athenaeus (second century C.E.), drew upon Xenophanes:

Of the myriad of evils across Greece
nothing is more evil than the pack of athletes.
First, they do not understand how to live properly,
nor would they be able to do so. How would someone
who is the slave of his jaw and loser to his belly
acquire wealth to increase his father's larder?
His kind cannot toil in poverty or help in hard times.
Unaccustomed as they are to noble habits,
hard for them to change in the face of adversity.
Magnificent in their prime, they come and go
like the city's crown jewels. But when bitter old age descends,
they discard their threadbare cloaks and leave.
I blame the custom of the Greeks
who call an assembly for these men
and honor their useless pleasures with a feast.
What benefit is he to the city, having a crown
for wrestling well or being swift of foot
or hefting a discus or whacking a jaw solidly?
Will they fight against the enemy hand-to-hand,
holding a discus or striking through shields?
Will they throw back the fatherland's enemies with bare hands?
No one who stands against iron is so foolish.
I believe that wise and brave men must
be garlanded with leaves and so, too, that man who guides the city
in the noblest way, a man of self-control and justice,
and that man who gets rid of evil deeds with his words,
removing fights and civil strife. Such things
are noble for the whole city and for all Greeks (Athenaeus *The Deipnosophists* 413c-f).

Euripides did not need to borrow from Xenophanes or be deeply adverse to athletes to have one of his characters conjure the stereotypic athlete, the overrated and pampered pet of misguided sports fans, gluttonous from his diet rich in meat, useless to his father thanks to time spent in training and competing and to his fatherland because of the insignificance of his endeavors for war, pretty in youth, poor and wretched in old age. This same Euripides, it may be noted, used athletic metaphors in his plays and composed an epinician ode for Alcibiades' chariot victories at Olympia (Plutarch *Alcibiades* 11.3).

In *Clouds* (423), Aristophanes lets the array of his comic muse—humor, ridicule, obscenity, social commentary, and inventive, often stirring, poetry—loose upon the way Athenian youths were being educated. Athenians had no public school system; education was the responsibility of the family whose means determined its manner and duration. The wealthy could afford to send their sons to sophists who were usually foreigners and who, for a fee, would teach them the way to success, especially through the art of persuasive speaking. Whatever Aristophanes the man thought about sophists, Aristophanes the poet, teacher of tradition, professed outrage over their deleterious effects upon the physical well-being and morality of the young. Contending that the Athenians let him down when his *Clouds* finished last in the competition at the Festival of Dionysus in the City (*Clouds* 518–527), he set out to rewrite the ending of his play for a second production. The revised *Clouds* never reached the theater, but it got into the libraries and remains extant. Its added speech by Better Argument argues badly, indeed, not at all, but expounds the good morality of the glorious days of the *Marathonomachai*, the warriors of Marathon. In the old-fashioned education, athletics made boys into ideal physical specimens of the sort portrayed on vases (see Dover, B65, B76, B271, R336):

> Glistening with oil and blooming with health, you'll pass time in *gymnasia*
> far from the coarse ribaldry they practice these days in the agora,
> far from being dragged off to court over some picayune lawsuit.
> No, you'll go down to the Academy and run under the sacred olives,
> garlanded with green reed and joined by a modest companion,
> smelling of the yew, leisure, and the white poplar, and
> delighting in the spring season when the plane tree whispers to the elm.
> If you do what I am telling you
> and apply yourself to what I say,
> you will always have
> an immense chest, a glistening complexion,
> large shoulders, a small tongue,
> big buttocks, and a little dickie (*Clouds* 1002–1014).

Worse Argument brands his opponent's view of the past as "old stuff, full of cobwebs, hoary poets, and primeval religious rites" (983–984). He espouses the new education that avoids exercise (1054), favors warm baths (1044–1052), innovative music (969–971), and facile speech (942–944), and rejects the religious beliefs, moral principles (1039–1040), and sexual conventions (1060–1062) of the community. This education, Better Argument contends, turns boys into pasty pansies:

> Should you practice what they are now advocating
> you will have
> a wan complexion, tiny shoulders,

> sunken chest, large tongue,
> small buttocks, and a large member,
> a long statue, and my opponent will seduce you
> into holding the disgraceful as noble,
> and the noble as disgraceful,
> and furthermore, he will stuff you
> with Antimachos' buggery (1015–1023).

Clarence A. Forbes sees in Aristophanes' nostalgia a historical decline in the appeal of physical exercise and athleticism that swept over Athenians of the late fifth century:

> In the latter half of the fifth century . . . there are distinct signs of a falling-off in interest. The sophists were turning the minds of youths and men into new and absorbing channels. This is written out plainly for all to read in the *Clouds* of Aristophanes (1002ff.) (85).

But Kyle rightly cautions against relying upon Aristophanes' pronouncements as evidence for Athenian athletics and physical education: "even as he claims that the *palaestrae* are empty, Aristophanes criticizes men who haunt these places seeking boys for pederasty" (1987, 133).

The demos continued to reward athletes who won at the Olympic and Isthmian Games, and widened the range of recipients to encompass victors at the Pythian and Nemean Games. When the Eleans added the chariot race for two horses at the ninety-third Olympiad (408) (Pausanias 5.8.10), the Athenians extended privileges to the winners as the Platonic Socrates recognizes in contending his greater right to the honor:

> What is fitting for a poor man who is your benefactor and who needs leisure to exhort you? There is nothing more fitting than that such a man dine in the Prytaneion, far more fitting than if some one of you has won at Olympia with a horse or two- or four-horse chariot (Plato, *Apology* 36D).

Chariot racing belonged to the wealthy who usually participated vicariously through a slave or hired charioteer. Nonetheless, the demos accepted that their victories benefited the community. In a pronouncement during the 430s known as the Prytaneion decree, the demos specified those eligible to receive the city's honor, the privilege of dining (*sitêsis*) at its hearth in the Prytaneion (*Inscriptiones Graecae* I^2 77.11–18). The stone is damaged, and the text has been subject to various restorations. The following translates the emendations of Edmond J. Morrissey:

> Whosoever
> won at Olympia or Pytho or Isthmos or Nemea or
> wins in the future, to them there shall be the *sitêsis* in the Prytaneion
> and other privileges in addition to the *sitêsis* according to what is
> written on the stele in the Prytaneion. Whosoever won
> in chariot and race for mature horses at Olympia or
> Pytho or Isthmus or Nemea or wins in the future, to them
> shall be the *sitêsis* according to what is written on the stele (125).

Winning athletes received the honor of *sitêsis* for life and, with it, probably the *prohedria* or privilege of sitting in front at the theater, assemblies, and athletic contests (Kyle 1987.147). The suggestion that the Prytaneion decree was intended to reaffirm civic honors for victors in the equestrian events in the face of resentment over their wealth and political exploitation of victory has not found acceptance (Morrissey 124; Thompson 1979.327). Kyle concludes that "[t]he policy of rewards was not a radical innovation pushed by a class of athletes, but an institutionalized expression of civic appreciation" (1987.147).

Athletics thrived at Athens throughout the classical period, and toward its end, the popularity of the *gymnasia* and palaestras encouraged public support for renovations to the Lyceum, overseen by the statesman Lykourgos. These included a palaestra and, after Lykourgos persuaded a citizen to donate the land in return for public honors, a stadium built in a ravine on the left bank of the Ilissos River ([Plutarch] *Moralia* 841C-D). The transfer of gymnastic events from the agora to a formal stadium required the approval of the demos and reflected the desire to bring athletics at Athens into line with other athletic sites as, unconsciously, Athenians moved toward the elaboration of athletic buildings characteristic of the Hellenistic period.

That athletics played a role in the lives of Greeks is beyond question. That their value was exaggerated by many among them cannot be denied. Yet all Greeks were deeply committed to their athletics, and even critics lived and breathed athletics in their own way. Athletes were idolized by some and branded by others as overfed and hypermuscled freaks. Their critics among the intelligentsia were dismissed as philosophizing windbags or feared as corrupters of the physical excellence admired in the athlete. The Roman Cicero (106–43), like all modern students of Greek athletics, was a foreigner, but a foreigner who strode the streets of Athens and visited its *gymnasia*. He has Crassus (ca.115–53), convey that experience in speaking to the issue:

> "All these matters," Crassus said, "I interpret differently. I think that
> the Greeks invented the palaestra, seats, and the colonnades
> themselves . . . for the purpose of exercise and pleasure and not for

philosophical discussion. For *gymnasia* were invented many generations before philosophers began to chatter in them, and at this very moment, when philosophers have taken over all the *gymnasia*, still their listeners prefer to hear a discus than a philosopher. As soon as it hums, they abandon a philosopher, who is discussing the most important subjects, in the middle of his speech to put on oil. Thus, they prefer the most frivolous pleasure to their most serious interests, as they themselves maintain" (*On the Orator* 2.21).

6.
Olympic Festival

The Eleans arrived too late for the battle near Plataea in southern Boeotia that crushed the retreating Persian army in 479. Stung with shame, they returned home and banished their leaders (Herodotus *Histories* 9.77.3). In the light of subsequent events, the episode manifests dissatisfaction with the oligarchs who had monopolized leadership in Elis from the time of its settlement. A few years later, in 471, the villages and small communities throughout Elis accepted the idea of a common political center and, adopting a democratic form of governance, founded the *polis* of the Eleans with Elis as its capital city (Strabo *Geography* 8.3.2). At the same time, the Eleans initiated a program of construction in the sanctuary at Olympia and reorganized their quadrennial festival which was attracting many visitors as indicated by the large number of wells dug in the first quarter of the fifth century (Mallwitz 1988, 98).

The Sanctuary during the Classical Period[1]

In 457, the Lacedaemonians dedicated to Zeus Olympios a golden shield in celebration of their victory at Tanagra in that year. The Eleans affixed it beneath a gilded Victory on the eastern end of Zeus's new temple (Pausanias 5.10.4). That sculptures were in place in the pediment shows that the structure, begun around 468, was near completion. Pausanias reports that "the temple and cult statue were made for Zeus from the spoils gained in the Elean defeat of Pisa and from those of their neighbors who supported the Pisans" (5.10.2). This war took place about 570, and unless the Eleans saved the spoils for a century, Pausanias must have been misinformed. Notably, Pausanias expresses no surprise

---

1. See Map 2, page 182.

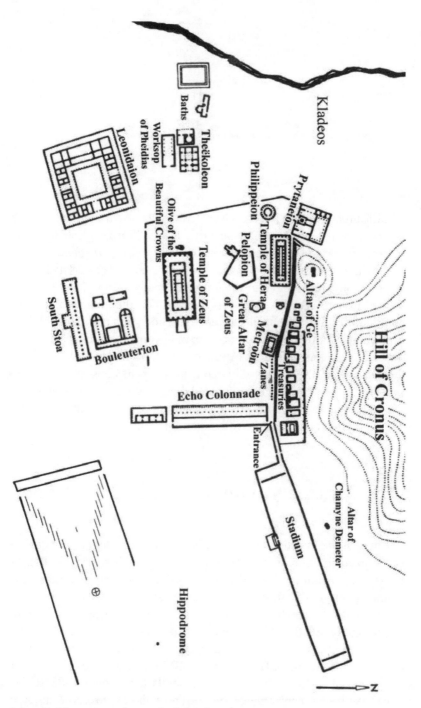

Map 2. Olympia at the end of the fourth century

or indignation that wealth Greeks looted from other Greeks funded the temple. The site in the southwest corner of the Altis, although unoccupied, required extensive preparation to raise and level the surface. The temple was of native limestone quarried across the Alpheios River and veneered with marble stucco and in the Doric order with an outer peristyle of six columns at the ends and thirteen along each side. Although the heaviest of any temple in Greece, the columns did not impart that impression because of the slight convexity of the shaft or entasis that ran throughout the structure. Vivid red, blue, and gold highlighted parts of its external architectural features. The plan of the temple adhered to traditional design in resting on three steps and having a central *cella*, an inner chamber surrounded by a porch at the eastern and front end, and a closed rear chamber. After 430, the *cella* enclosed the Athenian Pheidias' colossus of Zeus Olympios. Constructed from ivory and gold on a wooden frame, it represented the god sitting on a throne, his head nearly touching the roof. "If he stood up straight, they say, he would raise the roof" (Strabo *Geography* 8.3.30). Pheidias is alleged to have found his model for Zeus in Homer's description of the god Strabo *Geography* 8.3.30):

Beneath his dark brows the son of Cronus nodded assent,
and the lord's ambrosial locks flowed down
from his immortal head, and great Olympus quaked (*Iliad* 1.528–530).

When Pausanias visited the temple of Zeus, the panels above the columns displayed the gilded shields dedicated by the Roman general Lucius Mummius Achaicus to commemorate his destruction of Corinth in 146 (5.10.5). Until then, the panels were empty. Above them, the east pediment held sculptures illustrating the chariot race in which Pelops contends for Hippodameia against her father, Oinomaos (Apollodorus *The Library*, Epitome 2.2–7). Pausanias described the pediments in his travel guide from his, the observer's, point of view:

The contest of Pelops against Oinomaos is imminent, and both sides are readying for the race. About in the middle [of the pediment] is fashioned the statue of Zeus. Oinomaos is to the right of Zeus, his helmet resting on his head. Beside him stands his wife, Sterope, a daughter of Atlas. Myrtilos who drove the chariot for Oinomaos sits in front of the horses which are four in number. Behind him are two nameless men. They have been ordered by Oinomaos to tend the horses. At the very edge lies Kladeus. He among the rivers especially receives honors from the Eleans in other ways also, after Alpheios ,of course. The sculptures to the left of Zeus are Pelops, Hippodameia, the charioteer for Pelops, horses, and two men, grooms evidently for Pelops. The pediment narrows, and beneath the corner Alpheios has been represented (5.10.6–7).

Many fragments of these sculptures, some of them large, have been found where they fell after the destruction of the temple. Aided by Pausanias, scholars have reconstructed the scene in both pediments (Robertson, 1:71–291). As media for myths, the sculptures speak visually to those who know their story. Through their placement, gestures, and facial expressions, they can be fashioned, however, to direct and clue their audience to recall the myth in the way desired by their makers. The sculptures are larger than life not only to the eye but because they depict figures that loom larger than ordinary mortals.

Taller still than these stands Zeus in the middle of the east pediment beneath the peak of the roof. His head, now lost, was turned to his right (the observer's left), the direction of good omen (Robertson, 1:278). The mortals at his sides look away; they do not, cannot, see him, for, as Homer explains, "gods do not reveal themselves clearly to all men" (*Odyssey* 16.161). Zeus, present in the pediment but invisible to mortals, has arrived to be the sanction for the oath that governs the chariot race soon to begin. On his right stands his grandson Pelops, naked, and armed with a helmet, shield, and spear. Is he too fine and noble to have corrupted Myrtilos with a bribe, namely, half of his kingdom, as rumor reported (Hyginus *Fabula* 84)? Beside Pelops, Hippodameia adjusts the veil that marks her as a bride. She looks confident, because she has induced her father's charioteer, Myrtilos, to betray Oinomaos (Apollodorus *The Library*, Epitome 2.7). To Zeus's left, the thicker, older Oinomaos, naked except for a cloak draped over his shoulders and hanging down in long folds, strikes an arrogant, swaggering pose. He has already slain twelve or thirteen suitors whose heads Pelops saw nailed to his house (Hyginus *Fabula* 84). He evinces no signs of fear that he will die at the hands of his daughter's husband, the fate predicted by the oracle (Apollodorus *The Library*, Epitome 2.4). Beside him, his wife, Sterope, appears concerned. She must know that the rumors are true, the rumors of her husband's incestuous lust for his daughter, Hippodameia's resistance, and the contest rigged to keep his daughter for himself. The suitor must race to Corinth with Hippodameia at his side, and if he reaches the isthmus before Oinomaos overtakes him, he wins the girl. But he has no chance: Oinomaos' horses and weapons, gifts of his father, Ares, cannot be outrun or repulsed. Yet treachery is not his alone. Once Hippodameia saw Pelops, she desired him passionately. Playing on the lust that Myrtilos harbors for her, she persuaded him to leave the linchpins out of the axle ends. The race begins, the wheels spin off, and Oinomaos is dragged to his death by his own horses.

Inside the temple, the metopes placed above the doors of the porch and rear chamber depict Herakles' Twelve Labors (Pausanias 5.10.9). Herakles, the son of Zeus, plays a prominent role in founding the games, but his contests win for him the final victory, the immortality of the gods. His presence reminds the athletes that by their efforts in the games they can achieve the immortality conveyed by the olive of victory, but however great their achievements, they fall short of the bliss attained by Herakles, the man of contests and suffering, the ultimate *athletês*.

The games thrived during the 460s and 450s, and the increased attendance imposed unexpected demands upon the sanctuary. Stadium II, although a relatively new structure, proved inadequate after a single generation. Propelled by prosperity, the Eleans undertook a major renovation. The new track of Stadium III, covered with dirt and graced with starting and finishing lines of stone, was 192.27 meters (ca. 210 yards) long, 28.6 meters (ca. 31.3 yards) wide at the west end, and 29.7 meters (32.5 yards) wide at the east. The Eleans maintained the northeast orientation of Stadium II but moved the new facility 75 meters (ca. 82 yards) to the west. The shift allowed construction of an earthen embankment on the west end of the stadium and preserved the open spaces of the eastern part of the Altis. Stadium III was also located 12 meters (ca. 13 yards) closer to the Hill of Cronus. Excavation of the lower portion of the hill provided a steeper slope with better visibility and more room for spectators but ended its use as a source of well water (Mallwitz 1988, 98). With the eastern and southern embankments repositioned, seating capacity swelled to 40,000, but only the priestess of Demeter Chamyne, Demeter of the Earth, and the Hellanodikai enjoyed seats. The priestess sat on her altar on the north side of the stadium, and the judges, when they were not officiating, had chairs placed on a raised platform on the southern side opposite the altar (Pausanias 6.20.8–9). Everyone else sat cheek by jowl on the ground.

Hellanodikai and athletes entered the stadium from the northeast corner of the Altis through a passage cut in the embankment and lined with native limestone. The passage was open to the air during the classical period, but by Pausanias' time, it had become the "Hidden Entrance" (Pausanias 6.20.8), a vaulted tunnel buried beneath a higher and steeper slope. Those who entered it traversed a longish distance (31.1 meters or ca. 35 yards) to debouch dramatically into the dazzling light and searing heat of the stadium floor. Perhaps athletes were held up in the passageway and, while awaiting the signal to enter, scratched graffiti in the rocks like those found in the tunnel to the stadium at Nemea, for example, *Epikratos kalos*: "Epikratos is beautiful" (Miller 1990, 187–

191). Once inside the stadium, runners in the *stadion* crossed its length to the starting line in the east. Runners in the *diaulos* and *dolichos* began and finished in the west.

After 388, Hellanodikai and athletes approached the entrance to the stadium past the Zanes, bronze statues of Zeus mounted on stone bases at the foot of the Hill of Cronus (Drees, Ill. 8). The name is the plural of Zan, Zeus in the Doric and Ionic dialects. The Zanes were paid for by fines levied upon athletes "who acted with blatant disregard [*hybris*] for the rules of the contest" (Pausanias 5.21.2). The Eleans set up six statues in the ninety-eighth Olympiad (388) after Eupolos of Thessaly and his fellow competitors in boxing received fines, he for bribing the latter, and they for accepting his bribes. The Eleans inscribed four of the statues with elegiacs whose gist, Pausanias reports, was self-praise and the declaration that "not by money but by swiftness of foot and by strength of body is an Olympic victory gained" (5.21.4). After the 112th Olympiad (332), the Eleans erected another six statues with the fines for bribery in pentathlon imposed upon the Athenian Kallippos and his competitors (Pausanias 5.21.5). The Zanes, life-size and towering over those about to judge or compete, issue a stern warning against treating the games as one pleases.

Olympia did not have a formal palaestra until the end of the third or beginning of the second century, and its *gymnasion* could have been built as late as the first century. One amenity the Eleans did give the athletes during the fifth century was a swimming pool outside the Altis along the west bank of the Kladeus River. The pool, open to the air and measuring 24 meters long (ca. 26 yards) by 16 meters wide (17.5 yards) and 1.6 meters (1.75 yards) deep, drew its water from the Kladeus. In the following decades, it was joined by a hip bath and a heated bath (Drees, 49–50).

Traditional forms of construction continued during the fifth century. The Metröon, the small temple of Meter, Zeus's mother, Rhea, was erected in the early fourth century east of the Heraion along the northern edge of the Altis at the foot of the terrace for the treasuries (Pausanias 5.20.9). It reproduced the pattern of other temples in the sanctuary in having a porch leading to the door, a *cella*, and a walled-off rear chamber. The *cella* appears to have remained empty until filled with statues of Roman emperors (Pausanias 5.20.9). An altar stood before its western end, an indication that the temple, contrary to custom, may have faced the west. South of the Heraion was the Pelopeion, the sacred precinct of the hero Pelops, built about 390. Surrounded by a pentagonal fence of stone, it contained trees and dedicatory statues (Pausanias 5.13.1).

Northwest of the Heraion, the Prytaneion sheltered the fire that burned day and night on the communal hearth (Pausanias 5.15.9). Once a year, on the nineteenth of Elaphios (roughly March), the prophets removed the ash from the altar and, making a paste with water from the Alpheios River, smeared it on the great ashen altar of Zeus (Pausanias 5.13.11, 15.9). In the room opposite the hearth, the Eleans entertained the victors in the games (Pausanias 5.15.12).

The heated bath, a harbinger of the thermal baths of the Roman future, was not the only sign that the building program in the sanctuary was surrendering its Archaic simplicity. A long colonnade, erected along the eastern border of the Altis about 350–340, provided shade and rest for spectators. The Eleans, it seems, had begun to think of their sanctuary as an attraction that visitors would enjoy more by escaping the heat. On the north, the colonnade closely faced the Zanes (Pausanias 5.21.17) and extended southward where it met an existing colonnade, the so-called Southeastern Colonnade (ca. 400–350). The new colonnade severed cult and religious activities of the Altis from the games in the east without diminishing the sacredness of the games. The building was first called the Painted Colonnade after the pictures painted on its walls. Others called it the Echo Colonnade, because "when a man has shouted seven times, his voice is returned to him by the echo seven times or even more" (Pausanias 5.21.17).

The Macedonian king and new leader of the Greeks, Philip II, apparently funded construction of the Echo Colonnade, since its features resemble those of the later Philippeion, the king's circular temple dedicated in the years immediately after his victory at Chaeroneia in 338 to honor his athletic and military victories. Within stood statues of Philip, his son, Alexander, and his father, Amyntas (Pausanias 5.20.10). The temple asserted Philip's presence at the Panhellenic shrine, while his support of the colonnade appears aimed at promoting good relations with Greeks whose freedom his hegemony curtailed. The statues were made of gold and ivory, materials used for the colossal statues of Athena Parthenos and Zeus Olympios. Together with the presence of statues of humans in the *cella* of a temple, they "demonstrate the similarity— although not the identity—of the Macedonian kings and the Olympian gods" (Drees, 122) and foreshadow the ruler cult offered to Alexander.

The Eleans had always accepted votive dedications, and the gift of a temple from the new *hêgemon* or leader of the Greeks could hardly be refused, even though the Philippeion invaded the sanctum of a Panhellenic shrine with a display that promoted a single family of *barbaroi*, non-Greeks, as the Greeks characterized their Macedonian conquerors. The

Leonidaion, set in the southeast corner of the Altis, honored a much less widely known man but one of enormous wealth, Leonidas of Naxos. Built between 330 and 320, at 81 by 75 meters (88.5 by 82 yards) square, it covered an area larger than the temple of Zeus. Wealthy and distinguished visitors to Olympia strolled its inner and outer peristyles and luxuriated in its accommodations. Clearly, the Eleans courted the tourist trade, especially its constituents with drachmas. The sanctuary also included several other buildings of which little is known beyond their remains. These include the Southern Colonnade from which dignitaries perhaps watched the processions, the South Eastern Colonnade and the Thëekoleon (Pausanias 5.15.8).

As befitted a Panhellenic sanctuary, the cults of many gods besides those of Zeus received worship in the Altis, and their altars and shrines were everywhere. Once a month in Pausanias' time, the Eleans sacrificed at all of them (5.15.10). Scattered across the Altis were statues of the gods and victors. Although Pausanias does not attempt to describe all the statues of athletes, he mentions over two hundred (6.1–18). The Eleans permitted every victor to set up a statue of himself and, occasionally, of his trainer or horse. Their rule prescribed only that the statue must be life-size and not exaggerate the athlete's height (Lucian *Essay on Portraiture Defended* 11). Since the athlete or his friends paid for the making and transporting of the statue to Olympia (Pausanias 6.8.3), many victors did not avail themselves of the privilege (Frazer, 4:1). Inscriptions, in various dialects and often worn and faded from the elements by Pausanias' time, identified the victor's name, his city and event, and the name of the artist. The history of Greek athletics is particularly indebted to Pausanias for his diligence in deciphering these writings (Habicht, 64–94).

The Games: Making Ready

Ancient tradition unequivocally places the celebration of the games during the high summer after the summer solstice (Lucian *Herodotus* 8; Aelian *Historical Miscellany* 14.18; Diogenes Laertius *Lives of the Eminent Philosophers* 1.39; Censorius *De die natali* 21.6). A Pindaric Scholiast sets the date: "on the sixteenth while the moon is full, the Olympic festival is celebrated, that is, in the middle of the month of Parthenios or Apollonios" (on *Olympian Ode* 3.35a, in Drachmann

1:115). Despite these details, for the festival to be Panhellenic, the date of its celebration could not have been determined by the Elean calendar, or any *polis*'s calendar, since each followed its own (Miller 1975, 220). Rather, a universal system available to all Greeks was needed, and to find one, whoever knew the Olympic year had only to look to the heavens to calculate when the games would be held. As Miller points out (1975, 220), Greeks were aware of solstices since the time of Hesiod (see *Works and Days* 564, 663), and the cycle of the moon was evident. It is no surprise, then, that the Alexandrian boxer Apollonios Rhantes did not allege chronological ignorance in excusing his late arrival at the 218th Olympiad (93) (Pausanias 5.21.13). That athletes could be present at Elis thirty days before the festival suggests that the first full moon after the solstice was the marker for their arrival. Accordingly, the games fell under the second full moon after the solstice, with the Olympic or holy month the thirty days intervening between full moons (Miller1975, 221).

In anticipation of the games, the Eleans sent out ambassadors to declare the god's sacred truce. They could not reach everywhere Greeks were living, but their message served as a means of promoting safe travel for pilgrims to the games (Ziehen, 3–6). An inscription (ca. 460) announcing the truce for the mysteries of Demeter at Eleusis suggests its language: "there is a truce for the initiates and for the watchers and for the followers and for the possessions of the foreigners and for all Athenians" (Inscription 42, in Dittenberger 1:47). The truce was in effect before and after the festival for an unknown period and called for inviolability and personal safety for those traveling to and from, and while at, the festival, but it did not effect a general peace, contrary to a modern assertion extrapolated from Isocrates' declaration to his audience at Olympia: "You have concluded a truce with one another and settled your existing enmities and come together to this place" (*Panegyricus* 43). The Greeks waged war mainly during the summer. Such an armistice, as Harris points out, would have made warfare almost impossible (1964, 156). And that would hardly do.

The athlete set out on the grueling road to an Olympic crown under the strict supervision of the Hellanodikai (Philostratos *Gymnastic* 11, in Kayser, 266). Though Epictetus refers to his own day, his remarks drive home the rigor of the training:

> You must follow the rules, submit to a diet, refrain from goodies, exercise your body, whether you choose to or not, at a stated hour, in heat and cold. You must drink no cold water and sometimes not even

wine. In short, you must give yourself up to your master as to a physician (*Encheiridion* 29).

Hellanodikai were chosen by lot from the citizenry of adult male Eleans to conduct the office of Hellanodikes for one Olympiad (Pausanias 5.9.4; Plutarch *Lycurgus* 20.6). After 471 at the earliest when Elis was founded but surely later, they resided for the ten months preceding the games in Elis at the Hellanodikaion where they received instruction in their duties from the Guardians of the Laws (Pausanias 6.24.3). Their number had grown from one or two in the sixth century to nine after 400, three in charge of the horse races, another three overseeing the pentathlon comprising *stadion*, discus, jump, javelin, and wrestling, and the final three, all the other events. A tenth Hellanodikes was added in 392 and two more in 368, to represent each of twelve Elean tribes. After 364 when the Eleans lost territory in a war with the Aetolians, the number of Hellanodikai was reduced to eight to match the decreased number of tribes. In 348, the Eleans settled on ten Hellanodikai (Pausanias 5.9.4–6). While in office, the Hellanodikai wore a purple robe (*Etymologicum Magnum s.v. Hellanodikai*, in Gaisford, 331). The sight of them scurrying around the streets of Elis must have gladdened the Eleans, for their presence meant that the influx of visitors and wealth to the games in Olympia would soon begin. Most of what is known about their duties concerns the period after 471, but Hellanodikai of all periods must have fulfilled similar obligations.

In Pausanias' day, all athletes, the fathers and brothers of the boys, and the trainers had to assemble by the first full moon after the summer solstice at Elis on penalty of disqualification. For the next thirty days, the athletes who were accepted would train under the supervision of the Hellanodikai (Philostratos *Life of Apollonius* 5.43; Pausanias 6.23.1). When residency was first required is not known. Since it asserts Eleans' grip upon the Olympic Games, it may have been introduced after their loss of control in the war with the Aetolians (Xenophon *Hellenica* 7.4.28–32). The demand for a lengthy stay in Elis at the athlete's expense either contributed to, or was a product of, the rise of athletic professionalism during the classical period. Before they could commence training, however, the athletes first had be declared eligible. From the early fifth century, the Hellanodikai screened athletes (Herodotus *Histories* 5.22), a duty facilitated by the presence of competitors before the games. Since Greeks alone were eligible, Hellanodikai had to establish the parentage and descent of each athlete. Among the preliminaries, they would have barred from the assembly murderers, temple robbers, and violators of the Olympic truce, and administered the oaths of honesty to those accepted. According to Pausanias (5.24.9), the oaths were given at Olympia, but their content as well as the need for athletes to be bound from the outset support Ludwig Ziehen's contention that the swearing first took place at Elis (17). Hence, the ceremony at Olympia was a formality but entailed the same obligations:

> [I]t is customary for athletes, their fathers and brothers, and even their trainers to swear upon the cut pieces of a boar that "No misconduct will come from me into the Olympic Games." The adult athletes further swear that they have maintained their training regimen for ten consecutive months. Those who examine the boys or the colts swear that they will conduct their examination in accord with justice and without bribery and that any information acquired about someone, whether he is approved or not, will be kept guarded and secret (Pausanias 5.24.9).

The examiners had to determine whether an athlete who offered himself as a boy could fairly compete in that group, a decision which they typically based on age with size and appearance influencing factors (Pausanias 5.24.10; Golden, 106). The examiners seem to have considered everyone born in the same year to be the same age. During puberty, striking differences in size and appearance can emerge between a boy born at the beginning and one born at the end of a year. The examiners learned how to distinguish among them, but their task remained subjective, necessitating an oath of impartiality.

Boys from the ages of twelve to seventeen were eligible to compete (Crowther 1988, 304). For the seventy-eighth Olympiad (468), those judging the boys refused entry to Pherias [M 255] who had come from Aegina in the Saronic Gulf off Attica (Pausanias 6.14.1). His long voyage around the Peloponnesus and subsequent years of pondering his experience in Olympia were vindicated when he won boys' wrestling in the next festival and erected the statue announcing his deed. The twelve-year-old Damiskos [M 417] of Messene won the *stadion* in the 103rd Olympiad (368) (Pausanias 6.2.10–11). Because Pausanias wonders about his youthfulness but says nothing about any irregularity, Nigel B. Crowther concludes that twelve was the lower age limit for boys in fourth-century Olympia (1988, 306). The rejection of Nikasylos of Rhodes suggests that the upper age was seventeen (Pausanias 6.14.2). Nikasylos presented himself as a wrestler "in his eighteenth year." This could mean for the Greeks, who lacked precision in matters of age and chronology, that Nikasylos was seventeen and living in his eighteenth year or that he had already attained eighteen years of age. Candidates could be rejected for being too large, as was the son of Eualkes of

Athens (Xenophon *Hellenica* 4.1.40), or too small, as was Pherias (Pausanias 6.14.1). The examiners laughed at the sight Pythagoras [M 88] of Samos when he submitted himself as a boxer in the boys' event, though whether for his size (Diogenes Laertius *Lives of the Philosophers* 8.47) or for his effeminate Ionian appearance (Eusebius *Chronicles* in Schoene, 1:200) is uncertain. Pausanias, however, makes no reference to Nikasylos' size or appearance and speaks only of his age. It is assumed, therefore, that the examiners assessed Nikasylos to be eighteen and too old for the boys' contests and that seventeen years marked the upper limit for competition in such events (Crowther 1988, 306).

Hellanodikai were widely known for their impartiality (Plutarch *Lycurgus* 20.6). Herodotus tells the story of the Elean envoys who came to the Egyptians with a question:

> Envoys arrived to Psammis while he was king of Egypt, boasting that they held the games at Olympia in the most just and noble manner. They thought that the wisest of men, the Egyptians, could not discover anything to add. The Egyptians gathered and learned from the Eleans all about the manner in which they customarily conducted the games. After the Eleans explained everything, they said that they had come to find out whether the Egyptians could add anything fairer than their rules. The Egyptians deliberated and asked the Eleans whether their citizens competed in the games. The Eleans said that anyone of their own people and of the rest of the Greeks who wished were allowed to compete. The Egyptians replied that the Eleans had missed the mark of justice completely in holding the games in this manner, for it was impossible that they would not prefer a citizen who was competing and therefore wrong a foreigner. But if they wished to hold the games fairly and came to Egypt for that purpose, they would order the Eleans to hold the contest for foreign competitors and not to compete themselves. This was the Egyptians' advice to them (*Histories* 2.160; also, Diodorus Siculus *Bibliotheca* 1.95.2).

The story not only underscores the Eleans' concern for their games and their willingness to go to extremes to insure their impartiality. It also implies that after they adopted the advice of the Egyptians, their integrity as producers of the Olympic Games was above reproach and secured by the reputation and authority of the wisest men. Nonetheless, the Eleans continued to compete throughout the classical period, and Hellanodikai continued to be regarded as fair and honest judges.

On the other hand, Hellanodikai were Eleans, many winners were Eleans, and an individual Hellanodikes may not have been above favoring a fellow citizen in doubtful circumstances. Pausanias reports a stain upon their reputation for honesty that occurred in the ninety-sixth Olympiad (396) at the finish of the *stadion*:

> The statue of the Elean Eupolemos [M 367] was made by Daidalos of Sikyon. The inscription on it announces that Eupolemos gained a victory in the *stadion* for men at Olympia and two Pythian crowns in the pentathlon and one at the Nemean Games. The following is said about Eupolemos: three Hellanodikai were in authority at the race; two of them gave the race to Eupolemos and the third to Leon of Ambrakia; Leon secured a monetary fine from the Olympic council against the two Hellanodikai who determined Eupolemos the winner (Pausanias 6.3.7).

It is clear from this incident that the Hellanodikai decided the outcome of close finishes by a majority of those involved and that there was an appeal process for questioning their decisions to a council empowered to oversee the ceremonies (Pausanias 6.3.7). The council evidently could not overturn a decision, but it retained the competence to punish a miscreant Hellanodikes.

During training at Elis, the Hellanodikai began before dawn matching runners in the *gymnasion* beside the Peneios River and at noon the pentathletes and contestants in the heavy events (Pausanias 6.24.1). They paired the wrestlers for age and skill (Pausanias 6.23.2). Wrestlers also practiced in the Square, a palaestra named for its shape. Runners and pentathletes had separate tracks, and the boys practiced in their own *gymnasion*, called Maltho (soft) because of its sandy surface (Pausanias 6.23.5). How the owners prepared their teams is not known, but they may have followed local custom in training in the marketplace at Elis (Pausanias 6.24.2). Everyone labored under the fierce sun whose heat and glare would intensify.

At the end of the month's training in Elis, the athletes walked from Elis to Olympia along the Sacred Road (Pausanias 5.25.7) in a procession headed by the Hellanodikai. They probably took two days to complete the thirty-six miles. Along the way, the Hellanodikai harangued the athletes:

> If you have expended the effort worthy of entering Olympia and have done nothing slothful or ignoble, go in good cheer, but for those who have not trained in this way, depart wherever you like (Philostratos *Life of Apollonius* 5.43).

As the road passed through the plain toward Olympia, the Hellanodikai stopped at the spring Piera to purify themselves with pig blood and water. They celebrated this rite before performing any ritual duty

(Pausanias 5.16.8). Arriving at Olympia, the athletes saw to their own lodging (Ziehen, 10). Pausanias speaks of houses for the athletes near the *gymnasion* (6.21.2), but such accommodations, like the *gymnasion* itself, were yet to be built.

Crews of workmen had been readying the site for the games. After lying fallow for three years, the stadium and other athletic facilities needed refurbishment. The task at Olympia could not have been far different from that undertaken at Delphi and recorded in an inscription dated to the archonship of Dion (258) (Homolle, 565–567). The inscription lists the required work, the name of the contractor, and the allotted sum of money in staters, a coin worth two drachmas. A typical line reads, "cleaning out of the Pythian stadium and repair of the embankments, Smyrnaios: 15 staters." For this sum, Smyrnaios removed weeds and other debris from the stadium and repaired weather damage to the embankments. He also contracted for "the digging of the Pythian stadium and the digging and leveling of the jumping grounds" for 110 staters. His crew of workmen loosened the earth and rolled it level. Xenon received 83 staters 4 obols for covering the track with white sand, a sum that included the cost of 150 *medimnoi* of sand at 1¾ obols a *medimnos* (ca. 12 gallons). Other contractors dug up and rolled level the surfaces of the running tracks and hippodrome around the *kampteres*. Necessary repairs were contracted for a wall beside the shrine of Demeter, a wall in the ball-playing room in the palaestra, and the vaulted entrance to the stadium. Melission erected a pedestal in the stadium for 25 staters, Euthydamos, a fence for 10, and Nikon, the proscenium for 5. One contractor supplied 6 hoes, and another, turning posts for 36 staters. Funds probably came as part of the *leitourgiai* assessed wealthy citizens. Some monies may also have come from the treasury of the sanctuary and from a gate fee, as Harris speculates on the analogy with the admissions charge to the theater of Dionysus at Athens (1964, 152–153).

Meanwhile, the sanctuary was swelling with visitors come to watch the games or promote their own interests. As Cicero observes, some came to Olympia in search of the glory of a crown, but others "were induced by the profit and gain of buying and selling" (*Tusculan Disputations* 5.9). Spectators had to eat and offer sacrifices. Merchants peddled food and animals for sacrifice. Bronzesmiths and potters made objects for offerings, and poets created *epinikia* for victors. What everyone found at Olympia was an uncomfortable place, niggardly dappled by the shade of tree and edifice and crammed with tents and other makeshift accommodations. And everywhere there were people, competing for a good spot to roost for the night, jostling for position and attention, far more noisy than at home, and thirsty from the heat and dust. Eleans dug more wells in the east of their sanctuary than elsewhere; after the mid-fourth century, spectators could get water from open channels (Mallwitz 1988, 98). Epictetus gives an idea of the discomfort and its rewards:

> Unpleasant and harsh things happen in life. Do they not in Olympia? Aren't you scorching hot? Crowded? Don't you bathe poorly? Aren't you drenched when it downpours? Don't you get your fill of the commotion and shouting and other aggravations? But I think that balancing all this against the worth of the spectacle, you bear and endure everything (*Discourses* 1.6.26–27).

The spectators also found a cultural center. Herodotus gained his fame from reciting his *Histories* from the rear chamber of the temple of Zeus. "In one meeting, he won worldwide approval of Greece and was declared victor not by one herald, by Zeus! but by every city that had spectators at the games" (Lucian *Herodotus* 2). Other notables followed suit, Hippias of Elis, to be sure, but also the sophist Prodikos from Keos, and the philosophers Anaximenes of Chios and Polos of Agrigentum (Lucian *Herodotus* 3). The philosopher Anaxagoras called attention to his powers of prophecy by wearing a sheepskin into the stadium at Olympia as protection against the downpour impending at the time "when it rained the least" (Philostratos *Life of Apollonius* 1.2). Pindar and Bacchylides and surely others of their craft came in quest of clients. On the other hand, in 388, Dionysius, tyrant of Sicily, sent rhapsodes to recite his poetry along with several chariots. When the ship carrying the horses home was wrecked, the sailors blamed the disaster on the wretchedness of his poetry (Diodorus Siculus *The Library* 14.109; 15.7.2). Many famous men came to Olympia, among them, Aeschylus, Socrates, Pythagoras, and Lycurgus. "The prospect of appearing in Olympia before an audience which was numbered in tens of thousands must have been a very enticing one for the Greek intellectuals" (Drees, 62). Like any spectacle, Olympia during the games was a place to see and be seen.

A notable difference between audiences for the tragedies at Athens and crowds at the Olympia program was the absence of married women from the Altis during the days of the games. Scholars have long held that women were barred from the theater at Athens, but no ancient source reports their exclusion, and Plato allows that tragic discourse was addressed to women and children (*Gorgias* 502D; Henderson). Although married women were admitted in the Altis and on the lowest level of Zeus's monumental ashen altar (Pausanias 5.13.10), on the forbidden days, those of the festival, they were prohibited from crossing the Alpheios River much less joining the assembly for the games. The penalty was death by being thrown from Mount Typaion, "a precipitous mountain with lofty cliffs" to the south of Olympia (Pausanias 5.6.7). However, the priestess of Demeter Chamyne was permitted to see the spectacle. She sat on an altar of white marble in Demeter's sanctuary on the north side of the stadium (Pausanias 6.20.9). The honor of being the sole woman to watch the games perhaps derived from ancient fertility rites once conducted on the site of Demeter's altar, but for the priestess herself, confined to Demeter's stone altar in the open sun, it must have been a dubious and uncomfortable privilege.

Pausanias reports that virgin girls could observe the games (6.20.9), an assertion that has struck many as an error on his part. Understanding lies in the relationship of virgin girls to society. Unmarried, they exist in a state of savagery, their fertility and sexuality untamed and unframed by marriage (Tyrrell, 73–76). They are ordinary girls, of course, but in terms of their social status, they have yet to be civilized. This lack of status renders them liminal figures: no longer children, but sexually mature and unmarried; ripe to see men nude but necessarily restrained by such formal and public circumstances.

John Mouratidis (1984) attributes the exclusion of women from the Olympic Games to the prominence of Herakles at the sanctuary. He contends that Herakles was not only the founder of the games, as often told in the myths, but also their recipient, that is, the games were dedicated to him and not to Zeus. The primacy of Zeus at the sanctuary is confirmed by archeological evidence, but Herakles' prominence there may still be a factor in the taboo, since women were traditionally banished from Herakles' sanctuaries and cults across Greece.

Pausanias heard of one woman, called variously Kallipateira or Pherenike, who was apprehended at the games but who, out of respect for her family, was allowed to live. Her father, Diagoras [M252] of Rhodes, was the first in his family to win at Olympia in boxing in 464. His victory was followed by the victories of his son Damagetos [M 287, 300] in *pankration* (452, 448), his younger son, Akusilaos [M 299], in boxing (448), and youngest son, Dorieus [M 322, 326, 330], in *pankration* (432, 428, 424) and the family's distinction continued with his grandsons' victories in men's [M 356?] and boys' boxing [M 354?] in 404 (Pausanias 5.6.7–8; Scholiast on Pindar, *Olympian Ode* 7c, in Drachmann, 1:197). Widowed, the woman was free to disguise herself as her son's trainer and accompany him to Olympia. As her father's daughter, she would be well versed in the preparation of an athlete for competition. After her son Peisodoros [M 356?] won, she jumped over the barrier and exposed her sex. The Eleans made an exception for Diagoras' daughter but passed a law that all trainers henceforth had to enter the stadium in the nude. The incident passes as historical, and the details of the woman's early loss of her husband and so of a *kyrios* or master to watch over her as well as the uncertainty over her name add weight to its veracity. Respectable women were not spoken of by name in public (Shaps). The story itself may have floated around Olympia as a cautionary tale for women: "Beware of what you do if you lack such a family."

The Five Days of Competition

No ancient source recounts the order of athletic events, but there never was a monolithic schedule, because the slate of contests and their sequence kept changing throughout the games' thousand-year history (Lee 1992, 106). Notable progress toward a model schedule was made in 1904 when Ludwig Weniger published an article demonstrating that competitions took place before and after the religious ceremonies on the day of the full moon. Relying on a Pindaric scholiast, he proposed a six-day festival (150) that many scholars, including Ziehen (10), Mallwitz (1972, 69–70), and Gardiner (1910, 20; 1980, 224), adopted with few or no changes. Yet around 460, Pindar described the games as "five-day competitions" in an ode celebrating Psaumis:

> who, exalting your city, Coumarouna, nurturer of people,
> honored the twice six altars at the greatest festival of the gods
> with sacrifices of oxen and at the five-day competitions in the contests
> for chariots with horses, with mules, and in single horses (*Olympian Ode* 5.4–7).

The Scholiasts on the phrase "five-day competitions" define the period as extending from the eleventh to the fifteenth or sixteenth of the holy month (in Drachmann, 1:142). Weniger's reconstruction corresponds to a later time in the history of the Olympic schedule. For the fifth century, however, Pindar's authority, particularly in an ode sung before a knowledgeable audience, is too compelling to dismiss.

The most critical source for the Olympic schedule has a lacuna that must be emended, an expedient that compromises its authority:

> The order of the games in our time, with the victims sacrificed to the god after the pentathlon and horse races but *before the rest of the contests*, was instituted in the seventy-seventh Olympiad [472]. Before then, the Eleans held the games for the men and horses together on the same day. On one occasion, those competing in *pankration* continued into the night, since they were not summoned on time. The horses were responsible, but even more so, the competition in pentathlon. . . . In the future, neither the pentathlon nor the horses would interfere with the *pankration* (Pausanias 5.9.3).

The emendation, shown in italics, parallels the received text and, although more may have been lost, is satisfactory in itself. The text describes a minimum athletic program of three days with the horse racing and pentathlon falling before the religious ceremonies and the rest of the contests afterwards. "Before then" implies that after 472, the horse races and pentathlon took place on different days. This inference contradicts Xenophon's suggestion that the horse races and pentathlon occurred on the same day in 364 (*Hellenica* 7.4.29). An orator's commentary on the Athenian general and aristocrat Alcibiades' [M 416] victory at the ninety-first Olympiad (416), however, supports Pausanias in placing the horse races on the second day. After winning the four-horse chariot race, Alcibiades, as was custom, celebrated his triumph "on the day before the sacrifices" ([Andocides] *Against Alcibiades* 29). In this case, the Eleans offered the horse races on the second day—the first being given over to business and preparations—and in the early morning, for Bacchylides speaks of how "Dawn of the golden arms saw the chestnut Pherenikos, a colt swift as the storm winds, carry off the victory beside the wide-eddying waters of the Alpheios" (*Ode* 5.37–40). The pentathlon, which Xenophon places after the horse race (*Hellenica* 7.4.29), belonged to the same day and was necessarily conducted in the afternoon (Lee 1992, 107).

That Lachon [M 288] of Keos won boys' *stadion* at the eighty-second Olympiad (452) on the sixteenth of the holy month (Bacchylides *Ode* 7.3), the day after the full moon, fixes the *stadion* and surely the other boys' events, wrestling and boxing, on the day after the sacrifices. When the Eleans finished the boys' events, they called the men's (Plutarch *Moralia* 639A). These were probably the men's *dolichos*, *stadion*, and *diaulos*. Polites' victories in all three at an Olympiad of unknown date indicate that they were run in this order on the same day:

You could marvel about Polites. This Polites from Keramos in Karia
displayed at Olympia every excellence in running, for from the longest
and most demanding, he could switch to the shortest and swiftest.
Having won the *dolichos* and immediately afterwards the *stadion*, in
the same day, he added a third victory in *diaulos* (Pausanias 6.13.3).

Since the Argive Ageus [M 464] won the *dolichos* in the 113th Olympiad
(328) and announced his victory in person at Argos on the same day, the
footraces must have been held in the morning (Eusebius *Chronicles*, in
Schoene, 1:205).

The exception that the Hellanodikai granted Kleitomachos [M 589],
although happening after the classical period at the 142nd Olympiad in
212, struck such a cord in Olympic memory that the normal order of the
heavy events must have long been established:

> The Olympiad had Kleitomachos a contestant in *pankration* and
> boxing and Kapros of Elis intending to compete in wrestling and
> *pankration* on the same day. After Kapros won in wrestling,
> Kleitomachos apprised the Hellanodikai that it would be fair if they
> called the *pankration* before he received the wounds from boxing
> (Pausanias 6.15.4–5).

The exception shows that the fixed order of the heavy events, conducted
on the same day, was wrestling, boxing, *pankration*. The last event was
the hoplite race (Plutarch *Moralia* 639E; Artemidorus *Interpretation
of Dreams* 1.63).

The following schedule emerges for the games of the classical era:

> Day One: Taking of the oath and other preparations. Contests for
> heralds and trumpeters (beginning in 396).

> Day Two: Horse races in the morning. Pentathlon in the afternoon.
> Sacrifice to Pelops in the evening.

> Day Three: Procession to Zeus's altar and hecatomb of oxen. Feast
> in the evening in the Prytaneion.

> Day Four: Boys' events and men's running events in the morning.
> Men's heavy events in the afternoon. Hoplite race.

> Day Five: Crowning victors in the morning in the temple of Zeus.
> Feasting victors in the evening in the Prytaneion.

The first day was given over to the business conducted by the
Hellanodikai. They carried out sacrifices about which nothing is known.
These rituals were likely preceded by a rite of purification and a

proclamation forbidding murderers from entering the Altis or joining the festival (Ziehen, 16). The Hellanodikai administered the oath to athletes and judges. Although a formality, it must still have been momentous as the athletes, marvelous specimens of mortal men, faced Zeus of Oaths who stood outdoors in the *bouleuterion* holding a thunderbolt in each hand. Standing upon the pieces of the boar, the mortals again swore, this time before the god, that "No misconduct will come from me into the Olympic games" (Pausanias 5.24.9).

Beginning with the ninety-sixth Olympiad (396), the Eleans offered competitions on the first day for trumpeters and heralds who would perform at the games (Eusebius *Chronicles,* in Schoene, 1:204, 206). Before then, these contests had been reserved for Eleans (Pollux *Onomasticon* 4.92, in Bethe, 1:227). Competitors mounted an altar no longer used for sacrifices that stood in the Altis near the entrance to the stadium (Pausanias 5.22.1). This seems like a strategy to capitalize on the acoustics of the Echo Colonnade and, if so, belongs to the period after 338.

At Olympia, the Hellanodikai announced the order of the contests, perhaps as Cassius Dio records, by writing it on boards covered with white gypsum (*Roman History* 80.10). Although Dio's reference depends on an incident in the third century CE, Greeks used white boards for public notices during the fourth century (Lysias *On Behalf of a Soldier* 6). Athletes were summoned to compete by the "hot, competitive, and piercing" echo of the Olympic trumpet (Philostratos *Life of a Sophist* 10, in Kayser, 52), a custom attributed to Hermes, the god of contests, who was among a number of actors chosen by lot for a role in a comedy. After the others were hissed off the stage, the herald cried out for Hermes who had left the theater to practice. Not hearing the herald, he was fined for failing to appear. Hermes subsequently introduced the practice of summoning competitors by the trumpet (Pollux *Onomasticon* 4.88, in Bethe, 1:226). The Hellanodikai set byes in case of an odd number of entries (Lucian *Hermotimos* 41), disallowed athletes who appeared after the fixed time (Pausanias 5.21.14), and determined victors. They enforced the rules of a contest with the power to scourge athletes for violating them and fine anyone who had betrayed the Olympic Games by cheating and thereby perjuring his oath (Pausanias 6.2.2).

The clamor of pounding hooves and careening chariots in the hippodrome filled the morning of the second day. Horses and chariots were the toys of the rich. The horses, bred on their estates, tended to be small, hardy animals adapted less for riding than for the conditions of a chariot race, short spurts of speed punctuated at either end by a wrenching slide around the marker (Anderson, 37). Horse racing gave the wealthy an opportunity to compete against each other, free of the stigma of defeat to the farmer or tradesman. The fear of such ignominy motivated the reply Alexander the Great, who was swift of foot, gave when asked if he would wish to compete in the *stadion* at Olympia: "Yes, if I were going to have kings as my rivals" (Plutarch *Alexander* 4.5). Despite, or because of, their aristocratic glamour, horse races were popular as the Eleans' expansion of their equestrian program shows. For the seventieth Olympiad (500), they added a race for carts drawn by mules, the *apênê* (Yalouris 237, Ill. 137), and a trotting race for mares in the homestretch of which "the riders leaped from their mounts and ran with their horses, holding onto the reins" (Pausanias 5.9.1–2). They discontinued both events after the eighty-fourth Olympiad (444). Considering that religious scruple forbade breeding mules in Elis (Pausanias 5.5.2), the introduction of a race with mules, one devoid of gracefulness (5.9.2), hints at the enthusiasm for horse racing. Simonides scorned to write about mules for a victor in the mule race. After the victor offered more money, he complied by omitting the male donkey and referring to the mules as "daughters of storm-footed horses" (Aristotle *Rhetoric* 1405 b 24–27). In the ninety-third Olympiad (408), a race for chariot and two full grown horses called the *synôris* was added and in the ninety-ninth Olympiad (384), another for chariots drawn by four foals (Pausanias 5.8.10).

The hippodrome lay to the southeast of the stadium. It was bounded on the west by the Stoa of Agnaptos. Its longer northern side was abutted in the east by a low hill, an extension of the Hill of Cronus, where spectators stood; an embankment for seating bordered its southern side (Pausanias 6.20.15). Beyond, the Alpheios River flowed lazily by at its seasonal low. During the Middle Ages, the river spilled over its banks and eventually obliterated the hippodrome under alluvial mud that may never be removed. Excavation would not repay its costs, since the hippodrome was never more than a flat area with turning markers for racing horses. How large an area, in the absence of archaeological evidence, remains a question. An eleventh-century manuscript, discovered in the old Serapio in Istanbul, records the measurements at 1,900 feet (ca. 579 meters) by 400 feet (ca. 122 meters), but the text (in Ziehen, 22–23) is problematic and its value contested. Near a passage through the embankment stood the round altar of Taraxippos, Unsettler of Horses:

> As the horses run past this spot, they are seized with panic for no apparent reason. Confusion follows panic, and the horses generally crash the chariots, and the charioteers are injured. Consequently,

the charioteers offer sacrifices and pray that Taraxippos be gentle to
them (Pausanias 6.20.15).

A reference to the Athenian politician Cleon, the butt of Aristophanes'
Knights (424 B.C.E.   ), shows that Taraxippos haunted the hippodrome
near the first turn as early as the fifth century (247). Perhaps his effect
on horses derives from the sensitivity of the animals to their drivers'
panic on entering the first turn (Harris 1972, 170).

Nothing is said about limitations on the number of entries for a
race. Alcibiades sent seven chariots to Olympia in 416 (Thucydides
Histories 6.16.2), and the Eleans accepted all, a disparity that might
have elicited protest if restrictions were in place. Silence, however, in
view of the scant information about the horse races, bears little weight.
Forty chariots began a race at the Pythian Games of 460 (Pindar *Pythian
Ode* 5.49–51). The older and grander games could have accommodated
as many, had the need arisen.

Sophocles begins Orestes' chariot race in a simple fashion:

Taking their positions where judges in charge
positioned them by lots and stood their chariots,
at the brazen trumpet's signal, the charioteers tore away
(*Electra* 709–711).

Chariots were probably started in a similar fashion at Olympia for years.
Whether they shot forth at the clarion of the trumpet is not known, but
the trumpet did mark the second of the two laps in the single-horse race
(Pausanias 6.13.9).

Pausanias describes an elaborate starting mechanism invented by
Kleoitas, son of Aristokles:

As you pass out of the stadium where the Hellanodikai sit, you come
upon the hippodrome and the starting mechanism for the horses.
The starting mechanism has the shape of a prow with its beak pointed
into the course. Where the prow with its beak approximates the Stoa
of Agnaptos, the prow widens. A bronze dolphin on a rod has been
fashioned on the top of the beak. Each side of the starting mechanism
stretches more than four hundred feet in length. In it are stalls that
the entrants to the equestrian contests divide up among themselves
by lot. A rope is drawn in front of the chariots and single horse to
serve as a bar (*hysplex*). An altar of unbaked clay, plastered on the
outside, is constructed for each Olympiad as near as possible to the
center of the prow, and a bronze eagle, its wings fully extended,
stands on the altar. The official in charge of the races moves the
mechanism in the altar, and the eagle jumps upward so that it becomes
visible to those coming to the spectacle, and the dolphin falls to the
ground. The bars near the Stoa of Agnaptos on both sides are let
down first, and the horses standing behind them run out first. As they

run, they come abreast of those chariots that were allotted second place, and immediately the bars in the second-place stalls are released. It happens in this same way as I have described with all the horses until they are running equal with one another at the beak of the prow. From this point it becomes a display of the charioteers' skill and the speed of the horses (6.20.10–13).

Kleoitas erected an inscription at Athens that identifies him as "the first to invent the horse-starting mechanism at Olympia" (Pausanias 6.20.14). If Kleoitas' father, Aristokles, was the sculptor Aristokles known to have lived in the late sixth century, then Kleoitas and his innovation existed in the early fifth century (Frazer, 3:635).

The shift from dolphin to eagle announced the imminent beginning of the race. The starting gate addressed the problem of fairness in negotiating the first turn. The farther out from the center a chariot began, the farther it had to go in cutting toward the center for the turn to the left around the marker. By releasing the outer teams first and moving successively inward, the mechanism handicapped the inner teams, especially the final two which had the most direct course to the turn, since they were held to a slower start. The prow itself forced drivers to stay in their lane. Streipsiades' horse-mad son, Pheidippides, cries out in his sleep at Philon who was fouling, "Drive your own lane" (Aristophanes *Clouds* 25). At a point, perhaps signaled by a trumpet blast, the teams began to break toward the turn (Harris 1972,169), and the race got underway. From here on, it was a matter of human skill and animal speed. Charioteers driving mature horses faced twelve laps and twenty-two turns around the turning posts, while those with colts had to survive eight laps and fourteen turns for a chance at victory (Scholiast on Pindar *Olympian Ode* 3.59, in Drachmann, 1:122). The winner in 460 was the only chariot to last the race, offering clear testimony that getting a chariot around a turn had lost none of its peril since Homeric times.

The considerable skills of the charioteers and jockeys, the latter often boys riding bareback (Yalouris 233, Ill. 134), provided the competition and excitement of the race. Winning charioteers and riders were bound with fillets of wool by the owners of the horses (Thucydides *Histories* 5.50.4; Pausanias 6.2.2). Women, otherwise barred from Olympia during the games, could own, train, and enter teams. During the early fourth century, Kyniska [373, 381], daughter of the Spartan king Archidamos, was the first to win at Olympia (Pausanias 3.8.1, 6.1.6). The victorious owners, like every victor in the games, received a palm, placed in their right hand at the conclusion of the race after any challenge had been satisfied (Pausanias 8.48.2). Symbolizing victory, it was conferred upon the owners and their horses because both were the competitors. For this reason, the owner of Aura who threw her rider and finished first was declared victor (Pausanias 6.13.9).

In the afternoon of the second day, human strength and endurance came to the fore as the pentathlon tested the skills of men in a series of zero-sum, winner-take-all, competitions.

Pentathlon

The contest in pentathlon consisted of five events: discus, jump, javelin, a run assumed to be a *stadion* in length, and wrestling. Homer's warrior athletes compete in all these activities except the broad jump, and his Phaeacians jump (*Odyssey* 8.128), but there is no trace of an organized pentathlon in the epics. The contest was introduced to the Olympic program for men in the eighteenth Olympiad (708) and for boys in the thirty-eighth festival (628) (Pausanias 5.8.7). The boys' contest was immediately dropped after a Lacedaemonian youth, Eutelidas, won the wiild olve (Pausanias 5.9.1). Simonides, the earliest source, gives the order of the five events as jump, run, discus, javelin, wrestling, where the run is indicated by a metaphor, "swift-foot" (fr. 42, in Page, 262). Eustathius reproduces a different but commonly accepted order: "leap of feet, throw of discus, hurl of javelin, run, wrestling" (4:1320.18–19). The discus, jump, and javelin are the characteristic events of the contest, since they were held at athletic festivals only in pentathlon (Illustrations 24 and 25).

Discus

Diskos is often translated quoit, erroneously, since a quoit is a ring and the discus a solid disk thicker at the center than at the perimeter. Greeks first shaped discuses of stone and, by the fifth century, they were using bronze. One lead discus remains, found in Olympia (Gardiner 1907, 7). Lucian's Solon describes the discus for Anacharsis as "made of bronze, circular, like a small shield but not having a handle or straps. You tested it, since it lay there, and it seemed to you heavy and hard to

Illustration 24. Events of the pentathlon. Attic black-figure lekythos, sixth century B.C.E. The Metropolitan Museum of Art, New York, New York.

Illustration 25. Events of the pentathlon. Attic black-figure lekythos, sixth century B.C.E. The Metropolitan Museum of Art, New York, New York.

hold on to because of its smoothness" (*Anacharsis* 27). Solon goes on to say that the Greeks threw the discus for height and distance. Distance alone counted for the games. Pindar speaks of "discuses of stone" (*Isthmian Ode* 1.25), as befits the mythic times of first beginnings, and recalls that at Herakles' founding of the Olympic games:

> With a rock, Nekeus drove round his hand
> and hurled a distance beyond all (*Olympian Ode* 10.72).

Extant discuses vary in size from 6.5 to 13.5 inches in diameter and between 3 and 15 pounds in weight. Those of stone were likely votive offerings; most of the bronze discuses were used in the games.

Pausanias repeats a story he heard about the discovery of Ajax's bones that suggests boys did not throw the same discus as men. To convey its size, his informant compared Ajax's kneecap to "a boy's discus in the pentathlon" (1.35.5). At some point, the Eleans attained consistency in their pentathlon by using the same three discuses which they stored in the treasury of the Sikyonians (Pausanias 6.19.4). But Greek emphasis on the moment precluded notions of uniformity even if they had had an institution to impose it. Without such standards, how far Greeks threw the discus cannot be ascertained. Still, when "Phaÿllos leaped fifty plus five feet / and hurled the discus one hundred minus five" (Scholiast on Aristophanes *Acharnians* 214, in Dübner, 9), his cast must have been an outstanding performance. Mike Powell's modern world record of 29 feet, 4.5 inches pales before a leap of 55 feet, but Phaÿllos surely leaped so prodigiously only in words. On the other hand, his throw seems less spectacular and even mediocre compared to modern records.

In describing a picture of Hyacinthus' death by a discus, Philostratos gives what many believe the clearest literary account of how Greeks threw the discus (*Pictures in a Gallery* 1.24, in Kayser, 328). The first words of the received text, "a *balbis* has been heaped up" (*diakechôstai*), indicate that Greek athletes threw the discus from a raised platform. Out of respect for Philostratos, modern Greeks trained in this technique, and Pierre de Coubertin and the other founders of the modern Olympic movement adopted it for their first international games of 1896. Young recounts the results:

> The main foreign discus contender was Robert Garrett of Sloane's Princeton group. In America he had decided against entering the discus, since it was so unfamiliar to him. But in Athens he changed his mind and consulted Coubertin. Coubertin encouraged him to enter, so Garrett took his throws. He had never practiced the discus before,

according to all reports. Yet the Greek throwers were hampered by their training in a compulsory style, which Greek coaches had determined by depending on an unreliable ancient author, who misinterpreted Myron's famous ancient statue, the Discobolus. Greeks felt constrained to keep their feet planted in a particular way—almost like a statue—without using the shifting weight of the body to add impetus and centrifugal force. They threw mostly with the arm. Paraskevopoulos was leading when Garrett made his last throw, modifying the style to take better advantage of the leverage of the legs and body. Greeks began to celebrate as the event concluded, not knowing that Garrett had barely beaten Paraskevopoulos, 29.150 meters to 28.995. As the American flag went up for the second time, the mainly Greek crowd at first murmured in disbelief. But when they saw it was true, they gave Garrett a generous and roaring cheer of congratulation (1996, 147).

Philostratos, as Young points out, does not describe the movement of an athlete but rather that of the Discobolus or Discus Thrower, a bronze statue (Illustration 26) by the sculptor Myron (ca. 480–455) which survives in a Roman marble copy and on engraved gems. It captures the moment when the athlete is about to rise up for the release. Although Philostratos is not always a reliable source, in this instance it was the manuscript tradition that failed him by handing down *diakechôstai* for something like *diakechôristai* (has been marked off). With the first sentence emended, his text reads as follows:

> A starting line [*balbis*] has been marked off, small and accommodating only one standing man, except in the rear. The *balbis* supports his right leg. The upper body is bent forward, taking the weight of the left leg which must be thrown upward and go along with his right side. The posture of the man holding the discus must be this: he turns his head far to the right and bends the body so as to see his ribs and to throw upward as if drawing water and throwing with his whole right side. Apollo also threw the discus in this manner, for he could do so in no other way (*Pictures in a Gallery* 1.24, in Kayser, 328).

It is interesting to note that Philostratos' acceptance of the anthropomorphic qualities of the god Apollo confines to the limitations of the human body a deity strong enough to throw any weight with a fillip.

The event was held in the stadium and used a *balbis*, the starting line for the running contests, as the forward foul line (Gardiner 1907, 9–11). A low barrier confined the athlete on the sides; the back of the enclosure was left open (Harris 1961, 5). This throwing area was located in the middle of the stadium away from the crowds seated or standing along the sides of the stadium, insuring their safety from an errant throw

Illustration 26. Coiled for the delivery. Copy of the Discobolus by Myron, mid-fifth century B.C.E. Museo Nationale Romano, Rome, Italy.

such as killed Hyacinthus (Apollodorus *The Library* 1.3.3) or from an unseen flying discus such as killed Akrisios (2.4.4).

In the Greek style for a right-handed athlete, the thrower began, as does Statius' Phlegyas, by rubbing his hand and the discus with sand (*Thebaid* 6.670–671). He assumed a position facing the *balbis* and the stadium beyond it in which the discus had to land for the throw to be valid. His arms were extended before him with the discus in his right hand. The left steadied it and kept it snug against the right. His left leg was forward of the right which bore his weight, counterbalancing the discus (Illustration 25). With the discus in his right hand, he swung his arms up and down before him. The motion imparted the feel of the discus: "Phlegyas, knocking off the dust, turns the discus to see which side fits his fingers and which side fits more securely in the middle of his lower arm" (Statius *Thebaid* 6.671–672). It also generated centrifugal force that helped to drive the discus into his hand, reducing the desire to grip it. He wound the discus by turning his torso to the right. His throwing hand rotated so that the discus was held from above by his fingers over the rim and by the motion of his arm. He shifted his weight onto the toes of his right foot. At the same time, the left foot pivoted toward the right. Both feet remained in nearly constant contact with the ground. He continued the wind until his arm and the discus were fully outstretched behind his back. As he moved his arm, he bent his torso further to the right and at the waist and his knees toward the ground. His head turned backward with his body, allowing him to see his ribs. In the stance immobilized by Myron's Discobolus, he was now coiled for the delivery phase (Illustration 26).

The throwing technique did not involve the rotations of the modern athlete who spins through a 630–degree turn, but literary sources agree that the Greek athlete turned his body in throwing the discus:

> Brilliant Epeios took the lump
> and, whirling, set it forth (*Iliad* 23.839–840);
>
> Odysseus turned around and sent the discus from his stout hand,
> and the stone whistled (*Odyssey* 8.189–190);
>
> Phlegyas, confident in his technique, measured not
> the bristly acres of the plain but the sky. He bent
> each knee to the ground and, collecting his strength,
> he rotated and plunged the discus into the clouds.
> . . . .
> Phlegyas was already preparing a mighty throw,
> his neck already turned, and already his whole side was moving back:
> the weight slipped and fell before his feet (Statius *Thebaid* 6.678–681, 693–695);
>
> Do you mean the discus thrower, the one bent in the position of release, turned from the front toward the hand bearing the discus, crouching slightly with the other, like someone rising up with the throw? (Lucian *Lover of Lies* 18).

In delivery, the discus was unwound by being pulled around in a wide arc and accelerated by the rotation of body and right arm. The wider the arc, the more force generated. Long fingers and arms, both common attributes of the tall man Philostratus recommends for pentathlon, were an asset:

> The man competing in the five events should be heavy rather than light but not too heavy. He should be tall, well built, erect, not

excessively muscular but not stunted. He should have legs proportionally longer than the rest of his body. He should be fluid and limber because of the backward bending for the javelin and also the discus and because of the bending for the jump. He will jump with less pain and chance of injury if in letting down his hips, he supports them with his footing. He must have long hands and fingers, for he will throw the discus far better if, because of the size of his fingers, the edge of the discus is sent forth from a hollower hand, and the javelin will move more easily if the fingers, by not being short, touch the thong on its top surface (*Gymnastic* 31, in Kayser, 277).

The left arm guided the thrower through the arc as he turned clockwise to face the stadium. He shifted his weight forward and pivoted on his left foot. He cast his right side into the throw as he projected the discus upward. The discus rolled off his fingers, free of drag by being pressed against the palm—Philostratos' "hollower hand"—which caused it to spin and make the humming noise the Phaeacians heard from Odysseus' throw. The athlete's left arm, outstretched to the left, helped maintain balance. His was a flowing and seamless movement executed to the tempo of the orgiastic *aulos* that kept the timing for choruses in tragedies at the Festival of the City Dionysia. "It is more than likely that the discus thrower attempted to achieve almost a dance movement" (Swaddling, 52).

The use of the *aulos* in athletics makes "an obvious but unacknowledged link between the military and athletic activities of hoplites" who may be imagined "as adapting this music to the athletic field for comparable purposes of spiritual elevation and timing" (Raschke, 179). Philostratos (*Gymnastic* 55, in Kayser, 291) and Pausanias, who accounts for the *aulos* at the jump by the sacredness of the *aulos* song to Apollo, a repeated winner at Olympia (5.7.10), hint that the *aulos* attended only the jump, but the evidence of vases leaves no doubt that it was used throughout the triad in the pentathlon (Raschke, 185–186). A good *aulos* player was in demand. Pythokritos played for the pentathlon at six Olympic Games, and he or his kinsmen inscribed a stele to mark his achievement (Pausanias 6.14.10).

Jump

The jump in pentathlon was a broad jump following a short, powerful run. The pentathlete hit the take-off mark of stone or wood with his foot and threw himself into the air over a pit of loosened sand in the stadium. Athletes themselves dug up the pit to a suitable and safe depth; the inscription from Rhodes orders a depth of two feet (Bean 368). The sand was soft enough to receive the impression left by the feet on landing. Distance was measured by wooden rods, and pegs set in the sand recorded the jumps. A black-figure amphora of the mid-sixth century shows an athlete coming down ahead of three pegs (Illustration 27). The jumper is aided by an *aulos* player (Plutarch *Moralia* 1140D) and by the jumping weights or *halteres* that he grips (Illustrations 24 and 25). Philostratos explains the presence of both as a consequence of the difficulty of executing the jump:

> The jumping weight is an invention of the pentathletes and was invented for the jump from which it also takes its name. The rules acknowledge that the jump is more difficult than the other events in

Illustration 27. Jumping beyond the pegs. Attic black-figure neck amphora, ca. 575 B.C.E. © The British Museum, London, England

the contest by spurring the jumper with the *aulos* and further lightening the jumper with the jumping weight. The weight is a sure guide for the hands and leads him to the ground with a sure and well-marked impression. The rules make clear how important this is, for they do not measure the jump unless it has created a sharp impression (*Gymnastic* 55, in Kayser, 291).

The jumping weights were of lead or stone and came in various weights from 2.5 to 10 pounds. They were shaped or cut out for ease of grip. Pausanias describes the *halteres* held by a statue of Contest: "They are half of a circle, oval in shape, not a perfect circle, and have been so made that the fingers go through them as through the handle of a shield" (5.26.3). For Aristotle, "the pentathletes jump farther by holding the *halteres* than if they were not to do so, and runners run faster by swinging their arms, for in the extension of the arms a resistance builds against the hands and wrists" (*Progression of Animals* 705a 13–19). Aristotle believed that the *halteres* did not pull the athlete through the air with the momentum of their weight but moved the athlete by his pushing them off with his hands and wrists.

Literary sources have little to say about the jump. Commentators and scholiasts from the Roman period and later were fascinated by the expression "beyond the dug-up pit" found in Plato's *Cratylus*: "I ask questions longer than is fitting and jump beyond the dug-up pit" (413A), and in Lucian's dialogue *The Dream, or The Cock*. A cock addresses Mikullos whom he has aroused from dreaming with his crowing:

> By Herakles! You are talking about some special dream if, being winged, as they say, and having sleep as the limit of its flight, it leaps now beyond the dug-up pit and lingers in eyes that are open, being so honey-sweet and visible (6).

"Beyond the dug-up pit" became proverbial for accomplishing something extraordinary, a meaning that gave way to perpetrating something excessive, but critical fascination with it preempted serious discussion of the jump itself. Ancient scholars, the earliest of whom, Zenobios, lived in the early second century C.E., associated the expression with Phaÿllos' extraordinary fifty-five-foot leap (*Epitome* 6.23). Pausanias mentions Phaÿllos' victories at the Pythian Games, one in pentathlon and two in *stadion*, and his captaincy of a ship against the Persians and concludes that "this is all there is to the Krotonian athlete" (10.9.1). He omits the jump either because he did not know the story, or he did and dismissed it summarily. Scholars, however, have attempted to save the phenomenon by proposing that the jump consisted of two steps and a jump, but their theories collapse before Gardiner's battery of objections, among them, the difficulty of jumping on sand while holding *halteres* and the flippancy of the epigram with its arithmetical games (1904, 74–80). In accord with the shift in the meaning of the proverb, Phaÿllos' leap beyond measure brought him down on the hard surface beyond the pit where he broke his leg, his comeuppance for overdoing things (*Suda* 364, in Adler).

The jump begins with the athlete erect, his arms extended before him and *halteres* in his hands. One leg is advanced, and he leans back slightly to offset the weights. The smooth transition with the weights provides the thrust for the jump. The run is short but vigorous. At the takeoff, the jumper swings the weights up and down. Hitting the mark, he propels himself upward off one foot. As he ascends, he lifts the weights and holds them forward with his arms bent. At the same time, he folds his legs, calves against thighs. Reaching the apex, he extends the weights and his legs fully until his arms and legs are parallel. Shoving the *halteres* and legs forward pulls him forward. On the descent, he swings the weights down and toward his back, releasing them just before landing. He touches down with a firm impression of his feet, and the jump counts. But should he end indecorously on his knees or buttocks, he faults. As Gardiner says, "The Greek paid more attention to style than to records" (1980, 149).

Javelin

Like the jump and discus, the javelin event probably took place in the stadium and used a *balbis* as the foul line. The thrower executed his movements to the tempo of the *aulos*. For a throw to be valid, the javelin had to land inside the stadium. Had Greeks played baseball, out of respect for measure, they would not have had the home run:

> And I . . .
> . . . do hope
> not to cast wide of the course
> the bronze-cheeked javelin I whirl in my hand, but to throw it far
>   and beat out my rivals (Pindar *Pythian Ode* 1.42–45).

How many attempts were permitted is not known. Athletes have two or three javelins in vase paintings, a possible correlation with the number of throws allowed. Nor is it certain whether the javelin had to land on its point for a valid throw or how the throw itself was measured.

The javelin thrown in pentathlon was about as long as the thrower's height and roughly an inch in diameter. It was made of wood; Bacchylides specifies cornel (*Ode* 9.34). Other woods may have been used, provided they were light. The javelin, thrown for distance rather than for the accuracy and penetration of the war lance, was affected by the wind (Lucian *Anacharsis* 32) and, therefore, had to be light in weight. Pindar twice describes it as "bronze-cheeked" (*Nemean Ode* 7.71; *Pythian Ode* 1.44), implying that it was tipped with a bronze point. However, unless painters arbitrarily ignored the metal tips, javelins were not tipped in bronze. The vases show scenes, many of them practice sessions in the *gymnasion*, with athletes carrying or throwing a javelin that is blunted at the forward end (Yalouris, 199 Ill. 102). For competitions, the javelin was tapered to a point like the one the thrower on a red-figure cup is about to launch from behind the pillar marking the foul line (Yalouris, 199 Ill. 103).

The Greeks threw the javelin with the aid of a leather thong adopted from the military lance. The thong was attached near the shaft's center of gravity and formed into a loop of a size to impart tension and easy grip on the javelin. The thrower inserted his index or first two fingers into the loop in various ways (Gardiner 1980, 171). The device added to the leverage of the thrower's arm. The longer his fingers, the greater its effects (Philostratos *Gymnastic* 31, in Kayser, 277). Whether the thong was permanently attached or coiled around the shaft and secured with a hitch knot is uncertain. Both methods probably had their advocates. Harris finds marginal support for the free thong in vases depicting an athlete pushing the shaft "back with the left hand against the pull of the loop in the right" (1964, 95, Plate 11*b*). A fixed loop, he points out, would be tightened by the weight of the javelin as the hand draws back for the throw. The thong added distance to a throw or, with it coiled, spin that improved accuracy. Experiments with a modern javelin have proved that the javelin with a thong went farther and landed more consistently on its point than the javelin without a thong but cast doubt on the thong's effectiveness to add considerable distance or distance and spin on the same throw (Harris 1964, 93–95). In pentathlon, accuracy could be sacrificed in quest of distance as long as the javelin landed within bounds. If the javelin needed to land on its point for the throw to be valid, the worth of a thong is apparent.

Unlike the technique in jump and discus, that of the javelin closely resembles modern mechanics. The thrower approaches the *balbis*, the

Illustration 28. Casting the javelin. Red-figure amphora, ca. 500 B.C.E. Vase A Tf.204, 1f. Courtesy of Staatlich Antikensammulungen und Glyptothek, Munich, Germany.

same start/finish line used as a foul line in the discus, at a quick, short run. He aims at transferring the energy of the run smoothly through his rotating body into his arm and the throw. He keeps the javelin at a level with his ear, because this promotes better eye-hand coordination (Brown, Webb, and Sing, 252). A red-figure amphora (ca. 500) shows an athlete running with his javelin held in this position (Illustration 28). The transition begins for a right-handed thrower on the fall of his left foot at a point near the *balbis* but not near enough to induce a foul after release. His shoulders and head turn to the right, and his right arm is extended, drawing the javelin back behind him. He stretches his left arm forward to maintain balance. As he steps closer, trying not to decelerate, he rotates his arm so that the javelin rests in the palm of his hand, and the fingers hold on to the strap. Landing on his left leg, he rotates his right hip in the direction of the throw. The throw begins from this thrust and builds upward through his trunk to the arm that pulls the javelin from behind and whips it at full extension toward a point down the stadium. He releases the javelin at an angle of about thirty-five degrees from level for maximum distance.

Harris judges that a skilled athlete could throw a javelin with a thong "well over 300 feet" (196, 97). This is somewhat longer than the modern Olympic record of 89.66 meters or 294.16 feet. The ancient javelin was lighter than its modern counterpart, and the thrower benefited from the additional leverage from the thong.

The Sequence of Events in Pentathlon

The run has been considered the first event on the basis of Artemidorus' listing it first in his interpretation of dreams about the pentathlon (*Interpretation of Dreams* 1.57). Xenophon's account of the Eleans' attack in 364 securely places it before wrestling and thus as the fourth event, at least in that year:

> The Arcadians did not think that the Eleans would attack them, and, with the Pisatans, celebrated the festival themselves. They had already conducted the horse races and the running event of the pentathlon, and those who had reached the wrestling were no longer in the running track but were wrestling between the running track and the altar (*Hellenica* 7.4.29).

A fragmentary inscription from Rhodes (first century ?) rules out the run as the first event (Moretti 1956, 55; Bean, 368). In stating the rules for judges in charge of the pentathlon, the inscription indicates that in the first event athletes did something five times; that something could not have been the run. The Rhodians, it may be objected, did not set the pattern for all Greeks, some of whom may have begun the pentathlon with the run. This element of individuality cannot be discounted and in most cases escapes notice. Still, like other rituals, Greek athletics resisted change, with continuity reinforced by the period games and their imitators.

In an image of a losing javelin throw, Pindar implies that the javelin was fourth in his day, immediately preceding wrestling:

> O Sogenes from Euxenid fathers, I swear
> that I did not advance to the line and hurl my swift tongue
> like a bronze-cheeked javelin that keeps the neck

and strength from the wrestling, unsweated,
    before the limb was exposed to the blazing sun
(*Nemean Ode* 7.70–73).

Pindar assures Sogenes, winner of boys' pentathlon at Nemea (485?) and recipient of his ode, that he is a victor in his event, to wit, poetry, as Sogenes was in his, the javelin (Segal 1968, 45). The poet claims that he came up to the *terma* or starting line (see Lee, 1976) and sang on key, not like a losing thrower who hurled his javelin short, lost the event, and failed consequently to reach wrestling, so that he did not get the opportunity to wrestle in the heat of the Olympian summer (Segal 1968, 38–39). In other words, Pindar sends forth a winning throw with his song and is in quest of victory to the very end. Sogenes survived the preliminaries to win the pentathlon. He appears to have done so by winning the javelin and, reaching the wrestling, prevailing to win that contest. As Charles Segal notes, "it would be helpful, though not absolutely necessary, if the javelin contest came fourth, immediately before the wrestling" (39). Indeed, Gardiner places it fourth (1980, 177).

Bacchylides' phrase, "quick motion of final wrestling" (*Ode* 9.36), confirms that wrestling was the fifth and last event of the pentathlon. Teisamenos' experience in the pentathlon at the Olympic Games corroborates this position in the order. The Pythian priestess of Apollo's oracle at Delphi foretold to Teisamenos that he would win "five most glorious contests" (Pausanias 3.11.6). She means military victories, but Teisamenos assumes athletic ones. Three wins were essential for victory in pentathlon:

> After training in pentathlon for the Olympic Games, Tisamenos [*sic*] departed from there defeated, although he was first in two events. He overcame Hieronymos [173 ?] in the run and jump, but, thrown by Hieronymos in wrestling, he fell short of victory (3.11.6).

Over six hundred years before Pausanias, Herodotus told the same story:

> Teisamenos trained in pentathlon and, on entering the match with Hieronymos of Andros, came within one *palaisma* of winning the Olympic victory (*Histories* 9.33.2).

Teisamenos won in run and jump and Hieronymos in discus and javelin. Wrestling was the play-off to determine the victor. Whether *palaisma* is translated wrestling contest or fall does not matter in the sense that a match or a fall in the match brought final victory. Teisamenos came within one event, wrestling, or one fall in wrestling, from winning. A nail-biter results from translating *palaisma* as "fall." Each wrestler has scored two falls on his opponent, and everything has come down to the third fall. Yet wrestling as a play-off need not have had the same rules as the independent event, and one fall instead of three of five could have determined a winner. On balance, though, Greek conservatism attenuates such a solution. Pentathlon, with many entrants who repeated attempts in the jump and throws and with much organizational business, took time to complete. A preliminary and final in wrestling, each going to the fifth fall, could be lengthy. At the seventy-seventh Olympiad (472), it was primarily responsible for delaying the start of the horse races and *pankration* (Pausanias 5.9.3). Rather than changing its makeup, the Eleans responded by shifting pentathlon to an earlier day.

Determining the Winner of Pentathlon

The pentathlete who won three events was declared victor. Frequent comment on this testifies to its significance. The Scholiast to Aristeides' *Panathenaïkos* 3.339 states that "The pentathletes do not win completely, but it suffices for them to win three of the five" (in Bean, 361), and Pollux, a rhetorician living in the second century CE, cites a technical term for winning the pentathlon, *apotriazein*, based on the root for three (*tria-*): "they say that in pentathlon to win is 'to do the three completely'" (*Onomasticon* 3.151, in Bethe 1.201). A Scholiast on Aeschylus' *Agamemnon* 171 uses the same expression when he glosses the word *triaktêr* with "a victor from a metaphor of those who do the three completely [*apotriazontôn*] in the pentathlon" (in Fraenkel, 2:104). Finally, inscriptions speak of boys' pentathlon having been won "in the first triad" (Moretti 1953, Inscription 82).

The most vexed question in the study of ancient Greek athletics, how to determine the winner in pentathlon, is a modern problem. Greeks knew the procedure so well that apparently none cared to write it down. Two basic approaches have been taken: a progressive elimination in the triad that narrows the field to a maximum of three competitors, or systems that seek an overall winner through comparative victories, partial eliminations, and/or calculations of relative standings. Gardiner (1903) and George E. Bean review these systems and propose their own which, like all these proposals, are unduly complicated. Promoters of the second approach seek an outcome that reflects the athletes' ability in the combination of five events. Their goal is a system that allows overall performance to command the crown. They find support in the notion, expressed by the Greeks themselves, that pentathletes are jacks-of-all-events and masters of none:

> You seem to me to say what sort of men pentathletes are in the contest in comparison with runners and wrestlers. Pentathletes, inferior to those athletes in their events, are second to them, but in comparison with the rest of the athletes, they are first, and defeat them ([Plato], *Lovers* 135E);

and in the praise that pentathletes receive for their well-rounded athleticism:

> Beauty is a different thing at each stage of life. The beauty of a young man resides in a body useful for the toils of running races and deeds of brawn, a thing sweet to look upon for enjoyment. For this reason, pentathletes are the most beautiful because they are fit by nature for brawn and speed (Aristotle *Rhetoric* 1.5.11).

This dichotomy between generalists and specialists was applied to those in other endeavors who did not specialize or who consistently came in second. The philosopher Democritus is compared to a pentathlete because he was expert in several different areas, physics, ethics, mathematics, "common subjects," and the arts (Diogenes Laertius, *Lives of Eminent Philosophers* 9.37). Eratosthenes was dubbed Beta and Pentathlete because he was second-rate or second after the best (*Suda* s.v. *Eratosthenes,* in Adler 2.403).

A formidable influence in generating systems has been Philostratos' myth of the origin of pentathlon:

> Pentathlon is a combination of two kinds of events; wrestling and discus throwing are heavy, and javelin throwing, jumping, and running are light. Before Jason and Peleus, jump and discus were crowned separately, and the javelin was sufficient for victory at the time when the Argo sailed. Telamon was best with the discus, and Lygkeus with javelin. Peleus was second in both but surpassed all in wrestling. When they were holding contests in Lemnos, they say that Jason, to please Peleus, combined the five events, and Peleus in this way gathered the victory and was considered the most warlike of men because of the valor that he displayed in the battles and because

his training in the five was warlike, since he was throwing the javelin
in the contests (*Gymnastic* 3, in Kayser, 262–263).

Scholars have been uncommonly intrigued that Peleus was declared "most
warlike" because of his overall performance. The notion of overall
performance accords with modern scoring systems in multi-event contests
like decathlon "in which it doesn't really matter if the athlete finishes
first, third, or worse in a particular event. The score is the thing"
(Zarnowski, 3). One would be hard-pressed to find a trace of this outlook
among Greeks who normally ignored second-place finishers. When the
Athenians rewarded losers in the Panathenaea, it was to promote their
festival. Having the resources to suspend the zero-sum system, they
lavished amphoras of oil to draw athletes to the contests. As damaging
as the zero-sum mentality is to theories of overall performance, even
more so are the variation and complexity of the solutions themselves
that require of the judges in the heat of the moment certainty in the order
of finishers and in the calculations of relative standings. This smacks of
too much pencil and paper for Greeks who did not keep records of times
and distances (Bean, 363). The man who bested all in the event that
day was the winner—a clean and simple, elegant method.

Moreover, unlike its modern counterpart, the ancient pentathlon was
never intended to seek an overall winner, someone skilled in all five
events, if, as Kyle suggests, "when the event was introduced in 708
B.C. the run and wrestling were added to the three peculiar events for
the purpose of determining the best man of the possible winners from
the first three events" (1990, 299). The contest highlighted superior skill
in three separate and different activities, jump, discus, and javelin, while
running and wrestling served as a mechanism to ascertain a victor in the
case that no one swept the triad. An athlete especially good in the *stadion*
or wrestling would have an advantage only if he could survive the triad,
and, given the different skills needed by the first three events, practice
for them must have detracted from training in running and wrestling.
The ubiquity of wrestling insured that any athlete competitive in
pentathlon could wrestle well. Hugh M. Lee goes so far as to contend
that "The man who won the final event, the wrestling, was victor for the
entire pentathlon competition. Qualification for the wrestling was
determined by success in at least one of the four preceding events"
(1976, 70). Surely, this reduces the pentathlon to a glorified wrestling
match. The contest was about the triad, and any method for calculating
its winner that does not require a victory in at least one triad event must
be rejected (Harris 1972, 33).

Bean (364) finds confirmation for the quest for superiority in a curious topic in Plutarch's treatise *Questions at a Symposium* which is included among the *Moralia*:

> In three aspects, just as the athletes in pentathlon, alpha is superior and wins over the many 1) by being a vowel, and over vowels, 2) by having two quantities, long and short, and being over vowels with two quantities, 3) by never being second or following them (738A).

Unlike iota and upsilon that are second in the diphthongs oi and ou, alpha is always first in ai and au. Bean explains how alpha is superior to its rivals in the alphabet in the same way that superiority is determined in the pentathlon:

> the superiority described is not just a simple superiority in three respects: the 24 competitors are successively reduced in three stages as in the pentathlon, first to the seven vowels (as by the "first triad"), then to those which have two quantities (as by the foot-race), and finally to the letter A (as by the wrestling) (364).

Harris proposes a very attractive method of progressive elimination in three scenarios, each more complicated and speculative than the one before (1972, 34–35). The procedure for the first three events is the same in all the scenarios. In the first event, one man throws the discus the farthest; he is the victor and cannot be eliminated by losses in the next two events. The others, no matter how many, are losers in that event. All may enter the second event, the jump. The one who jumps the farthest is declared victor. Again, all other competitors are losers. In the third, all who wish enter, and the man who hurls the javelin the farthest wins; everyone else loses.

In Harris's first scenario, the same competitor wins the first three events, and the pentathlon has been decided. The second scenario has two men emerge from the triad, for a victor in one event is not eliminated despite losses in the other two. One man has two victories, and the other, one. The two winners alone stand for the run, and should the man with two victories win the run, the contest is over. If not, they move to the wrestling where, with three falls out of five, one gains the third and decisive victory. Automedes' victory came this way. He lost the jump and run but, winning in discus, javelin, and wrestling, he triumphed:

> To Automedes now victorious,
> the triennial garland the god gave.
> In pentathlon he stood out conspicuous
> as the brilliant moon in the night

at mid-month outshines the light of the stars.
Such a man throughout the boundless assembly
of Greeks did he appear in his marvelous physique.
Hurling the round discus
and sending forth the branch of dark-leaved
elder from his hand through the lofty sky,
or in the quick motion of final wrestling,
he roused the host to cheering (Bacchylides *Ode* 9.25–36).

Three men, each with one victory, have reached the run in the third scenario, surely a common occurrence. The run gives one athlete a second victory as the three head into the wrestling. How to reduce three to a pair for the final wrestling?—the vexing problem at the heart of the vexed question. Harris proposes a preliminary wrestling match with the winner of the run having a bye:

> If after the triad there were three athletes with one win each, these three ran the race. One of them, A, now had two wins, while B and C still had one each. B and C now wrestled in a semi-final; in virtue of his two wins, A was given a bye and sat by as *ephedros*. He then wrestled with the winner of the semi-final, who now also had two wins, and the winner of this bout was the victor of the whole event (1972, 34–35).

Despite the lack of evidentiary support, the third scenario demands a semi-final.

Commonplace in wrestling were several rounds with byes given in case of an odd number of competitors; the *ephedros* received the bye and thus sat out a match waiting to meet its winner (Poliakoff 1987, 21–22). Wrestling was the quintessential Greek athletic contest in pitting two men against one another in a tight embrace that demanded physical strength (*bia*) and cunning (*mêtis*). In fact, the sheer ordinariness of a preliminary match in wrestling may account for the silence of sources. Kyle advances another run as the preliminary. With everything in place, a second run would be easy to mount and leave the winner fresher for the final in wrestling than would a preliminary match in wrestling. "The man with two wins in a sense had earned a bye but having him face an already tired opponent would make for a one-sided final and poor spectator sport" (Kyle 1990, 303). That more *stadion* runners are known to have won the pentathlon than winners in heavy events favors a second run (Golden, 72). Yet the events of the triad called for brief explosions of effort that in no way corresponded to the continuous drain of the opening rounds in wrestling where any unfairness in the bye was tolerated. Kyle's appeal to spectator interest, however, introduces into hidebound athletics a desire not elsewhere evinced. Greek athletics were driven by the belief that the man who defeats all his competitors is the best man. Today, a sanctioned fight between a lightweight and a heavyweight is impossible because of modern weight classes, but such a spectacle would not displease the Greeks who wanted to see the best man, not necessarily the best fight. Otherwise, they would not have permitted bruisers to dominate and skew the athleticism of wrestling, boxing, and *pankration*.

In the evening of the second day, victors and their friends celebrated by donning garlands and cruising about the Altis singing songs of triumph. They feasted and drank much wine. The full moon lighted their carousing as well as the rituals for Pelops in his sanctuary. As befitted a chthonic hero, the Eleans sacrificed a black ram, an offering of blood to appease his spirit (Pausanias 5.13.2; Pindar *Olympian Ode* 1.90).

Under the rising sun of the third day, Eleans, members of the official delegations from the *poleis*, and others formed themselves into a procession. Setting forth perhaps from the Prytaneion outside the Altis, the procession escorted victims, at least a hundred bulls for the hecatomb, to a god's altar. It followed the processional road along the western and southern walls of the sanctuary. The participants wore festive clothing and had bedecked themselves with garlands and fillets. Specific individuals carried the instruments and paraphernalia needed for the sacrifice. It was imperative that the animals walk calmly. Any disturbance or balking could be interpreted as unwillingness to offer themselves, a recalcitrance that could corrupt the ceremony and endanger the participants. They entered the Altis at its southwestern corner (Pausanias 5.15.2, 6.20.7; Heberdey) and wended their path through the sanctuary, arriving at Zeus's altar. Elean priests sacrificed the bulls and carried their thighs to the top of the ashen altar for burning. There, the ashes, mixed with water from the Alpheios, were smeared on the mound, a visible monument to the worshipers' piety (Pausanias 5.13.9–11). After the ceremony, the celebrants offered sacrifices and prayers of their own and made merry, while slave crews of butchers, cooks, and their helpers cut up the meat and vegetables and prepared the stews and soups for the grand feast to be held that night in the Prytaneion. Given the scarcity of water in the sanctuary, the roaring fires under the Olympic sun, and the hordes of flies spawned by "the hot climate and the low damp situation" (Frazer, 3:558) at Olympia, this was unpleasant work.

The morning of the fourth day was spent in the stadium where the boys' events were held and, at their conclusion, men's running events. In the afternoon, men were called for the heavy events, wrestling, boxing, and *pankration*. The athletic program closed with the hoplite race, a sign that the Olympic truce was drawing to an end.

Glorious Day, Day of Glory

For an experience burned into the memory of every Olympic victor, that moment when he received his crown of wild olive (Illustration 27) has left few traces in the tradition. The ceremony took place before the temple of Zeus where the athletes and Hellanodikai had gathered before the assembly. Many spectators probably were already contending with the crowds leaving the sanctuary, but many others, including the members of the official delegations, remained to witness the final act of the festival. Branches had been cut from Zeus's sacred olive that stood behind his temple, by a boy with living parents (Pausanias 5.15.3; Scholiast on Pindar *Olympian Ode* 3.60, in Drachmann 1:122). The wreathes were laid out on a tripod covered with bronze (Pausanias 5.12.5) and later,

Illustration 29. Victor is crowned. Attic black-figure amphora of Panathenaic shape. Vase B 138. © The British Museum, London, England.

perhaps during the time Pheidias was working at Olympia, on a table of gold and ivory made by his student Kolotes (5.20.2). The herald called out the victor's name, his city, and his father's name, and the Hellanodikes placed the crown of olive on his head. Before Zeus who wore the crown of his victory over Cronus, the athlete became an Olympic champion, and the smell of sweat began to fade, to be replaced over the years by the glow of youthful glory remembered.

Bibliography

Adkins, Arthur W. H. 1960. *Merit and Responsibility*: *A Study in Greek Values*. Oxford: Oxford University Press.

Adler, Ada, ed. 1967–1971. *Suidae Lexicon*. Stuttgart: B. G. Teubner.

Alexandris, O. 1968. The Topography of Athens. *Athens Annals of Archaeology* 2: 101–107.

Anderson, J. K. 1961. *Ancient Greek Horsemanship*. Berkeley: University of California Press.

Andrewes, A. 1963. *The Greek Tyrants*. New York: Harper and Row.

Arieti, James A. 1975. Nudity in Greek Athletics. *The Classical World* 68: 431–436.

Babbitt, Don. 2000. Discus. In *USA Track & Field Coaching Manual*. Authored by USA Track & Field and Joseph L. Rogers, Project Coordinator. Champaign, IL: Human Kinetics.

Bailey, Peter. 1978. *Leisure and Class in Victorian England: Rational Recreation and the Contest for Control, 1830–1885*. London: Routledge & Kegan Paul. Toronto: University of Toronto Press.

Bean, George E. 1956. Victory in the Pentathlon. *American Journal of Archaeology* 60: 361–368.

Bekker, Immanuel, ed. 1814. *Harpocration et Moeris*. Berlin: G. C. Nauck. Reprint, Graz, Austria: Akademische Druck-u.Verlagsanstalt.

Bethe, Ericus, ed. 1967. *Pollucis Onomasticon. E codicibus ab ipso collatis*. Fasciculus Prior Lib. I-IV Continens. Stuttgart: B. G. Teubner.

Boardman, John. 1974. *Athenian Black Figure Vases: A Handbook*. London: Thames and Hudson.

―――. 1975. *Athenian Red Figure Vases: The Archaic Period: A Handbook*. London: Thames and Hudson.

―――. 1985. *Greek Sculpture: The Classical Period: A Handbook*. London: Thames and Hudson.

Bonfante, Larissa. 1989. Nudity as a Costume in Classical Art. *American Journal of Archaeology* 93: 543–570.

Boring, Warren J. 1975. *Science and Skills of Wrestling*. Saint Louis: C. V. Mosby.

Bowie, E. L. 1986. Early Greek Elegy, Symposium and Public Festival. *The Journal of Hellenic Studies* 106: 13–35.

Broneer, Oscar. 1956. An Archaeological Enigma. *Archaeology* 9: 134–137.

―――. 1956. The Enigma Explained. *Archaeology* 9: 268–272.

―――. 1956. The Scene of International Athletic Meetings 2700 Years Ago: An Enigma Solved During the Excavations of the Isthmian Site At Corinth. *The Illustrated London News* 229 (September 15): 430–431.

———. The Isthmian Victory Crown. *American Journal of Archaeology* 66: 259–263.

———. 1973. *Isthmia: Excavations by the University of Chicago, under the Auspices of the American School of Classical Studies at Athens.* Vol. 2: *Topography and Architecture.* Princeton, NJ: American School of Classical Studies at Athens.

———. 1972. Starting Devices in Greek Stadia. *American Journal of Archaeology* 76: 205–206.

Brophy, Robert H., III. 1978. Deaths in the Pan-Hellenic Games: Arrachion and Creugas. *American Journal of Philology* 99: 363–390.

Brown, C. Harmon, Bill Webb, and Bob Sing. 2000. Javelin. In *USA Track & Field Coaching Manual.* Authored by USA Track & Field and Joseph L. Rogers, Project Coordinator. Champaign, IL: Human Kinetics.

Brulotte, Eric L. 1994. The "Pillar of Oinomaos" and the Location of Stadium I at Olympia. *American Journal of Archaeology* 98: 53–64.

Burn, Andrew Robert. 1960. *The Lyric Age of Greece.* New York: St. Martin's Press.

Burkert, Walter. 1983. *Homo Necans: The Anthropology of Ancient Greek Sacrificial Ritual and Myth.* Translated from the German by Peter Bing. Berkeley: University of California Press.

———. 1985. *Greek Religion.* Translated from the German by John Raffan. Cambridge, MA: Harvard University Press.

Carne-Ross, D. S. 1985. *Pindar.* New Haven: Yale University Press.

Carey, C., ed. 1989. *Lysias: Selected Speeches*. Cambridge: Cambridge University Press.

Cartledge, Paul. 2001. The Mirage of Lykourgan Sparta: Some Brazen Reflections. In *Spartan Reflections*, 169–184. Berkeley: University of California Press.

Cohen, Steven D. 1980. More Than Fun and Games: A Comparative Study of the Role of Sport in English and American Society at the Turn of the Century. Ph.D. diss., Brandeis University.

Coldstream, J. N. 1977. *Geometric Greece*. London: Ernest Benn.

Cook, Arthur Bernard. 1925. *Zeus God of the Dark Sky (Thunder and Lightning.* Vol. 2 of *Zeus: A Study in Ancient Religion*. Cambridge: Cambridge University Press.

Coulson, William and Helmut Kyrieleis, eds. 1922. *Proceedings of an International Symposium on the Olympic Games, 5–7 September 1988*. Lucy Braggiotti Publications for the Deutsches Archäologisches Institut Athen: Athens.

Crowther, Nigel B. 1985. Male Beauty Contests in Greece: The Euandria and Euexia. *L'Antiquité classique* 54: 285–291.

———. 1985. Studies in Greek Athletics, Part I. *The Classical World* 78: 497–558.

———. 1985. Studies in Greek Athletics, Part II. *The Classical World* 79: 73–135.

———. 1988. The Age-Category of Boys at Olympia. *Phoenix* 42: 304–308.

———. 1990. The Evidence for Kicking in Greek Boxing. *American Journal of Philology* 111: 176–181.

Darwin, Bernard. 1929. *The English Public School.* London: Longmans, Green, and Co.

Davies, John K. 1981. *Wealth and the Power of Wealth in Classical Athens.* New York: Arno Press.

Davison, J. A. 1958. Notes on the Panathenaea: I. Nomenclature. *The Journal of Hellenic Studies* 78: 23–41.

Delorme, Jean. 1960. *Gymnasion: Étude sur les Monuments Consacrés a l'Éducation en Grèce.* Paris: E. de Boccard.

De Ste. Croix, G. E. M. 1972. *The Origins of the Peloponnesian War.* London: Duckworth.

Detienne, Marcel and Jean-Pierre Vernant. 1978. *Cunning Intelligence in Greek Culture and Society.* Translated from the French by Janet Lloyd. Hassocks, UK: Harvester Press and Atlantic Highlands, NJ: Humanities Press. Reprint, Chicago: The University of Chicago Press, 1991.

Dibble, R. F. 1925. *John L. Sullivan: An Intimate Narrative.* Boston: Little, Brown, and Company.

Dickie, Matthew W. 1984. Fair and Foul Play in the Funeral Games in the *Iliad. Journal of Sports History* 11: 8–17.

Diels, Hermannus. 1958. *Doxographi Graeci.* 3rd ed. Berlin: Walter de Gruyter.

———. 1952. *Die Fragmente der Vorsokratiker, griechisch und deutsch.* 6th ed., ed. Walther Kranz. Berlin: Weidmann.

Dindorf, Wilhelm, ed. 1853. *Harpocrationis Lexicon in Decem Oratores Atticos.* Vol. 1. Oxford, 1853. Reprint, Groningen: Bouma's Boekhuis, 1969.

Dittenberger, Wilhelm. 1898–1901. *Sylloge Inscriptionum Graecarum*. 3 Vols. Leipzig: S. Hirzel. Reprint, Hildesheim: Georg Olms, 1982

Dodds, E. R. 1951. *The Greeks and the Irrational*. Berkeley: University of California Press.

Donland, Walter. 1980. *The Aristocratic Ideal in Ancient Greece: Attitudes of Superiority from Homer to the End of the Fifth Century B.C.* Lawrence, KS: Coronado Press.

Dover, K. J. 1978. *Greek Homosexuality*. Cambridge, MA: Harvard University Press.

Dowden, Ken. 1992. *The Uses of Greek Mythology*. London: Routledge.

Drachmann, A. B., ed. 1964. *Scholia Vetera in Pindari Carmina*. 3 vols. Amsterdam: Adolf M. Hakkert.

Drees, Ludwig. 1968. *Olympia: Gods, Artists, and Athletes*. Translated from the German by Gerald Onn. New York: Frederick A. Praeger.

Dübner, Friedrich. 1877. *Scholia Graeca in Aristophanem cum Prolegomenis Grammaticorum. Varietate Lectionis Optimorum Codicum Integra, Ceterorum Selecta, Annotatione Criticorum Item Selecta, Cui Sua Quaedam Inseruit*. Paris. Reprint, Hildesheim: Georg Olms, 1969.

Dunning, Eric and Kenneth Sheard. 1979. *Barbarians, Gentlemen and Players: A Sociological Study of the Development of Rugby Football*. New York: New York University Press.

Dürrbach, Félix and Pierre Roussel, ed. 1935. *Inscriptions de Délos*. 5 vols. Paris.

Edmonds, J. M., ed. and trans. 1931. *Elegy and Iambus*. 2 vols. London: W. Heinemann and Cambridge, MA: Harvard University Press. Reprint: 1961.

————. 1959. *The Fragments of Attic Comedy*. Vol. 2. Leiden: E. J. Brill.

Edwards, G. Roger. 1957. Panathenaics of Hellenistic and Roman Times. *Hesperia* 26: 320–349.

Edwards, Mark W. 1987. *Homer, Poet of the Iliad*. Baltimore: The Johns Hopkins University Press.

Erbse, Hartmut, ed. *1977. Scholia Graeca in Homeri Iliadem (Scholia Vetera)*. Vol. 5. *Scholia ad Libros* Υ–Ω *Continens*. Berlin: Walter de Gruyter.

Eustathius. 1827-1830. *Eustathii, Archiepiscopi Thessalonicensis, Commentarii ad Homeri Iliadem. Ad fidem exempli romani editi*. 4 vols. Lipsiae: sumptibus Joann. Aug. Gottl. Weigel.

Farnell, Lewis Richard. 1896-1909. *The Cults of the Greek States*. Oxford: Clarendon Press.

Fiechter, E. 1929. Stadion (der Bau). *Paulys Real-Encyclopädie der classischen Altertumswissenshaft*. Edited by Wilhelm Kroll and Karl Mittelhaus, Ser. 2, vol. 3., cols. 1967–1973. Stuttgart: J. B. Metzler.

Fine, John V. A. 1983. *The Ancient Greeks: A Critical History*. Cambridge, MA: Belknap Press of Harvard University Press.

Finley, John H., Jr. 1978. *Homer's Odyssey*. Cambridge, MA: Cambridge University Press.

Finley, M. I. 1975. *The Use and Abuse of History*. London: Chatto and Windus.

———— and H. W. Pleket. 1976. *The Olympic Games: The First Thousand Years*. New York: Viking Press.

Fitzgerald, Jim. 1980. *Boxing for Beginners*. New York: Atheneum.

Fleischer, Nat and Sam Andre. 1981. *A Pictorial History of Boxing*. Revised by Sam Andre and Nat Loubet. New York: Bonanza Books.

Fontenrose, Joseph. 1959. *Python: A Study of Delphic Myth and its Origins*. Berkeley: University of California Press.

————. The Cult of Apollo and the Games at Delphi. In *The Archaeology of the Olympics: The Olympics and Other Festivals in Antiquity*. Edited by Wendy J. Raschke. Madison: The University of Wisconsin Press.

Forbes, Clarence A. 1929. *Greek Physical Education*. New York and London: The Century Co. Reprint, New York: AMS Press, 1971.

Forrest, George. 1956. The First Sacred War. *Bulletin de Correspondance Hellénique* (1956): 33–52.

Fraenkel, Eduard, ed. 1950. *Aeschylus: Agamemnon*. Oxford: Oxford University Press.

Frazer, J. G. 1898. *Pausanias's Description of Greece*. 6 vols. London: Macmillan and Co. and New York: The Macmillan Company. Reprint, New York: Biblo and Tannen, 1965.

Frost, K. T. 1906. Greek Boxing. *The Journal of Hellenic Studies* 26: 213–225.

Gantz, Timothy. 1993. *Early Greek Myth: A Guide to Literary and Artistic Sources.* 2 vols. Baltimore: The Johns Hopkins University Press.

Gardiner, E. Norman. 1903. The Method of Deciding the Penthalon. *The Journal of Hellenic Studies* 23: 54–70.

———. 1903. Notes on the Greek Foot Race. *The Journal of Hellenic Studies* 23: 261–191.

———. 1904. Phayllus and his Record Jump. *The Journal of Hellenic Studies* 24: 70–80.

———. 1904. Further Notes on the Greek Jump. *The Journal of Hellenic Studies* 24: 179–194.

———. 1905. Wrestling. I. *The Journal of Hellenic Studies* 25: 14–31.

———. 1905. Wrestling. II. *The Journal of Hellenic Studies* 25: 263–293.

———. 1906. The Pankration and Wrestling. III. *The Journal of Hellenic Studies* 26: 4–22.

———. 1907. Throwing the Discus. *The Journal of Hellenic Studies* 27: 1–36.

———. 1907. Throwing the Javelin. *The Journal of Hellenic Studies* 27: 249–273.

———. 1910. *Greek Athletic Sports and Festivals.* London: Macmillan.

———. 1929. Regulations For A Local Sports Meeting. *The Classical Review* 43: 210–212.

————. 1930. *Athletics of the Ancient World.* Oxford:
Clarendon Press. Reprint, Chicago: Aries, 1980.

Gebhard, Elizabeth R. 1987. The Early Sanctuary of Poseidon at
Isthmia. *American Journal of Archaeology* 91: 475–476.

————. 1988. The Sanctuary of Poseidon on the Isthmus of Corinth
and the Isthmian Games. In *Mind and Body: Athletic Contests
in Ancient Greece.* Edited by Olga Tzachou-Alexandri. Athens:
Ministry of Culture: National Hellenic Committee I.C.O.M.

————. 1992. The Early Stadium at Isthmia and the Founding of
the Isthmian Games. In *Proceedings of an International
Symposium on the Olympic Games, 5–7 September 1988.*
Edited by William Coulson and Helmut Kyrieleis. Lucy Braggiotti
Publications for the Deutsches Archäologisches Institut Athen:
Athens.

Glass, Stephen L. 1988. The Greek Gymnasium: Some Problems.
In *The Archaeology of the Olympics: The Olympics and
Other Festivals in Antiquity.* Edited by Wendy J. Raschke.
Madison: The University of Wisconsin Press.

Golden, Mark. 1998. *Sport and Society in Ancient Greece.*
Cambridge: Cambridge University Press.

Gomme, A. W., A. Andrewes, and K. J. Dover. 1981. *A Historical Commentary on Thucydides.* Vol. 5. *Book VIII.* Oxford:
Oxford University Press.

Gordon, Cyrus H. 1950-1951. Belt-Wrestling in the Bible World.
Hebrew Union College Annual 23: 131–136.

Gouldner, Alvin W. 1965. *Enter Plato: Classical Greece and the
Origins of Social Theory.* New York and London: Basic Books.

Greene, William Chase. 1938. *Scholia Platonica*. Philological Monographs 8. Haverford, PA: Haverford College, 1938. Reprint, American Philological Association, 1981.

Guttman, Allen. 1978. *From Ritual to Record: The Nature of Modern Sports*. New York: Columbia University Press.

Habicht, Christian. 1998. *Pausanias' Guide to Ancient Greece*. Berkeley: University of California Press.

Hammond, N. G. L. 1959. *A History of Greece to 322 B.C.* Oxford: Clarendon Press.

Hanson, Victor Davis. 1989. *The Western Way of War: Infantry Battle in Classical Greece*. Oxford: Oxford University Press.

Harris, H. A. 1960. Stadia and Starting-Grooves. *Greece and Rome* 7: 25–35.

———. 1961. Philostratus, *Imagines* 1.24.2. *The Classical Review* n.s. 11: 3–5.

———. 1964. *Greek Athletes and Athletics*. Introduction by The Marquess of Exeter. London: Hutchinson.

———. 1968. The Starting-Gate for Chariots at Olympia. *Greece and Rome* 15: 113–126.

———. 1972. The Method of Deciding Victory in the Penthalon. *Greece and Rome* 19: 60–64.

———. 1972. *Sport in Greece and Rome*. London: Thames and Hudson.

Havelock, Eric A. 1963. *Preface to Plato*. Cambridge, MA: Belknap Press and Harvard University Press. Reprint, New York: Grosset and Dunlap, 1967.

Heberdey, Rudolf. 1983. Die olympische Altarperigese des Pausanias. *Eranos Vindobonensis* (1983): 34–47.

Henderson, Jeffrey. 1991. Women and the Athenian Dramatic Festivals. *Transactions and Proceedings of the American Philological Association* 121: 133–147.

Herrmann, Klaus. 1988. Olympia: The Sanctuary and the Contests. In *Mind and Body: Athletic Contests in Ancient Greece*. Edited by Olga Tzachou-Alexandri. Athens: Ministry of Culture: National Hellenic Committee I.C.O.M.

Heston, Charlton. 1995. *In the Arena: An Autobiography*. New York: Simon and Schuster.

Hicks, E. L. and G. F. Hill. 1901. *A Manual of Greek Historical Inscriptions*. Oxford: Clarendon Press.

Homolle, Th. 1899. Le Gymnase de Delphes (1). *Bulletin de Correspondance Hellénique* 23: 560–583.

Honey, J. R. de. S. 1977. *Tom Brown's Universe: The Development of the Victorian Public School*. London: Millington Books.

Hoyle, P. 1967. *Delphi*. London: Cassell.

Hughes, Thomas. 1988. *Tom Brown's School Days*. Mahwah, NJ: Watermill Press.

Humphreys, S. C. 1974. The Nothoi of Kynosarges. *The Journal of Hellenic Studies* 94: 88–95.

Inscriptiones Graecae, consilio et auctoritate Litterarum Borussicae editae. 1913–. Berlin: Akademie der Wissenschaften.

Jackson, Donald F. 1991. Philostratos and the Penthalon. *The Journal of Hellenic Studies* 111: 278–181.

Jacoby, Felix. 1962. *Die Fragmente der griechischen Historiker.* 2nd Part: *Zeitgeschichte.* B: *Spezialgeschichten, Autobiographien und Memoiren. Zeittafeln.* Leiden: E. J. Brill.

—, ed. 1904. *Das Marmor Parium.* Berlin. Reprint, Chicago: Ares, 1980.

Jebb, Richard C. 1907. *Sophocles: The Plays and Fragments.* Part 6: *The Electra.* Cambridge: Cambridge University Press.

Jeffery, L. H. 1976. *Archaic Greece: The City-States c. 700–500 B.C.* London and Tonbridge: Ernest Benn.

Johnston, A.W. 1987. *IG* II^2 2311 and the Number of Panathenaic Amphorae. *Annual of the British School at Athens* 82: 125–129.

Jones, Henry Stuart. 1900. *Thucydides: Historiae.* 2 vols. Oxford: Clarendon Press. Reprint: 1959.

Judeich, Walther. 1931. *Topographie von Athen.* 2nd edition. Munich: C. H. Beck.

Jüthner, Julius. 1949. Pale. In *Paulys Real-Encyclopädie der classischen Altertumswissenschaft.* Edited by Wilhelm Kroll and Karl Mittelhaus, Vol. 36, Part 2, cols. 82–89. Stuttgart: Alfred Druckenmüller.

—. 1949. Pankration. In *Paulys Real-Encyclopädie der classischen Altertumswissenschaft.* Edited by Wilhelm Kroll and Karl Mittelhaus, Vol. 36, 2nd third, cols. 619–625. Württ.: Albert Druckenmüller.

————. 1968. *Die athletischen Leibesübungen der Griechen.* Vol. 2. *Einzelne Sportarten: 1. Lauf-, Sprung- und Wurfbewerbe.* Edited by Friedrich Brein. Graz-Wien-Köln: Hermann Böhlaus.

———— and Erwin Mehl. 1962. Pygme. In *Paulys Real-Encyclopädie der classischen Altertumswissenschaft.* Edited by Wilhelm Kroll and Karl Mittelhaus, Supplment 9, cols.1306–1352. Stuttgart: Alfred Druckenmüller.

Kamerbeek, J. C. 1974. *The Plays of Sophocles.* Part 5: *The Electra.* Leiden: E. J. Brill.

Kayser, C. L. 1871. *Flavii Philostrati Opera.* 2 vols. Leipzig: Teubner. Reprint, Hildesheim: Georg Olms, 1964.

Keaney, John J., ed. 1991. *Harpocration: Lexeis of the Ten Orators.* Amsterdam: Adolf M. Hakkert.

Kells, J. H. 1973. *Sophocles*: Electra. [London]: Cambridge University Press.

Kitchell, Kenneth F., Jr. 1998. "But the Mare I Will Not Give Up": The Games in *Iliad* 23. *The Classical Bulletin* 74: 159–171.

Kühn, C. G., ed. 1964–1965. *Claudii Galeni Opera Omnia.* 20 vol. in 22. Leipzig. Reprint, Hildesheim: Georg Olms, 1964–1965.

Kurke, Leslie. 1991. *The Traffic in Praise: Pindar and the Poetics of Social Economy.* Ithaca, NY: Cornell University Press.

Kyle, Donald G. 1987. *Athletics in Ancient Athens.* Leiden: E. J. Brill.

———. 1990. E. Norman Gardiner and the Decline of Greek Sport. In *Essays on Sport History and Sport Mythology by Allen Guttmann, Richard D. Mandell, Steven A. Riess, Stephen Hardy, and Donald G. Kyle.* Edited by Donald G. Kyle and Gary D. Stark. College Station: Texas A & M University Press.

———. 1992. The Panathenaic Games: Sacred and Civic Athletics. In *Goddess and Polis: The Panathenaic Festival in Ancient Athens.* Edited by Jenifer Neils. Hanover, N.H.: Hood Museum of Art and Princeton, NJ: Princeton University Press.

———. 1995. Philostratos, *Repêchage*, Running and Wrestling: The Greek Penthalon Again. *Journal of Sport History* 22: 60–65.

———. 1998. Games, Prizes, and Athletes in Greek Sport: Patterns and Perspectives (1975–1997). *The Classical Bulletin* 74: 103–127.

———. 1990. Winning and Watching the Greek Penthalon. *Journal of Sport History* 17: 291–305.

Lee, Hugh M. 1976. The TERMA and the Javelin in Pindar, Nemean vii 70–3 and Greek Athletics. *The Journal of Hellenic Studies* 96: 70–79.

———. 1992. Some Changes in the Ancient Olympic Program and Schedule. In *Proceedings of an International Symposium on the Olympic Games, 5–7 September 1988 = Praktika symposioy olympiakon agonon, 5–9 septembrioy 1988.* Edited by William Coulson and Helmut Kyrielis, 105–111. Athens: Deutsches Archäologisches Institut Athen.

———. 1993. Wrestling in the *Repêchage* of the Ancient Pentathlon. *Journal of Sport History* 20: 277–279.

Liddell, Henry George and Robert Scott. 1940. *A Greek-English Lexicon*. 9th ed. Edited by Henry Stuart Jones, with the assistance of Roderick McKenzie. Oxford: Clarendon Press.

Lynch, John Patrick. 1972. *Aristotle's School: A Study of a Greek Educational Institution*. Berkeley: University of California Press.

McGregor, Malcolm F. 1941. Cleisthenes of Sicyon and the Panhellenic Festivals. *Transactions and Proceedings of the American Philological Association* 72: 266–287.

Macleod, C. W. 1982. *Homer, Iliad, Book XXIV*. Cambridge: Cambridge University Press.

Mahaffy, J. P. 1913. *Rambles and Studies in Greece*. New York: Macmillan.

———. May 1877 to October 1887. Old Greek Athletics. *Macmillan's Magazine* 36: 61–69.

Malcolmson, Robert W. 1973. *Popular Recreations in English Society 1700–1850*. Cambridge: Cambridge University Press.

Mallwitz, Alfred. 1988. Cult and Competition Locations at Olympia. In *The Archaeology of the Olympics: The Olympics and Other Festivals in Antiquity*. Edited by Wendy J. Raschke. Madison: The University of Wisconsin Press.

Mangan, J. A. 1981. *Athleticism in the Victorian and Edwardian Public School: The Emergence and Consolidation of an Educational Ideology*. Cambridge: Cambridge University Press.

Mann, J. C. 1974. GYMNAZO in Thucydides 1.6.5. *The Classical Review* 24: 177–178.

Meiggs, Russell and David Lewis. 1969. *A Selection of Greek Historical Inscriptions to the End of the Fifth Century.* Oxford: Oxford University Press.

Miller, Stella G. 1988. Excavations at the Panhellenic Site of Nemea. In *The Archaeology of the Olympics: The Olympics and Other Festivals in Antiquity.* Edited by Wendy J. Raschke. Madison: The University of Wisconsin Press.

Miller, Stephen G. 1979. The Date of the First Pythiad. *California Studies in Classical Antiquity* 11: 127–158.

————. 1975. The Date of Olympic Festivals. *Mitteilungen des Deutschen Archèaologischen Instituts, Athenische Abteilung* 90: 215–231.

————. 1978. Excavations at Nemea, 1977. *Hesperia* 47: 58–88.

————. 1979. Excavations at Nemea, 1978. *Hesperia* 48: 73–103.

————. 1980. Excavations at Nemea, 1979. *Hesperia* 49: 178–205.

————. 1980. Turns and Lanes in the Ancient Stadium. *American Journal of Archaeology* 84: 159–166.

————. 1982. Kleonai, the Nemean Games, and the Lamian War. In *Studies in Athenian Architecture, Sculpture, and Topography: Presented to Homer A. Thompson*, 100–108. Princeton, NJ: American School of Classical Studies at Athens.

————. 1988. Nemea and the Nemean Games. In *Mind and Body: Athletic Contests in Ancient Greece.* Edited by Olga Tzachou-Alexandri. Athens: Ministry of Culture : National Hellenic Committee I.C.O.M.

————, ed. 1990. *Nemea: A Guide to the Site and Museum*. With contributions by Ana M. Abraldes, Darice Birge, Alison Futrell, Michael Goethals, Lynn Kraynak, Mark Landon, and Jeannie Marchand. Berkeley: University of California Press.

————. 1991. *Arete: Greek Sports from Ancient Sources*. Berkeley: University of California Press.

————. 1992. The Stadium at Nemea and the Nemean Games. In *Proceedings of an International Symposium on the Olympic Games, 5–7 September 1988*. Edited by William Coulson and Helmut Kyrieleis. Lucy Braggiotti Publications for the Deutsches Archäologisches Institut Athen: Athens.

Mommsen, August. 1878. *Delphika*. Leipzig: B. G. Teubner.

Moretti, Luigi. 1953. *Iscrizioni agonistiche Greche*. Roma: Istituto Italiano per la storia antica.

————. Un regolamento rodio per la gara del pentatlo. *Rivista di Filologia e di Istruzione Classica* 34: 55–60.

————. 1957. *Olympionikai, I Vincitori negli Antichi Agoni Olimpici*. Mem Lincei ser. 8.8.2. Rome: Accademia Nazionale dei Lincei.

Morgan, Catherine. 1990. *Athletes and Oracles: The Transformation of Olympia and Delphi in the Eighth Century BC*. Cambridge: Cambridge University Press.

Morrissey, Edmond J. 1978. Victors in the Prytaneion Decree (*IG* I² 77). *Greek, Roman, and Byzantine Studies* 19: 121–125.

Mosshammer, Alden A. 1979. *The* Chronicle *of Eusebius and Greek Chronographic Tradition*. Lewisburg, PA: Bucknell University Press.

————. 1982. The Date of the First Pythiad—Again. *Greek, Roman and Byzantine Studies* 23: 15–30.

Mouratidis, John. 1984. Heracles at Olympia and the Exclusion of Women from the Ancient Olympic Games. *Journal of Sport History* 11: 41–55.

————. 1985. The Origin of Nudity in Greek Athletics. *Journal of Sport History* 12: 213–232.

Muellner, Leonard. 1996. *The Anger of Achilles : Mênis in Greek Epic*. Ithaca, NY: Cornell University Press.

Nagy, Gregory. 1996. *Homeric Questions*. Austin: University of Texas Press.

Neils, Jenifer. 1992. Panathenaic Amphoras: Their Meaning, Makers, and Markets. In *Goddess and Polis: The Panathenaic Festival in Ancient Athens*. Edited by Jenifer Neils. Hanover, NH: Hood Museum of Art, Dartmouth College; Princeton, NJ: Princeton University Press.

Nilsson, Martin P. 1927. *The Minoan-Mycenaean Religion and its Survival in Greek Religion*. 2nd ed., revised, Lund: C. W. K. Gleerup. Reprint, 2nd revised edition. Lund: C. W. K. Gleerup, 1950.

Page, D. L., ed. 1981. *Further Greek Epigrams*. Revised and prepared for publication by R. D. Dawe and J. Diggle. Cambridge: Cambridge University Press.

Parke, H. W. 1977. *Festivals of the Athenians*. London: Thames and Hudson.

Paton, W. R., trans. 1916–1918. *The Greek Anthology*. 5 vols. Cambridge, MA: Harvard University Press and London: William Heinemann.

Perlman, P. 1989. The Calendrical Position of the Nemean Games. *Athenaeum* 90: 57–90.

Picard, Olivier. 1989. Delphi and the Pythian Games. In *Mind and Body: Athletic Contests in Ancient Greece*. Edited by Olga Tzachou-Alexandri. Athens: Ministry of Culture: National Hellenic Committee I.C.O.M.

Pleket, H. W. 1976. Games, Prizes, Athletes and Ideology: Some Aspects of the History of Sport in the Greco-Roman World. *Stadion* 1: 48–65.

Poliakoff, Michael B. 1980. The Third Fall in the *ORESTEIA*. *American Journal of Philology* 101: 251–159.

———. 1986. *Studies in the Terminology of the Greek Combat Sports*. 2nd ed. Frankfurt am Main: Anton Hain.

———. 1987. *Combat Sports In the Ancient World: Competition, Violence, and Culture*. New Haven, CT and London: Yale University Press.

Raschke, Wendy J. 1985. Aulos and Athlete: The Function of the Flute Player in Greek Athletics. *Arete* 2: 177–200.

Raubitschek, Antony. 1988. The Panhellenic Idea and the Olympic Games. In *The Archaeology of the Olympics: The Olympics and Other Festivals in Antiquity*. Edited by Wendy J. Raschke. Madison: The University of Wisconsin Press.

———. 1992. Unity and Peace through the Olympic Games. In *Proceedings of an International Symposium on the Olympic Games, 5–7 September 1988 = Praktika symposioy olympiakon agonon, 5–9 septembrioy 1988*. Edited by William Coulson and Helmut Kyrielis. Athens: Deutsches Archäologisches Institut Athen.

Reed, John R. 1964. *Old School Ties: The Public Schools in British Literature*. Syracuse, NY: Syracuse University Press.

Reed, Nancy B. 1990. A Chariot Race for Athens' Finest: The Apobates Contest Reexamined. *Journal of Sport History* 17: 306–317.

Richardson, Nicholas. 1993. *The Iliad: A Commentary. Volume VI: Books 21–24*. Cambridge: Cambridge University Press.

Richter, Gisela M. A. 1965. *The Portraits of the Greeks*. 2 vols. London: Phaidon Press.

Robertson, Martin. 1975. *A History of Greek Art*. 2 vols. London: Cambridge University Press.

Roller, L. E. 1981. Funeral Games for Historical Persons. *Stadion* 7: 1–18.

Roos, Paavo. 1965. The Start of the Greek Foot-Race. *Opuscula Atheniensia* 6: 149–165.

Rose, H. J. 1922. The Greek Agones. *Aberystwyth Studies* 3: 1–24. Reprint, *Arete* 3 (1985): 163–182.

Rostoker, W. and E. R. Gebhard. 1980. The Sanctuary of Poseidon at Isthmia: Techniques of Metal Manufacture. *Hesperia* 49: 347–363.

Sansone, David. 1988. *Greek Athletics and the Genesis of Sport*. Berkeley: University of California Press.

Scanlon, Thomas F. 1982–1983. Greek Boxing Gloves: Terminology and Evolution. *Stadion* 8–9: 31–45.

———. 1984. The Footrace of the Heraia at Olympia. *Ancient World* 9: 77–90.

————. 2002. *Eros and Greek Athletics*. Oxford: Oxford University Press.

Schoene, Alfred, ed. 1875. *Eusebi Chronicorum Libri Duo*. 2 Vols. Berlin. Reprint, Zürich: Weidmann, 1999.

Segal, Charles. 1968. Two Agonistic Problems in Pindar, *Nemean* 7.70–74 and *Pythian* 1.42–45. *Greek, Roman, and Byzantine Studies* 9: 31–45.

————. 1981. *Tragedy and Civilization: An Interpretation of Sophocles*. Cambridge, MA: Harvard University Press.

Serwint, Nancy. 1993. The Female Athletic Costume at the Heraia and Prenuptial Initiation Rites. *American Journal of Archaeology* 97: 403–422.

Shapiro, H. A. 1992. *Mousikoi Agones*: Music and Poetry at the Panathenaia. In *Goddess and Polis: The Panathenaic Festival in Ancient Athens*. Edited by Jenifer Neils. Hanover, NH: Hood Museum of Art, Dartmouth College and Princeton, NJ: Princeton University Press.

Shaps, David M. 1977. The Woman Least Mentioned: Etiquette and Women's Names. *Classical Quarterly* 27: 323–330.

Shear, T. Leslie, Jr. 1975. The Athenian Agora: Excavations of 1973–1974. *Hesperia* 44: 362–365.

Snell, Bruno, ed. 1959. *Pindari Carmina cum Fragmentis*. Vol. 1: *Epinicia*. 3rd ed. Leipzig: B. G. Teubner.

————. *Pindari Carmina cum Fragmentis*. 1975. 2 vols. Edited by Hervicus Maehler. Leipzig: B. G. Teubner.

Snodgrass, A. M. 1965. The Hoplite Reform and History. *The Journal of Hellenic Studies* 85: 110–122.

———. 1971. *The Dark Age of Greece: An Archaeological Survey of the Eleventh to the Eighth Centuries BC.* Edinburgh: Edinburgh University Press.

———. 1980. *Archaic Greece: The Age of Experiment.* Berkeley: University of California Press.

Spears, Betty. 1984. A Perspective of the History of Women's Sport in Ancient Greece. *Journal of Sport History* 11: 32–47.

Storace, Patricia. 1996. *Dinner With Persephone: Travels in Greece.* New York: Vintage Books.

Sturtevant, E. H. 1912. GYMNOS and NUDUS. *American Journal of Philology* 33: 324–329.

Swaddling, Judith. 1980. *The Ancient Olympic Games.* London: British Museum Publications.

Sweet, Waldo E. 1983. A New Proposal for Scoring the Greek Pentathlon. *Zeitschrift für Papyrologie und Epigraphik* 50: 287–290.

———. 1987. *Sport and Recreation in Ancient Greece: A Sourcebook with Translations.* New York and Oxford: Oxford University Press.

Tersini, Nancy D. 1987. Unifying Themes in the Sculpture of the Temple of Zeus at Olympia. *Classical Antiquity* 6: 139–159.

Thierfelder, Andreas. 1968. *Philogelos.* Munich: Heimeran.

Thorne, Will. 1925. *My Life's Battles.* London: G. Newnes. Reprint, London: Lawrence and Wishart, 1989.

Thompson, H. A. 1961, The Panathenaic Festival. *Archäologischer Anzeiger* 76: 224–231.

Thompson, Wesley E. 1979. More on the Prytaneion Decree. *Greek, Roman, and Byzantine Studies* 20: 325–329.

Tigerstedt, E. N. 1965. *The Legend of Sparta in Classical Antiquity*. 3 vols. Stockholm: Almquist and Wiksell.

Tod, Marcus N. 1948. *From 403 to 323 B.C.* Vol. 2 of *A Selection of Greek Historical Inscriptions*. Oxford: Oxford University Press.

Trollope, Anthony. 1868. *British Sports and Pastimes*. Edited by Anthony Trollope. London: Virtue and New York: Virtue and Yorston..

Turner, Frank M. 1981. *The Greek Heritage in Victorian Britain*. New Haven: Yale University Press.

Tyrrell, Wm. Blake. 1984. *Amazons: A Study in Athenian Mythmaking*. Baltimore: The Johns Hopkins University Press.

———— and Frieda S. Brown. 1991. *Athenian Myths and Institutions: Words in Action*. Oxford: Oxford University Press.

Tzachou-Alexandri, Olga, ed. 1989. *Mind and Body: Athletic Contests in Ancient Greece*. Athens: Ministry of Culture: National Hellenic Committee I.C.O.M.

Verdenius, W. J. 1987. *Commentaries on Pindar*. Vol. 1: *Olympian Odes 3, 7, 12, 14*. Leiden: E. J. Brill.

Vernant, Jean-Pierre. *1980. Myth and Society in Ancient Greece*. Translated from the French by Janet Lloyd. Sussex, England: Harvester Press and Atlantic Highlands, NJ: Humanities Press.

————. 1991. A "Beautiful Death" and the Disfigured Corpse in Homeric Epic. In *Mortals and Immortals: Collected Essays*. Edited by Froma I. Zeitlin. Princeton, NJ: Princeton University Press.

Veyne, Paul. 1988. *Did the Greeks Believe in Their Myths? An Essay on the Constitutive Imagination*. Translated from the French by Paula Wissing. Chicago and London: The University of Chicago Press.

Wade-Gery, H. T. 1932. Thucydides, The Son of Melesias. *The Journal of Hellenic Studies* 52: 205–227.

———. 1925. King Pheidon. In *The Cambridge Ancient History*. Volume 3: *The Assyrian Empire*. Edited by J. B. Bury, S. A. Cook, and F. E. Adcock. New York: Macmillan.

Webster, T. B. L. 1972. *Potter and Patron in Classical Athens*. London: Methuen.

Wheeler, Robert W. 1975. *Jim Thorpe, World's Greatest Athlete*. Norman: University of Oklahoma Press. Revised edition,1979.

Wells, Margot. 1983. *The Allan Wells Book of Sprinting*. EP Publishing: Wakefield, West Yorkshire, England.

Weniger, Ludwig. 1904. Das Hochfest des Zeus in Olympia. *Klio* 4: 125–151.

Whitney, Caspar W. 1895. *A Sporting Pilgrimage: Riding to Hounds, Golf, Rowing, Football, Club and University Athletics. Studies in English Sport, Past and Present*. New York: Harper & Brothers.

Willcock, M. M. 1973. The Funeral Games of Patroclus. *Bulletin of the Institute of Classical Studies of the University of London* 20: 1–11.

———. 1984. *The Iliad of Homer, Books XIII–XXIV*. New York: St. Martin's Press.

———. 1995. *Pindar, Victory Odes: Olympians 2, 7, 11; Nemean 4; Isthmians 3, 4, 7*. Cambridge: Cambridge University Press.

Winkler, John J. 1990. *The Constraints of Desire: The Anthropology of Sex and Gender in Ancient Greece*. New York and London: Routledge.

Woodford, Susan. 1981. T*he Parthenon*. Cambridge: Cambridge University Press.

Wycherley, R. E. 1962. *How the Greeks Built Cities*. 2nd ed. London: Macmillan. Reprint, New York and London: W.W. Norton, 1976.

———. 1978. *The Stones of Athens*. Princeton, NJ: Princeton University Press.

Yalouris, Nicolaos, ed. 1979. *The Eternal Olympics: The Art and History of Sport*. Introduction by Manolis Andronicos. New Rochelle, NY: Caratzas Brothers.

Young, David C. 1985. *The Olympic Myth of Greek Amateur Athletics*. Chicago: Ares Publishers.

———. 1996. *The Modern Olympics: A Struggle for Revival*. Baltimore: The Johns Hopkins University Press.

Zarnowski, Frank. 1989. *The Decathlon: A Colorful History of Track and Field's Most Challenging Event*. Champaign, IL: Leisure Press.

Ziehen, Ludwig. 1939. Olympia. In *Paulys Real-Encyclopädie der classischen Altertumswissenschaft*. Edited by Wilhelm Kroll and Karl Mittelhaus. Vol. 35, cols. 1–71. Stuttgart: J. B. Metzler.

Index

A

Achilles *9, 10*
  as director of funeral games
    11, 18, 27
  wrath of *8, 12, 17, 18*
Aeschines
  Against Timarchus 11 *168*
  Against Timarchus 158–159 *173*
Aeschylus
  Agamemnon 168–175 *107–108*
  Agamemnon 342–343 *71*
  Eumenides 589 *111*
aethla 9
Agamemnon *8, 10, 11, 12, 20*
  contest in throwing a spear *27*
  geras (prize) *17*
Agesilaos *71, 85, 96*
Ageus of Argos (runner) *199*
Ajax, son of Oïleus *16*
  running contest *25*
Ajax, son of Telamon
  contest in throwing lump of iron
    26
  wrestling contest *24*
akoniti 111
  Eleans, and *118*
Alexander the Great *187, 201*
Alkinoös *27*
Alpheios River *33*
Altis
  Olympia *31*
  trees in *35*
Amateurism
  and Greeks
    and Victorian classism xv
Ambrose
  Commentary to Psalm 36.55 *134*
anephedros 111
Anonymous Iamblici, 2:400 *171*

[Andocides]
  Against Alcibiades 29 *198*
Antilochos *15*
  mêtis of *18–19, 21*
Apollo
  and Diomedes *14*
  as boxer *123*
  Daphne *76*
  Delphi *1, 75–76*
  Hyacinthus *208*
Apollo Lykeios *163*
Apollo Pythios *76*
Apollonius Rhodius
  Argonautica 2.43–44 *128*
  Argonautica 2.65–85 *130*
  Argonautica 2.88–97 *132–133*
  Polydeukes vs. Amykos
    130, 133
aptôs 111
Aratos of Sikyon *96*
aretê 15
  athlete, of *2, 8*
  ideology of *58, 59*
  warrior, of *2–3, 10*
Aristophanes
  Archarnians 483 *60*
  Clouds 1002–1008 *161*
  Clouds 1002–1014 *177*
  Clouds 1015–1023 *177–178*
  Frogs 1089–1098 *155*
  Knights 1159 *63*
  Knights 571–573 *110*
  Wasps 1381–1386 *136*
aristos 15
Aristotle
  Lyceum *164*
  Progression of Animals 705a 13–
    19 *212*
  Progression of Animals 705a 18
    62

Rhetoric 1.5.11 *219*
Rhetoric 1361b 23–24 *62*
Arrachion or Arrichion of Phigalia
    (pankratiast) *138*
Artemidorus
    Interpretation of Dreams 1.61
    119
Athena
    Diomedes *14, 15*
    Odysseus *25*
    Panthenaic amphora *146*
Athenaeus
    Deipnosophists 413c–f *176*
    Deipnosophists 609d *159–180*
Athens
    agora *141*
athletics
    critics of *175–180*
    "polis-oriented athletics" *142*
    war, and *59, 174*
aulos 210

B

Bacchylides
    Ode 37–40 *198*
    Ode 9.2–36 *222*
    Ode 9.6 *217*
Baer, Max *124*
balbis (bar)
    discus, and *206, 207*
    javelin *213*
balbis (bar) *61, 63, 67*
Bean, George E. *219, 221*
Bonfante, Larissa *70*
boxing *118–122*
    clinching *106, 120*
    Epeios vs. Agelaos *129*
    "head-hunting" *119, 124*
    how to win *119, 123*
    inauguration at Olympia *34*
    Onomastos of Smyrna *118*
    Polydeukes vs. Amykos *129*
    stance *126*
    strips *120*

"ants" *122*
    technique *128*
    vs. street fight *128*
boys' boxing
    inauguration at Olympia *53*
boys' *pankration*
    inauguration at Olympia *53*
boys' pentathlon
    inauguration at Olympia *53*
boys' *stadion*
    inauguration at Olympia *53*
boys' wrestling
    inauguration at Olympia *53*
Broneer, Oscar *63, 72*
Brophy, Robert H., III *125, 140*
Butler, Montagu xiv

C

chrematitês (monetary game) *58*
Cicero
    On the Orator 2.21 *179*
    Tusculan Disputations 5.9 *194*
Clytemnestra *71, 78, 79, 111*
Corbett, Jim ("Gentleman") *127*
Corinth *87*
Coubertin, Pierre de, *206*
Cronus
    as wrestler *108*
Crowther, Nigel B. *191*

D

Damaretos of Heraia
    hoplite race *6*
Damiskos of Messene (boy athlete)
    191
Damonon *86*
Damoxenos of Syracuse (boxer) *125*
Daphne *76*
Delorme, Jean *159, 167*
Delphi *74*
    Apollo *1*
    athletic contests at *76*
    First Sacred War *57, 75*
    musical contests *76, 77*

Mycenean period 75
  oracle at 44
  sanctuary 75
  site for athletic contests 77
Delphi Charioteer 86
Detienne, Marcel 12
Diagoras of Rhodes (boxer) 196
diaulos
  inauguration at Oympia 34, 71
  turning post in 71
Dio Chrysostom
  Eighth Discourse 5 92
  Eighth Discourse 6–7, 9–10,
    11–13, 15 93
  Eighth Discourse 19 138
  Ninth Discourse 10–12 93
  Ninth Discourse 22 93
Diogenes Laertius
  Lives of the Eminent Philoso-
    phers 6.54 92
  Lives of the Eminent Philoso-
    phers 6.60 92
Diogenes the Cynic 89, 92
Diomedes 11, 14, 15
  contest in arms 26
  winner of chariot race 18
Dionysus
  as wrestler 116
dolichos
  ideal runner for 72
  inauguration at Olympia 34
  inauguration of at Olympia 72
  number of laps in 60, 72
Dorieus of Rhodes (boxer) 111
Dromeus of Mantineia (pankratiast)
  111

E

Eleans 6
  boys' events 54
  mythmaking Olympia 44
  Pisatans 37
  polis of 181
Epeios 23

ephedros (bye) 222
epic (Homeric or oral) poetry
  as encyclopedia 1–2, 12
  simile in 10
Epictetus
  Discourses 1.6.26–27 195
  Discourses 3.14.14 136
  Discourses 3.15.5 135
  Encheiridion 29 189–190
Epikrates
  fr. 11 162–180
Eualkes of Athens (boy athlete) 191
Eumelos 19
Euripides
  Electra 953–956 60
  Electra 955–956 72
  Hecuba 29 72
  Hippolytus 1224 83
  Hippolytus 87 72
  on athletes 176
Eusebius
  Chronicles 1:201 140
Eustathius
  4:1320.18-19 204

F

First Sacred War 57, 75, 77
Forbes, Charles A. 178
four-horse chariot race
  inauguration at Olympia 34, 53
funeral games 10, 141
  for Patroclus 8–27

G

Galen
  On Protecting One's Health
    6:141-142 K. 114
  On the Natural Faculties 2:80 K.
    110
Gardiner, E. Norman 28, 171, 213,
    217, 218
  on "head-hunting" in boxing 124
Gebhard, Elizabeth R. 89
Gellius, Aulus

Attic Nights 13.28 *135*
Glass, Stephen L. *157*, *158*
Glaukos of Karystos (boxer) *123*, *152*
Golden, Mark *54*
Gordon, Cyrus H. *24*
Gouldner, Alvin W. *3*
grammê (scratch-line) *60*, *66*, *67*
gymnasion
  Academy *158*, *160–161*
    Charmos *161*
    Cimon *161*
    cults in *160*
    Eros *154*
    Hipparchos *159*, *161*
    Plato *162*, *170*
    Prometheus *154*
    Socrates *162*
    Sulla *161*
    trees in *161*
  administration of *165*
  culture of *156–160*
  description of *157*
  education and training in *167–168*
  Eros *167*
  etymology of term 157
  gymnastes (trainer) *168*, *169*
  Herakles *167*
  Hermes *166*
  hoplite *160*
  idelogy of *171–173*
  Kynosarges *158*, *164*
    bastards of Themistocles *164*
    Herakles *164*
  legislation *158*
  legislation, and *158*
  Lyceum *158*
    Apollo Lykeios *163*
    Aristotle *164*
    founders *163*
    Socrates *163*
    the military *163*
  paidotribês *167*, *169*
  palaestra *167*

pederasty *170*, *171–173*
  Socrates *170*
  the military *159*
  use of term *106*
gymnastês (trainer) *168*, *169*
gymnos (naked) *69*

H

halter (jumping weight) *134*
Harris, H. A.
  72, *189*, *214*, *216*, *221*
heats *65*
"heavy events" vs. "combat sports" *105*
Hekademos *16*
Heliodorus
  Aethiopica 10.31 *112*
  Aethiopica 10.31–32 *113*
  Aethiopica 10.32 *110*
  Aethiopica 4.3 *61*
Hellanodikai *119*, *185*, *189*, *190*
  rules of *44*
Hera
  at Olympia *38*
  SixteenWomen *50*
Herakles *42*
  as athlete *185*
  Idaean
  Kynosarges *164*
  Nemean lion *133*
  son of Amphitryon *40*
  temple of Zeus Olympios
hero, hero cults
  epic (Homeric or oral poetry) *36*
Herodotus *59*, *195*
  Histories 2.160 *192*
  Histories 6.27 *110*
  Histories 8.26.3 *58*
  Histories 8.59 *63*
  Histories 9.33.2 *217*
Heston, Charlton *80*, *82*
Hierokles
  Philogelos 72 *122*
Hipparchos *159*

Homeric epics *149*
Hippias of Elis *44*
Hippodameia *183*
   Sixteen Women *50*
Homer
   Iliad 1.528–530 *183*
   Iliad 12.310–328 *2*
   Iliad 22.158—166 *10*
   Iliad 23.257–261 *9*
   Iliad 23.306–321 *12*
   Iliad 23.334–343 *13*
   Iliad 23.362–372 *13*
   Iliad 23.420–441 *15*
   Iliad 23.474–481 *16*
   Iliad 23.534–538 *18*
   Iliad 23.570–585 *20–21*
   Iliad 23.711–715 *25*
   Iliad 23.839–840 *209*
   Iliad 5.440–442 *15*
   Odyssey 8.189–190 *209*
   Odyssey 16.161 *184*
hoplite *4–5*
   gymnasion *160*
hoplite race *6–7, 199*
   inauguration *6*
   start of *60*
Horace
   Epistles 2.2.45 *161*
horse racing
   chariot *81*
   Lacedaemonians *85*
hybris
   Zanes *186*
hysplex (starting mechanism) *63, 67, 74*

I

Illustration 1. Bronze statuette of a
   female runner *50*
Illustration 10. Theseus and
   Kerkyon *114*
Illustration 11. Wrestlers practice
   before a trainer *115*
Illustration 12. Shoulder throw *117*

Illustration 13. Boxer signals defeat
   119
Illustration 14. Boxer wearing sharp
   thongs *121*
Illustration 15. Boxers before a
   trainer or umpire *126*
Illustration 16. A forbidden act in
   pankration *135*
Illustration 17. Roman bronze
   statuette *137*
Illustration 18. Striding Athena *144*
Illustration 19. Inscription *146*
Illustration 2. Bronze statuette of a
   male runner *61*
Illustration 20. Racing chariot *147*
Illustration 21. Torch race *154*
Illustration 22. Proposition *172*
Illustration 23. Proposition *172*
Illustration 25. Events of the
   pentathlon *205*
Illustration 26. Discus Thrower *208*
Illustration 27. Jumping beyond the
   pegs *211*
Illustration 28. Casting the javelin
   215
Illustration 3. Starting gate with
   balbides *64*
Illustration 30. Victor Crowned *224*
Illustration 4. Victor pulls away from
   the field *68*
Illustration 5. Footrace *68*
Illustration 6. Runners in the
   dolichos *73*
Illustration 7. Front view of a four-
   horse chariot *81*
Illustration 8. Charioteer nearing turn
   82
Illustration 9. Youthful wrestler *112*
Inscriptio Graeca II 2311 *148, 153–155*
Inscriptiones Graecae I² 77 11–18
   179
Iphitos *43*
   discus of *44*
Iros *118, 124*

Isocrates
  Panegyricus 43 *189*
isolympic *57*
Isthmian Games *49*, *87–89*
  Athenians at *91*
  inauguration of *57*, *87*, *88*
  prize at *58*
  stadium *62*

K

kalos thanatos (beautiful death)
  140
kampter (turning post) *6*, *71*
kelês race
  inauguration at Olympia *53*
Kirrha *75*
Kladeos River *31*
Kleitomachos *111*
Kleitomachos (boxer) *118*
Kleitomachos (pankratiast and
  boxer) *199*
Koroibos of Elis *42*
Kreugas of Epidamnos *125*
Kyle, Donald G.
  143, *153*, *178*, *179*, *220*, *222*
Kylon *141*, *142*
Kyniska *85*, *86*, *203*

L

Lacedaemonians
  agoge of and athletics *49*
  and Olympia *45–47*
  at Olympia *44*
  pankration, and *137*
  Spartan mirage *47*
  wrestling, and *119*
Lachon of Keos (runner) *198*
Lee, Hugh M. *74*, *220*
Lucian
  Anacharsis 1 *107*
  Anacharsis 10 *58*
  Anacharsis 24 *113*
  Anacharsis 27 *66*, *204*

Anacharsis 31 *139*
  Herotimus 40 *65*
  Life of Demonax 49 *134*
  Lover of Lies 18 *209*
  Slander 12 *67*
  The Dream, or The Cock 6 *212*
  Timon 20 *67*
Lucillius
  Greek Anthology 11.75 *123*
  Greek Anthology 11.78 *122*
Lygdamis of Syracuse (pankratiast)
  105, *133*
Lykourgos
  Athenian athletics *179*

M

Mahaffy, John *161*
Mallowitz, Alfred *35*
Map 1. Early Olympia *31*
Map 2. Olympia at the End of the
  Fourth Century *182*
Mardonius *58*
Melikerte *90*
Menelaos *11*, *15*, *18*, *20*
Meriones *26*
Messenia *46*
mêtis *24*, *25*
  Antilochos *12*
  vs. bia *127*, *130*, *222*
Miller, Stephen G. *6*, *71*, *95*, *189*
Milo of Croton (wrestler) *77*, *105*,
  110, 152
Mosshammer, Alden A. *45*
Mouratidis, John *196*
Mycenean Period *1–2*
myth
  functions of *38–39*
myth and mythmaking *90*
  foundation myth *7*, *39–41*
    athletic nudity *69*
    Daphne and Apollo *77*
    Herakles *59, 101, 102*
    Hermes *200*
    Isthmian Games *89*

Opheltes 95
Palaestra 108
pankration 133
pentathlon 219
Phorbas 108
Sisyphus 89
stadion at Olympia 59
Theseus 91, 108
Melikertes 89
temple of Zeus Olympios
Herakles 185
Oinomaos and Pelops 183

N

Nemea
sanctuary 95, 97
sanctuary at 94
stadium 88
diaulos 6
Nemean Games 49, 94–97
Argives, and 96
contests 92, 97
inauguration of 57, 94
prize at 58
stadium
starting lines in 62
Nemean lion 94
Nestor 22–23
as adviser 11
Nikasylos of Rhodes (wrestler) 191
Nilsson, Martin P. 36
Nonnus
Dionysiaca 37.557-567 113
Dionysiaca 48.138-146 116
Dionysiaca 48.152-164 116
Dionysiaca 48.216 116
nudity, athletic 69–70
Orsippos 69
Thersites 70

O

Odysseus
Iros 118
Phaeacians 27–29

running contest 25
wrestling contest 24
Oinomaos 183
Old Oligarch
Constitution of the Athenians
2.10 157
Ollier, Francois 47
Olympia
Altis 31
Mycenaean period 35
Pelops 35
and Hera 38
and Pelops 38
as shrine 32–34
battle between Eleans and
Arcadians in 95
black substratum 33
black substratum at 32
Bouleuterion 53
boxing
inauguration of 53
boys' boxing
inauguration of 53
boys' pankration
inauguration of 53
boys' stadion
inauguration of 53
boys' wrestling
inauguration of 53
Echo Colonnade 187
festival at 34–35
four-horse chariot race
inauguration of 53
heat at 32, 34
Heraion 49
Herakles 196
keles race
inauguration of 53
Kladeos River 31
Olive of Beautiful Crowns 102
pankration
inauguration of 53
Pelopeion
date of 36
priestess of Demeter Chamyne

185
Sanctuary
  Leonidaion *188*
sanctuary
  ashen altar of Zeus *187*
  Metroon *186*
  Pelopeion *186*
  Philippeion *187*
  Prytaneion *187*
  temple of Zeus *181–183*
  Zanes *186*
stadium
  Hidden Entrance *185*
stadium II *185*
stadium III *185*
statues of athletes *188*
swimming pool *186*
temple of Zeus
  date of *34*
treasuries at *49*
wells *181, 195*
wells at *34*
Olympic Games
boxing
  inauguration of *105*
boy athletes
  eligibility of *191*
boys' *pankration*
  inauguration of *133*
date of *188, 189*
equestrian events *200–202*
  inauguration of two-horse
  chariot race *178*
  starting mechanism *202–203*
  Taraxippos *201*
Hellanodikai *189*
  duties of *190, 193, 200*
  impartiality of *192*
  Kleitomachos *199*
  number of *190*
oath of *191*
pankration
  inauguration of *105, 133*
pentathlon *204–209*
  aulos in 210

discus *204–206*
how to win *218–219*
inauguration of *204*
javelin *213*
jump *210–211*
jumping weight *(halter)* *134, 211*
sequence of events *216*
thong in javelin *214*
pentathlon for boys *204*
preparations for *188–192*
prize at *58*
prizes, awarding of *224*
running events *59–62*
schedule of events *197*
spectators *194–195*
stadion (passim) *59–61*
stadium
  preparations of *194*
  starting lines in *62*
truce for *59, 189*
trumpeteers and heralds *200*
two-horse chariot race
  inauguration of *201*
virgin girls at *196*
women,
  absence of *195–196*
  Kallipataeira/Pherenike *196*
wrestling
  inauguration of *105*
Onomastos of Smyrna *118*
Opheltes *95*
Orestes *77–78, 111*
Orikadmos *109*
Orsippos of Megara
  athletic nudity *69*
Ouranos
  as pankratiast *108*
Oxyrhynchus Papyrus 3.446 *169*

P

paidotribês (wrestling instructor)
  167, 168, 169
palaestra *106, 167*

vis-a-vis *gymnasion* 157
Panathenaea
early *142*
inauguration of *142*
Panathenaic Games *145–149*
amphoras of oil as prize
143, 145
iconography of *146–147*
value of *150*
inauguration of *142*
rhapsodes *149*
tribal contests *153–155*
Panhellenic
definition of *49*
Panhellenic games *98*
pankration 133–134
Arrichion *138*
definition of *133*
foul play *134*
foundation myth *133*
iconography of *115*
inauguration at Olympia *53*
Lacedaemonians, and *137*
Leukaros of Akarnania *133*
stance *135*
technique *136*
Patroclus *9*
Pausanias, *Geography of Greece*
1.30.2 *155*
1.35.5 *206*
1.39.3 *108*
1.44.1 *69*
1.44.7-8 *90*
3.11.6 *217*
5.10.2 *181*
5.10.6-7 *183*
5.15.2-4 *50*
5.21.17 *187*
5.21.2 *186*
5.21.5 *186*
5.24.9 *191*
5.4.6 *42*
5.7.6-8.4 *40–41*
5.9.3 *198*
6.10.2 *124*

6.13.3 *199*
6.13.4 *65*
6.15.4-5 *199*
6.20.10-13 *202–203*
6.20.14 *203*
6.20.15 *201*
6.3.7 *193*
8.40.1-2 *138*
8.40.3-5 *125*
10.9.1 *212*
Peisistratos *154, 159, 163*
Pelops *35, 183*
at Olympia *38*
Sixteen Women *50*
pentathlon
inauguration at Olympia *34*
Pericles *163*
Odeion *148*
periodos (period games)
Panhellenism of *57–58*
timing of *57*
Perizoma Group (vases) *70*
Phaÿllos of Croton (pentathlete)
152, 206, 212
Phaÿllos of Kroton *77*
Pheidias *183, 225*
Pheidon of Argos *36*
Pherias of Aigina (boy athlete) *191*
Philip II *187*
Philo
On Agriculture 113 *109*
Philostratos
Gymnastic 3 *219–220*
Gymnastic 5 *59*
Gymnastic 9 *48–55*
Gymnastic 10 *120*
Gymnastic 11 *117–118, 134*
Gymnastic 31 *210*
Gymnastic 32 *66, 72*
Gymnastic 33 *66*
Gymnastic 34 *124*
Gymnastic 50 *109*
Gymnastic 55 *211*
heavy events *105*
hoplite race *7*

ideal boxer *124*
ideal pankratiast *134*
ideal pentathlete *210*
ideal runner *66*
ideal runner for *dolichos 72*
Life of Apollonius 1.2 *195*
Life of Apollonius 5.43 *193*
Pictures in a Gallery 1.24 *207*
Pictures in a Gallery 2.6
     136, 138–139, 140
Pictures in a Galley 2.32 *108*
Phlegon
     Olympiads 42–43
     Olympic truce *59*
pick
     iconography of *106*
Pindar
     biography of *98*
     epinician odes *98–99*
     fr. 6.5 *89*
     Isthmian Ode 4.65-66 *136*
     Nemean Ode 11.22–29 *54*
     Nemean Ode 7.70–73 *217*
     Olympian Ode 10.64–65 *60*
     Olympian Ode 10.72 206
     Olympian Ode 3 *99*
     Olympian Ode 5.4–7 *197*
     Olympian Ode 8 53–63 *168*
     Pisa and Pisatans *37*
     Pythian Ode 1.42-45 *213*
     Pythian Ode 8.81–84, 88–92 *111*
Pisans/Pisatans *181*
Pisatans *37, 44, 51*
[Plato]
     Hipparchus 228B 149
     Lovers 135E *219*
Plato
     Apology 36D *178*
     Cratylus 413A *212*
     Crito 47B *169*
     Euthydemos 277D *111*
     Lysis 203A *163*
     Lysis 203A-204E *165–166*
     Phaedrus 256B *111*
     Protagoras 326B *167–168*

Plutarch
     Alexander 4.5 201
     Aratus 28.4 96
     Lycurgus 14.3 *52*
     Lycurgus 19.9 *120*
     Moralia 224F *62*
     Moralia 638D *134*
     Moralia 638E *120*
     Moralia 738A *221*
     Pericles 13.11 *148*
     Themistocles 1.3 *164*
     Theseus 25.5 *91*
Poliakoff, Michael B. *8*
     combat sports *105*
polis 70, 156
     and hero cults *36*
     formation of *33*
     gymnasion, and *156*
     origin of *1*
Polites of Keramos (runner) *198*
Polites of Keramus *73*
Pollux
     Onomasticon 3.151 *218*
Polydeukes (boxer)
     "head-hunting," and *124*
Polymester of Miletus *152*
Poseidon *88, 89*
Powell, Mike *206*
Prometheus *155*
Prytaneion decree *179*
Pythagoras of Ionia (boxer) *127*
Pythagoras of Samos (boxer) *192*
Pythian Games 49, 74–75
     inauguration of *77*
     inauguration of athletic contests
       at *57*
     prize at *58, 76*
     stadium
       starting lines in *62*

Q

Quintus Smyrnaeus
     Fall of Troy 4.345–348 *129*
     Fall of Troy 4.479–480 *133*

S

Sarpedon *2–3, 5*
Scanlon, Thomas F. *123*
Scholiast on Pindar
    Nemean Ode 5.89 *133*
    Pythian Ode 9.209 *61*
Scholiast on Plato
    Laws 796 Kerkyon *108*
Scholiast to Aeschylus
    Agamemnon 171 *218*
Scholiast to Aristeides
    Panathenaikos 3.339 *218*
Scholiast to Aristophanes
    Acharnians 214 *206*
    Knights 1159 *65*
    Peace 353 *159*
    Peace 879 *88–89*
Scholiast to Pindar
    Isthmian Odes, hypothesis b *90*
    Isthmian Odes, hypothesis b *91*
    Olympian Ode 3.35a *188*
Segal, Charles *217*
Seneca
    On Benefactions 5.3 *111*
Serwint, Nancy *52*
Simonides 69
    fr. 42 *204*
    Greek Anthology 16.24 *106*
Snodgrass, Anthony, *6*
Socrates *166*
Solinus
    Collectanea Rerum
        Memorabilium 7.14 *88*
Solon *91, 142, 159*
Sophocles
    Antigone 130–132 *61–62*
    Electra 47–50 *78*
    Electra 681–695 *78*
    Electra 698–708 *79*
    Electra 709–711 *202*
    Electra 709–719 *80*
    Electra 720–723 *81*
    Electra 724–733 *83*
    Electra 734–748 *83–84*

    Electra 749–763 *84*
    Philoctetes 874 *79*
Sostratos of Sikyon (pankratiast)
    135
s*tadion*
    heats for *65*
    herald *65*
    technique in *62, 67*
    warm-up for *66*
Statius
    Thebaid 6.587–592 *66–67*
    Thebaid 6.593–595 *63*
    Thebaid 6.678–681, 693–695 *209*
    Thebaid 6.878–880 *109*
    Thebaid 6.899–904 *109*
stephanitês (crown game) *58*
Strabo
    Description of Greece 8.3.30 *41–42*
    Geography 8.3.30 *183*
    Geography 8.6.23 *87*
strigil *107*
Sullivan, John L. *127*

T

Table 1. *47*
Table 2. *85*
Teisamenos (pentathlete) *217*
terna (marker) *6*
Teukros *26*
Theagenes of Thasos *77*
Theagenes vs. the Ethiopian *109*
Themistocles *148*
    Kynosarges *164*
    on "jumping-the-gun" *63*
Theocritus
    22.101–106 *131*
    22.109–130 *131*
    22.44–52 *127*
    22.80–86 *128*
    22.88–97 *129*
    24.111–116 *105*
    Polydeukes vs. Amykos
        127, 131, 132

Theognis
  Elegies 1335–1336 *158*
Theophrastus
  Inquiry into Plants 1.7.1 *164*
Thersites *70*
Theseus *91*
  Kerkyon *108, 115*
  pankration *133*
Thucydides
  Histories 1.103.4 *92*
triaktêr
  definition of *108*
Trollope, Anthony xiv
truces for festivals *189*
Tyrtaios
  fr. 10.31–32 *4*
  fr. 12.1–2, 9–20 *7–8*

V

Vernant, Jean-Pierre *17*
Vitruvius *167*
  On Architecture 5.9.1 *148*
  On Architecture 5.11.1–2 *157–180*

W

Wade-Gery, H. T. *38*
war
  and athletics *7–8, 23*
warrior
  aretê of *2–3*
  as athlete 9
  mediated immortality of *4*
  shame of *3*
  valor of *9*
Wellls, Allan *62*
Wells, Margot *67*
Weniger, Ludwig *197*
Wheeler, George *74*
Winkler, John J. *171, 173*
wrestling *107–109*
  akoniti 111
  anephedros 111
  aptôs 111

clinching *114*
Dionysus vs. Pallene *116*
Eleans on *116*
how to win *109*
inauguration at Olympia *34*
Lacedaemonians, and *119*
opening stance *112*
Orikadmos *109*
rules of *109*
shoulder throw *116*
Theagenes vs. the Ethiopian *112*
Tydeus vs. Agylleus *109*
upright vs. ground *108*
Wycherley, R. E. *163*

X

Xenophanes *175*
Xenophon
  Anabasis 4.8.26 *107*
  Constitution of the Lacedaemonians 1.3–4 *52*
  Hellenica 4.5.2 *96*
  Hellenica 7.4.29 *216*
  Memorabilia 3.7.1 *174*
  Memorabilia 3.7.9 *174*

Y

Young, David C. *150, 151, 153, 206*
  social standing of athletes *152*

Z

zero-sum game
  3, 20, 112, 152, 204, 220
Zeus
  as *triaktêr 108*
  Averter of Flies *32*
  Olympios *32, 35*
  cult of *32*
Zeus Nemaios *94*
Zeus Olympios
  Pheidias *183*
Ziehen, Ludwig *191*